THE KRAYS

THE PRISON YEARS

DAVID MEIKLE
KATE BEAL BLYTH

arrow books

7 9 10 8

Arrow Books
20 Vauxhall Bridge Road
London SW1V 2SA

Arrow Books is part of the Penguin Random House group of companies
whose addresses can be found at global.penguinrandomhouse.com.

Penguin
Random House
UK

First published by Century in 2017

www.penguin.co.uk

A CIP catalogue record for this book is available from the British Library.

ISBN 9781784757229

Typeset in 11.48/16.41 pt Baskerville MT by Jouve (UK), Milton Keynes

Penguin Random House is committed to a sustainable future for
our business, our readers and our planet. This book is made from
Forest Stewardship Council® certified paper.

MIX
Paper from
responsible sources
FSC® C018179

Printed and bound in Great Britain by Clays Ltd, Elcograf S.p.A.

To our families for their unwavering support
throughout the project

Contents

Foreword

By Fred Dinenage

For some years I shared many hours of the Kray twins' prison years with them, conducting face-to-face interviews.

Every couple of weeks I would visit Ron at Broadmoor Hospital for the criminally insane at Crowthorne in Berkshire. I visited Reg in prison at either Parkhurst on the Isle of Wight, Lewes in Sussex, Gartree in Leicestershire or – towards the end of his life – in the Category 'C' Wayland Prison at Griston in Norfolk.

The authorities liked to keep Reg on the move. They felt that, if he was left in one place for too long, he would set up his own criminal network in a particular 'nick'. They were right, of course. He always did! I never had any problems gaining access to Reg. The authorities were always helpful – though the 'welcome' one received at the various prisons tended to vary.

In contrast, my relationship with the authorities at Broadmoor began with some difficulty. They were wary of my media connections and it was some months before

I was able to gain access to Ron. On my first visit the chief medical officer took me to his office and explained that Ron, as a chronic paranoid schizophrenic, was on powerful medication which tended to last for about forty days.

'Unfortunately for you,' he told me, 'he's now on day thirty-nine. You'll find he's easily upset. If you ask him a question and his leg begins to shake, you'd do well to change the subject.'

As it happens, Ron and I got on well. And, eventually, I got on very well with the authorities ... so much so that Ron and I were eventually allowed to have our conversations in a private room and I was able to take a tape recorder with me.

The Broadmoor authorities, in fact, eventually trusted me so much they allowed me to take TV cameras into the hospital to film inmates who were talented artists. It was on one of these occasions that my cameraman actually shot footage of Ron himself outside his cell.

On my first visit to see Ron I had parked my car and was walking towards the intimidating black doors at the entrance to Broadmoor when I became aware of an expensive limo alongside me. One of the darkened rear windows slid down, a puff of cigar smoke drifted out, and a quiet but firm voice questioned: 'Fred Dinenage?'

'Yes,' I replied.

The Voice continued: 'I'm a friend of Ron Kray's. I believe you're going to be writing a book about him?'

'That's right,' I answered, wondering what was coming next.

'OK,' said The Voice. 'Just make sure it's honest and fair, won't you?'

'Of course,' I replied.

'Good,' said The Voice, 'because I'll be watching.'

And with that, the window closed – and the limo drove off.

It was an encounter I've never forgotten. I later discovered that the sinister voice belonged to Joey Pyle, the then overlord of London's gangland and a man who was much feared in the capital.

When *Our Story* was eventually published I received a phone call from him. 'I've read your book. It's fair and honest. Thank you.'

My first visit to see Reg in Parkhurst was with the twins' older brother, Charlie, and a dear friend of theirs, Wilf Pine. Reg, as always, was flanked by his 'minders': young toughs who were there to protect him from any punk who thought he could make a name for himself by toppling a Kray twin.

Reg liked people around him. Ron didn't. When we met at Broadmoor his only companion was his trusty aide Charlie – a double murderer – who poured me coffee from a silver pot, opened endless cans of non-alcoholic lager for Ron, and lit his endless stream of cigarettes. Ron would take two or three puffs and then stub the cigarette out.

Often on those earlier visits we would sit with Peter

Sutcliffe. The so-called 'Yorkshire Ripper' sat just yards away from us, always with a couple of young 'groupies' holding his hands. Sutcliffe was not permitted to talk to Ron – not even to look at him. The Krays had no time for sex offenders. On arrival at Broadmoor, Sutcliffe was told by an intermediary: 'Stay away from Ron Kray – or you are dead.'

I think it's fair to say that both Reg and Ron were held in high esteem by both fellow inmates and by prison and hospital staff. They were respected. And that, for Reg and Ron, was the most important word in the world: respect. It's what they valued above all else. And I have to say it's what they always showed to me over the years.

We had our disagreements, mainly over the content of their autobiography. I've never known two blokes change their minds so often!

But I have to say they always showed me respect.

The prison years weren't easy for Reg. I always felt he was like a caged animal. Always prowling, always thinking, always planning, always tense. I don't believe he found a day of happiness in all his many years in prison. His sexuality was always a problem for him, although never admitted and never discussed.

Fellow gang members have told me Reg struggled coming to terms with his sexual leanings, which went back to his youth. Ron was different. Ron's sexuality was never a problem for him. He was a homosexual from the day he was born. It never bothered him. And life in Broadmoor was never an issue. It was what he'd wanted from the moment he was sent down. With his mental illness, prison was never going to work for him.

In Broadmoor they called him 'The Colonel'. He marched everywhere. Never walked. Always immaculate, hair slicked back, well shaven, beautifully dressed in fine suits, shirt and tie. Brogue shoes, always so highly polished you could see your reflection in them.

He spoke sometimes of getting out of Broadmoor and of moving to Morocco. The mountains, the sun, the sea, the sand – and, of course, the young boys. But he knew it was never going to happen. 'Get married, Ron,' people used to say to him. 'You'll get out of Broadmoor easier that way.' So Ron did. A couple of times. But it made no difference.

It just cost him a few quid.

Money was never a problem for Reg and Ron. They made, and spent, a small fortune. Much of it went to the senders of dozens of begging letters. Some were genuine, some not. The twins were always a soft touch. Ironically, both died virtually penniless. But both would have been thrilled with the way the Kray name lives on – in books, films and television documentaries.

For them that would have been the proof that they'd achieved what they craved more than anything. Respect.

The Krays: The Prison Years is no ordinary 'true crime' book. Far from it. David and Kate have written in a dramatic, creative style from start to finish, using key information from people who knew the twins while they were in prison.

I have been delighted to help with some of the finer details about their time behind bars. As you read the book, you will find that the legend lives on . . .

Chapter 1

Arrested at Dawn

A dull, grey morning greeted the East End of London. Spring had not yet sprung, and several days of rainfall had spread a general chill over the capital. The drizzle was relentless. As dawn broke on the morning of 9 May 1968, all was quiet in Bunhill Row, Shoreditch.

Reg and Ron Kray were still drunk. A boozy evening at the Astor Club in the West End had left them on the brink of consciousness. Other members of the Firm, the trusted group of followers loyal to the twins, had drifted off into the night. The Krays' driver brought the pair back, with company, after a typical evening of merriment alongside the rich and famous.

Their mother's council flat, in towering Braithwaite House, loomed large over the deserted streets, as grey as the damp morning. Two miles from their previous headquarters in Vallance Road – demolished to make way for a new development – the twins felt they were untouchable. As usual, they felt that no one could ever bring them down.

Ron dozed in one bedroom, with a young male admirer, possibly in his late teens. Reggie, in another bedroom, snuggled up to an attractive young blonde lady. Mother Violet was spending a couple of days away with grumpy Charlie senior at a Suffolk country house, provided for them by the twins.

In the surrounding streets, the forces of law and order gathered for the biggest operation of its type ever carried out by Scotland Yard. Detective Chief Superintendent Leonard Ernest 'Nipper' Read, tasked with bringing the Krays to book, took charge of proceedings. All over the East End, detectives lay in wait, poised to make their move.

Nipper and his main men took the lift up to the ninth floor and surrounded the flat, on the lookout for any signs of life. Shortly afterwards a bemused milkman, complete with crates, appeared from the lift, with his daily deliveries. Within seconds a couple of officers had him back in the lift, destination ground floor and none the wiser.

With a crash, the glass door of number 12 Braithwaite House, on the ninth floor overlooking Old Street, was kicked open. An array of gun barrels pointed inside.

Ron woke, up, startled. Almost before he had time to rub his eyes, his bed was surrounded by armed police, led by Nipper Read. Ron recognised .45 Webley pistols being aimed at him. He froze.

'Get out of bed, hands in the air.'

'You're under arrest,' Nipper announced calmly, reeling

off a few more procedural details and saving plenty of key elements for later.

Ron accepted his situation, requesting only that he always needed to have his antipsychotic drugs on hand.

The notorious gangster's young friend was of no interest to the uninvited guests. He was allowed to scamper off into the darkness. Reg's companion also wanted nothing more to do with the Krays' criminal organisation.

After a few seconds, Reg, now separated from his young lady, appeared in the room under heavy escort. The pair were being arrested on suspicion of murder and other offences.

Violet's beloved twins were led away, barely dressed. Within minutes, Ron and Reg, bleary-eyed and hungover, were in the back of a Jaguar 340 3.8, handcuffed and slowly waking up to reality. The car, a sleek icon of the sixties, sped through the deserted streets. They were no strangers to this type of motor, resplendent in British Racing Green; however, they weren't normally handcuffed in the back seat.

The bewildered twins prepared themselves for the usual grilling at their destination, West End Central police station. They were used to interrogations and nearly always came out on top. Nipper had anticipated this, preparing a detailed list of charges that covered every possible angle.

Ron said any suggestion of murder was ridiculous, and gave another reminder about his pill-taking requirements.

Reg told his inquisitors that they'd been expecting a frame-up, but plenty of people would help them.

Next stop: remanded in custody at HMP Brixton.

A phone call shortly afterwards from Reggie's blonde lady friend to Chris Lambrianou, a trusted member of the Firm, provided more information. Reggie had taken some 'speed' and chatted her up in the nightclub. The amphetamines had helped to 'loosen him up a bit' before they returned to Braithwaite House.

Chris, also a friend of the anxious lady caller, was brought up to speed with developments: 'They crashed through the door of the flat and got Reggie out of bed, not too politely. They called me a name and ordered me to get out of bed too. I said they should never talk to me like that, and they told me just to get out of the bed. I said I didn't have any clothes on, but they insisted I should get up because I might have a gun or something.

'I put on a dressing gown. I said Reg was going to be very annoyed, and one of the coppers told me that "Mr Kray isn't coming back". They were tipping drawers out on the floor and chucking things everywhere.'

'You're innocent, and that raid could have happened at anytime, anywhere,' Chris tried to reassure her.

In a nearby street, eldest brother Charlie Kray, forty-one, lay in bed with his wife Dolly. The marriage was nearly at an end. For Charlie, freedom was about to end, too. Again, the door was broken down; this time the police decided against handcuffs, and Charlie prepared to leave with his accusers. He insisted on a cup of tea before getting into a second Met Jag.

Ultra-reliable friend and newspaper model Maureen Flanagan, then a hairdresser, saw the twins' latest arrest in 1968 as no surprise because of so many previous brushes with the Old Bill. The first she knew about it was from the newspaper the next morning. She was married at the time and her husband, reading the paper, said the Krays had been taken into custody after a series of dawn raids.

'Oh, they've been arrested before,' she told him, recalling the previous cases, and knowing that the Krays usually managed to find some alibi or other.

'No, this is serious,' her husband insisted. 'They've been arrested for murder.'

A quick scan of the newspaper confirmed Maureen's worst fears. She could see mentions of the Blind Beggar pub, a dawn raid and a jumble of details. Her first instinct was to head straight for Violet's home at Braithwaite House and find out what was happening. Violet was a valued customer as well as being a close family friend.

When Maureen arrived, Violet was crying in the arms of her sister, May, as they looked at the remains of a smashed-in door – the entrance to the Krays' mother's flat.

'What happened, Violet?'

'I was in the house in the country, but the boys were here. It seems the police arrived at six in the morning and did this. They didn't even knock. They just kicked the door in and took my boys away. Can they do that?'

'They probably can if they're from Scotland Yard or higher up,' Maureen explained. 'Normal policemen wouldn't do this, but these weren't normal policemen.'

'They've taken the twins away and I can't see them until tomorrow.'

'Do you want me to come with you?'

'No thanks, that's OK. May is coming.'

'Isn't Charlie going with you?'

'No, he's been arrested as well,' Violet wept.

Maureen didn't know about Charlie's arrest. She always got on well with the affable eldest brother, who looked like a film star with his flowing blond hair and immaculate suits. She couldn't believe that he had committed a murder as well! No one wanted to be in Ronnie's company when he was in one of his dark moods, but Charlie . . . well, that was totally different. 'Champagne Charlie' always seemed to be a decent bloke.

Downcast, Maureen climbed into her white Mini and drove back to her home in Islington, a few streets away. She decided to go away and return the next day. However, when she returned, Violet was crying again.

'Bail's been refused for the three of them,' the doting mum groaned.

That was a crushing blow for Violet, May, Maureen, and all other friends and relatives; it was an indication of the authorities' desire to ensure that the twins were never allowed to roam free. The door would have to be replaced by her boys, or through insurance, because the police no doubt 'had justifiable cause'. The cost was immaterial; the loss of her sons meant everything.

As it happened, there were so many reasons why the twins could have been arrested, but for a long time they were left alone.

Gathering evidence against them was a long, slow and painstaking process, suited only to the meticulous methods of Nipper Read. He was highly respected by police throughout the land and, grudgingly, by his adversaries. The twins knew what they were up against.

News updates were broadcast from Braithwaite House: 'The 34-year-old ex-boxer brothers, Reginald and Ronald, were arrested by Flying Squad officers early this morning. They were in bed when the officers called to their home. They have wide interests in theatre and entertainment and they are well known for their fundraising work for charity. Up to a few years ago they were well known West End theatre first nighters and hosts to some of the newer big names in showbusiness.'

At West End Central police station, TV reporters provided more information: 'The Kray twins, Reginald and Ronald, aged thirty-four, have been arrested after a series of dawn raids in London. They are among eighteen men currently helping with enquiries relating to offences including conspiracy to murder, fraud, demanding money with menaces and assault.'

Duncan Campbell, former crime correspondent for the *Guardian*, remembers the day of the arrests: 'I think the Krays' initial reaction to being arrested was: they would get off with it. They had got off before, and that was the impression they gave to people around them. They had good lawyers and they believed that nobody would dare to give evidence against them.

'I'm sure there was a feeling of relief amongst the police that they finally had enough evidence to take them to court because there were unsolved murders.'

Throughout the East End, events were unfolding at a rapid pace. Sirens blared. Tyres screeched. Guns pointed, their metal dull in the gloom of that May dawn.

Uniforms. A myriad of voices. Shouting. Almost screaming. Hands in the air. No escape. No hiding place for the Krays' inner circle.

Freddie Foreman, a major figure in the underworld at the time, stumbled on the renewed police interest purely by accident.

Freddie was known as 'Brown Bread Fred', the Cockney rhyming slang for 'dead'. He was known as the Godfather in London's criminal circles, and they actually used to say: 'Don't mess with Brown Bread or you're dead!'

Freddie was a formidable character. Anyone who broke the strict code of conduct in the underworld faced the wrath of Freddie, who appeared at first to be a softly spoken gentleman; yet he had a brutal reputation.

Freddie was born in 22 Sheepcote Lane, Battersea, a typical two-up-two-down terraced house, on 5 March 1932. It was nineteen months before the Krays arrived on the planet, and seven and a half miles from their birthplace in Hoxton.

The fledgling Foreman was the youngest of five brothers, brought up in an area where crime took centre stage.

Freddie's dad had an Irish background, with a typically large family. His father was one of thirteen children. Ironically, his mother came from a middle-class family in London, but she joined the ranks of the poor in Sheepcote Lane.

Crime was a way of life during the Great Depression, when Britain's world trade halved. During the year of Freddie's birth, three and a half million people were unemployed in the UK. Survival instincts took over.

Still trying to stay a few steps ahead of the law in the sixties, Fred dropped in at Braithwaite House, hoping to see the twins and Charlie to discuss some business on the day of the arrest.

The police were there, all over the block; the street was full of uniforms. Freddie was on the run at the time. He decided to act normally, hoping that the coppers would have no idea who he was, with everything else going on.

'I walked straight past them into the flats. They just looked surprised and let me through.'

Freddie took the lift to the ninth floor. He carried on walking along the corridor, as far as he could, until the end. He arrived at the last door, before the fire exit.

The unexpected visitor knocked and a young woman

answered with a baby in her arms. He asked if she could 'do him a big favour' and let him in for a couple of minutes. The startled young mum listened to Freddie's plea that he was coming to see the Krays, but now police were everywhere.

'OK, come in quick,' the confused resident of Braithwaite House said.

Freddie enjoyed a cup of tea and a playful few minutes with the baby. 'If I could stay a little while until it calms down, then I'll be out of your way.'

And that was what happened. He stayed for half an hour, thanked his unexpected hostess with a 'cheerio, goodbye' and he was gone . . . to find a safer hiding place. Freddie, 'on his toes' and trying to evade capture, stayed at different addresses all over London. A picture of the notorious safe-blower and armed robber had been circulated everywhere in the capital.

Of course they were after Freddie big time, whether he was described as on the run, on his toes or on the trot – although they had missed this one golden opportunity. After the massive publicity surrounding the Krays' arrest, Freddie decided to lie low as much as possible.

Eventually, though, the long arm of the law under Nipper's guidance caught up with him. He ran a pub at the time, the Prince of Wales in Southwark, and received misinformation that it was safe to go there on one particular day. He was inside for half an hour, met some friends and left to get into his Mercedes. The Old Bill smothered the entire area.

'The police appeared out of nowhere and swooped on me. There were guns pointing at me, at my head.'

Chris Lambrianou, living in Birmingham during the police swoops, wasn't overly worried about his own position, despite the 'heads up' from Reggie's lady friend. He assumed, as always, that the Firm would stick together with no chance of any leaks. He did believe, though, that he was being followed. He came out of the Elbow Room nightclub and spotted two police officers in a car.

'I rang the police station and reported that two coppers were in a vehicle, joking, smoking and drinking when they should be out on the streets catching criminals. Within a matter of minutes they were gone.'

Chris became more and more suspicious. When he went to the Cedar Club or other venues in Birmingham, he was convinced that police were hovering around. He was right to be on his guard.

'I'd just been to Johnny Prescott's club, the Ponderosa. I was driving down to the Elbow Room when I was surrounded by unmarked cars. I had a big American Ford Galaxie then. There must have been fifteen coppers, with guns and everything. I got out and put my hands on top of the car.

'I thought at first another firm had come to kill me. But then when they showed their badges, some of them, I got the message that they were the police. I didn't feel safe with all those unmarked cars. Things were getting out of hand and out of control.'

Chris was searched, handcuffed and taken to a police station in Birmingham. His pride and joy, the oversized pale blue Ford, with its gigantic seven-litre engine, was left on the kerbside for an associate to reclaim.

'When I got to the station I could see some of the Old Bill in a side room playing darts. There was a picture of Reg and Ron on the dartboard!'

'What's that going to do?' Chris asked. 'You're not frightening me.'

'No,' they said, 'but Mr Read will.'

Chris was driven to London, in similar style to the Krays. He was surprised not to be arriving at Scotland Yard. Instead, a reception committee was waiting at Tintagel House, a Met Police building on the Embankment, between Vauxhall Bridge and Lambeth Bridge. That was where Nipper preferred to operate, away from the spotlight of the Yard.

Chris had cleaned up the flat where Jack 'The Hat' McVitie was killed by Reggie and Ronnie in October the previous year, and allegedly helped to move the body. Detective Chief Superintendent Read had worked full-time on the case and was looking for a breakthrough. Chris was given the full treatment.

He recalled: 'Nipper Read was sitting at a big desk. Behind him on a board were all the photographs of the main members of the firm and associates. I sat down and he was very polite and amicable.'

'Look, I know you weren't involved, but tell us about it,' the determined detective had said.

'Tell you about what?'

'Tell us about McVitie.'

'I don't know what you're talking about.'

'Oh yes, you do. You were there, but you left. What happened when you were there?'

'Look, I don't know what you're talking about. Maybe you can tell me instead?'

'Well, you went to the Regency Club where you met McVitie. You went from the Regency Club down to Evering Road, to Blonde Carol's flat there, where there was supposed to be a party. But there was an altercation. McVitie died. You weren't there when it happened, but you went with him to the flat.'

'Mr Read, I don't know anything you're talking about. As far as I'm concerned it's a non-event – it didn't happen.'

Chris, looking back, in his late seventies, was surprised that this high-ranking officer had so much detail; all those accusations, although denied, were worrying. He realised that Nipper was at the top of his game, totally in charge, and circling his prey. Chris stood his ground and assessed this confident police chief on the other side of the desk.

At five foot seven inches, Nipper had been considered too short for the standard police uniform. He became a plain clothes officer, and his supreme organisational abilities were quickly recognised. There were a few theories as to his nickname. Most believed it was because of his small stature. Some thought it was because, as a young boxer, he nipped in to deliver a hammer blow. Chris could see that another knockout blow was coming.

Nipper Read wasn't finished: 'Look, we're going to let you go. I'm going to give you my card, and I want you to go away and think. Give me a call and I promise that neither you nor any of your family will suffer any consequence over this. We'll support you, and we'll protect you, but just tell us what happened.'

Chris had heard that incredible deals were being offered to secure convictions against the Krays. He knew that this high-flyer, at the pinnacle of his career, would be open to negotiation.

However, he couldn't say anything to the inquisitive Nipper; not a word. 'It's the culture I grew up with.'

In Chris's world, you were a footballer, a boxer or a criminal. All he wanted to do was to escape from poverty and accumulate enough money to live a straight life. He thought that, perhaps, crime could pay after all. Did he think about the consequences of a criminal life? No.

After the meeting with Nipper, Chris was free to go, clutching the Detective Chief Superintendent's card. He decided to visit Violet and explain what was going on, with the police closing in on her beloved sons' criminal network.

'You must let the twins know what has happened,' the twins' mum urged.

Chris weighed up the situation. His own mother would have said the same: to tell Reg and Ron about the new developments. He was in a 'no win, no win' situation.

At that moment in time, he could see everyone losing everything. How would the twins react to news that Nipper was undermining the Firm, from top to bottom?

Chris set off in a taxi from Violet's home in Bunhill Row, towards Jebb Avenue, Brixton. The basic black London cab felt like a box on wheels with poor suspension compared to the luxuries of his American beast, now being cared for by pals up in Birmingham.

Chris disembarked outside the dismal front gate of HMP Brixton, paid his fare and made himself known to the prison officers. He signed in as Mickey Mouse; there was a much lower level of security in the sixties.

Chris was led to the visiting room, where the three brothers were sitting behind a glass partition, in separate cubicles. He could see 'a small speaker thing' at the bottom.

Charlie whispered, possibly hoping the twins wouldn't hear: 'You shouldn't have come, Chris. Bad move.'

A different approach from Reggie: 'Hello Chris, how you going? Nice to see you.'

Ronnie: 'How's everything out there, what's happening?'

Chris: 'It's not good at all. It's bad.'

'What do you mean?' the twins both demanded to know.

'Nipper Read had me brought to London. They know about McVitie and everything.'

'Keep schtum,' Reggie whispered. 'Don't say nothing. We've got it under control. We'll sort out a good lawyer for you.'

The three Krays, individually, thanked Chris for coming, for remaining loyal and keeping them up to date with Nipper's activities.

Back at Braithwaite House, Violet was keen to hear about her sons' welfare. Chris confirmed they were in good spirits. They appeared to be in good health, but he was more than a little concerned about everything else that was going on. Chris kept wondering if he had done the right thing.

'Maybe I shouldn't have told them, Vi. Maybe it wasn't a good move on my part, saying about Nipper and everything.'

'At least they're not in the dark,' Violet assured him.

Everything went quiet. Friends and associates of the twins urged Chris to stay loyal, despite the increasing pressure from Nipper. Everyone told him to stay sound. He headed north once more, wondering what the future held for the Firm.

Any hopes of evading Nipper's clutches were dashed. Back in Birmingham, another dawn raid. This time the target was Chris's flat, and the well-rehearsed arrest procedure took place once more. Chris was whisked down the motorway again, back to London. It was a fast journey. The M1 in the sixties had no speed limit, no central reservation and no lights. The restless Nipper lay in wait at Tintagel House.

'I'm going to give you this chance once again,' Nipper told him, although not so friendly on this occasion.

Nipper had more or less prepared a speech for all the arrested associates. It was a 'take it or leave it' offer.

'This is your one opportunity. You will never get another. You have the opportunity, if you choose, to come on the side of law and order. Make a statement and tell me all you know about the Krays. This is the only chance you will get.'

Chris stared straight ahead, determined not to give any signs of cooperation.

'I did tell you that you and your family would not be in any trouble. Just tell me the truth about McVitie. You were there at the beginning of the evening, so tell me about it. What happened?'

Chris remained polite, and tried not to look startled. 'As I said, it's a non-event. I don't know who you've been listening to.'

Nipper span round in his chair with a sudden burst of energy, and pointed to pictures of Kray associates on the wall: 'I'm listening to him. I'm listening to him. And I'm listening to him.'

Krays' driver Scotch Jack Dickson and several others had accepted the offer. 'There was no chance for me, so I admitted everything. I just told them all that I knew,' Dickson said later.

But Chris was made of stronger stuff. Nipper worked hard at hiding his frustration. Chris was a potential witness who operated not in London, but in Birmingham, Liverpool, Manchester and Blackpool. Here was a man, not too well known in the city, who would stand up well in the dock against the Krays. Nipper's expression appealed once more for a hint of help. Chris's uncooperative brother Tony was involved in the London scene, but a fresh voice from the outside could make all the difference.

'I still don't know what you're talking about.'

Nipper gave up. He nodded to one of the other officers in the room. They had been met with a wall of silence and a seemingly impregnable wall of fear. It was time to tackle the Krays and their devoted supporters head on.

'He wants to be on their side. He'll get the same result as them. You're going down. I gave you a chance. Charge him with murder.'

Chris always believed that Nipper was 'dead against' nicking him. The other witnesses were steeped in crime in London. Even though some were saving their bacon, their credibility was questionable. Their reputations had the potential to be exploited by clever defence lawyers.

Without hesitation, Chris was handcuffed and taken to Bow Street Magistrates' Court. He was led straight to a cell. As the door clanged shut, he heard a voice coming from the barred room next door. It was his brother Tony.

'Is that you?' Chris shouted out.

'Yeah, Chris. Who else? Ronnie Bender is next door to me. We've both been charged with murder.'

The next day, the trio appeared before Bow Street Magistrates and were remanded in custody. Despite Nipper's pressure, Chris felt that the Krays' lawyers would win the day. He wondered about Ronnie Bender. Ronnie was a decent guy and an all-round sportsman, with a kind heart.

He trusted the Krays too; yes, he put his total faith in them. And yet, what would Ronnie Bender gain from remaining loyal, apart from a long sentence? What was going through his friend's mind?

Chris knew it wasn't the first time the Krays had been detained. Three years earlier they had been charged with demanding money with menaces from club owner Hew McCowan. The twins were accused of seeking protection money from the Hideaway Club in Gerrard Street. The accusation was that they threatened to hurt him and damage the club if money wasn't forthcoming. The Krays claimed they were owed cash, and merely tried to retrieve it. They were only interested in securing investments for a project to build houses and factories in Nigeria.

At that time, Ron and Reg were remanded in prison for several weeks, awaiting trial. Their friend Lord Boothby told the House of Lords that the Krays were being held indefinitely without trial and something had to be done.

The case against them started to weaken. There were reports that McCowan had been seen in the Hideaway Club talking to a member of the Firm. McCowan's manager, also due to give evidence, changed his story. Suddenly, he had a revelation from God. He was told from above that the statement he had made was false. He wanted to confess to a priest that he had told the wrong story and the truth must come out.

The case against the twins collapsed, and they were cleared of all charges. There were rumours of jury 'nobbling'; whatever the case, the Krays were free men again. The celebration party in Vallance Road was on a scale never to be repeated in the East End again.

The twins gave a television interview in which Ron said the trial had cost them £8,000. Reg said it was a lot of money to spend for no reason at all. Ron said it didn't leave them broke, but it was a lot to pay 'when one is innocent'.

Why didn't they give evidence themselves?

Their legal representative: 'The law of this country is well established. The onus is on the prosecution to prove its case. Counsel for these two men and the third defendant were quite satisfied in their own minds, as I was in my own humble way as well, that the prosecution had not proved its case. There was no obligation on these men to make any answer to any of the allegations against them.'

Reg said he was going to concentrate on family life: 'I intend to get married in the near future. I did before, but it was put back over this case.'

Ron: 'I'd like to go abroad for a short while and then I'd like to be left alone.'

Ronnie had also been linked with Lord Boothby in a homosexual scandal. It was well known that Ronnie was gay.

The *Sunday Mirror* had obtained a picture of Ron with the Old Etonian and former aide to Winston Churchill. They didn't print it; instead, they ran a story headlined 'The

Picture We Must Not Print'. And they decided not to name names, but readers were given strong hints the previous week:

> A top level Scotland Yard investigation into the alleged homosexual relationship between a prominent peer and a leading thug in the London underworld has been ordered by Metropolitan Police Commissioner Sir Joseph Simpson.
>
> The peer concerned is a household name, and Yard detectives are inquiring into allegations that he has a 'relationship' with a man who has criminal convictions and is alleged to be involved in a West End protection racket.

Lord Boothby wrote to *The Times*, saying he had only met Ron three times to discuss business matters, and always in company. He also denied being homosexual. The *Sunday Mirror*, fearing a massive libel payout, apologised profusely to Ron Kray and Lord Boothby, and paid the peer £40,000 – the equivalent today of £500,000. Not only that, the newspaper editor was sacked.

After that debacle, other newspaper proprietors were understandably apprehensive about writing anything criticising the twins. After the Boothby case, Reg and Ron were generally referred to as 'successful businessmen'.

Boothby's relationships with the Krays were closer than he admitted. He was even having an affair with Dorothy, the wife of former Prime Minister Harold Macmillan.

Nipper knew all of that background, having suffered the bitter disappointment of the Hideaway Club result. He was determined to have a bombproof case next time around.

As well as dealing with the McVitie murder, Nipper had to prove that Ronnie Kray shot George Cornell in the Blind Beggar pub, Whitechapel, on 9 March 1966.

Cornell was an associate of the Richardson gang, a rival firm from south of the Thames. Witnesses were few and far between; in fact, it appeared that Ronnie had carried out the killing while everyone else in the pub was blindfolded.

Ronnie had the romantic idea that, in the underworld, you simply didn't grass. It couldn't happen. Grassing was the ultimate sin in that shady, sinister world where loyalty was the measure of all men.

Duncan Campbell: 'Cornell came from the other side – the Richardsons' side of the river. It had been suggested that he'd mocked Ronnie Kray and that he'd called him a fat poof.

'But I think the feeling is that, when Cornell found himself in the Blind Beggar, he was on the wrong side of the tracks. Ronnie Kray marched in and shot him in the head and that was the beginning of the end in a way for the Krays, even though the police had no luck in nailing Ron immediately.

'Nobody would give evidence against him at that time and nobody had seen anything. Everyone hit the floor and Ronnie marched off.'

Freddie Foreman's faith in loyalty was shattered as soon as a dedicated, determined team of officers compiled the evidence about the Firm's activities. Freddie, like Chris, was helpless as the Old Bill offered deal after deal. Previously trusted associates squealed and squealed.

'They just kept rolling over, one after the other,' Freddie recalled bitterly. 'Once they started rolling over, nothing surprised me. A whole lot of them did the same. There were about thirty statements inside a few weeks.'

It was nearly the end of the road for the Krays' empire. Still, they believed they would get away with it. Still, they thought they would walk free. But this time, the trump card belonged, not to the Krays, but to their main adversary . . . Nipper Read.

Chapter 2

Memories of Jack 'The Hat'

The persistent Nipper knew the truth about the murder of Jack 'The Hat' McVitie all along. The earlier denials, like those from Chris Lambrianou, were testament to the accepted code, 'thou shalt not grass'. Honour among criminals meant that this 'eleventh commandment' had to be obeyed, even if staying quiet meant decades in jail.

Chris, despite all of his denials to Nipper, knew exactly how the pest, Jack 'The Hat', had met his bloody end.

'What happened was, we all met together at a pub on the corner of Vallance Road. It was Vi's birthday. There were celebrations going on. We were having a drink, saying hello and all the rest of it.'

Major and minor members of the Firm were enjoying themselves on 29 October 1967 as the juke box competed with the hubbub. 'Happy Jack', by The Who, was an inappropriate choice on the playlist. The celebration was typical of the East End, with hard men in expensive suits dominating the place, admired by their dolled-up wives and girlfriends.

Chris knew everything about all of the main venues in the East and West End. As it happened, the twins had actually bought the Carpenter's Arms in Cheshire Street, just round the corner from Vallance Road, in 1967, as a gift for their beloved mother.

Brother Tony's preference for the next drink was the Queen's Arms in Hackney Road. Chris's oversized American convertible purred all the way towards one of Tony's favourite boozers. Chris had been mixing vodka and lemonades with amphetamines, making him feel hyper, and needing a change of scene.

Chris fancied moving on from the Queen's Arms to the Best Cellar in Leicester Square, where he'd made a lot of friends. He was also more than familiar with the Regency Club, a couple of miles away in Hackney, part-owned by the Krays. Chris didn't fancy going there. He preferred other local clubs where there were plenty of birds, drink and all the rest of it.

Tony insisted on going to the Regency. For a start, he wanted to show the Mills brothers round. They were good friends of Chris from Birmingham. The brothers wanted to sample the bright lights of London.

Chris recalled: 'I said not to go to the Regency because of the Saturday night gangsters. They would all be dressed up, looking like hard men, so it was best avoided. I knew the place would spell trouble. Anyway, we all went and

Jack "The Hat" turned up, shaking hands with different people.'

Jack always had his head covered to hide his bald patch. Apparently he even wore a hat in the bath. Jack had a reputation as a tough villain who drank a lot, took drugs, and was basically a menace. He was usually so high on various concoctions that he often stayed awake twenty-four hours a day.

Chris knew that Jack 'The Hat' had caused problems in the club before. On another evening he had brandished a gun and threatened to shoot a rival. He also cut a man down in the club basement, then reappeared upstairs to wipe the blood from the knife on the dress of a woman who had been enjoying a drink and a dance. Not only that, Jack had threatened to shoot the main owners of the Regency, the Barry brothers. Jack also owed the Krays money, said to be for a contract killing that wasn't carried out, so his life expectancy appeared to be limited.

The weekend gangsters mingled, everyone mingled, and Tony suggested yet another venue. He'd heard that a party was going on at Blonde Carol's flat. The idea was accepted unanimously. Outside, Chris's American convertible was blocked in, so the unsuspecting McVitie offered to take everyone in his battered old blue Ford Zodiac.

This was Blonde Carol's flat at 65 Evering Road, mentioned over and over again by Nipper Read. Also in the flat, Chris remembers, was Cornelius Whitehead, or Connie, a thirty-year-old member of the Firm.

'We got there, had a drink and straight away an argument started between Jack "The Hat" and Reggie.'

Jack had walked into a trap. There were no women at the so-called party. All that awaited the boozed-up victim was the grim reaper, normally a bleak figure brandishing a scythe, who this time would acquire a different blade.

'Reggie pulled a gun out, he pressed the trigger but it didn't work, so to me it looked like a bluff. I turned round to Connie Whitehead and said I didn't want this. I thought there was going to be a party, not this. I told Connie I just wanted out of there.

'Ronnie Kray appeared and asked if there was a problem. Connie told him I was a bit drunk and wanted to go home. Ronnie said Connie should take me. So Connie drove me to my dad's house in Queensbridge Road, about a couple of miles away. I began to think about Tony, who I imagined was still back at Blonde Carol's. I'd sobered up a bit by then.'

Back at the flat, Reg, undeterred by the gun's failure, grabbed a knife from a plate and launched it into Jack's chest. Encouraged by Ronnie, Reg stabbed Jack in the face and in the chest again. One version of events says that, with all of Reggie's stabbing, Jack's liver came out and had to be flushed down the toilet. Within minutes the twins were gone, and the clearing-up work began.

'I had a gun in Dad's house, a Webley automatic pistol.

I phoned a taxi and went to get Tony out of there. I thought, if they've hurt Tony, I would use the gun. I wasn't frightened to use it. I'd fired a gun before and knew exactly what I was doing.'

Chris knew that some of the group including Ronnie Bender, one of the twins' drivers, would still be in the vicinity and presumably at the flat. Also, hopefully, things would have calmed down.

'When I got there I knocked at the door. Ronnie Bender appeared and I asked where Tony was. Ronnie said Tony had gone, so I asked where to. Ronnie pleaded with me not to go and I asked him what he meant. Again, he asked me not to go. He said they'd killed Jack.'

Chris recalled more of the conversation with Ronnie Bender.

'What, they've killed him in front of all those people?'

'Yeah, they've done him.'

'Oh no! Where is he?'

'Downstairs.'

'Look, Ronnie, I don't want to . . .'

'Help me, Chris, please . . .'

'What are your instructions?'

'I've got to get the body, put it over my shoulder and take it a hundred yards up to the railway bridge on Evering Road, then throw it over so it gets mashed up. There'll be no evidence. The body will be scattered everywhere.'

'Where are the twins?'

'They've gone. Please help me.'

That was Chris's downfall. At that moment, he strayed over the line. He became involved in cleaning up after the main event. He was implicated.

'I went in to the kitchen, found some socks, and got cleaning stuff. We cleaned the whole place up. McVitie's body was just lying there. It had to be moved. In the meantime, Tony arrived back from wherever he'd been so now the three of us were involved.'

The option of dumping the body over the railway bridge didn't appeal to Chris. For a start, taxi drivers used to gather at a bagel shop across the road from Blonde Carol's flat. They could appear at any time, day or night, to get their bagels – and no doubt catch sight of a bloodied body being carried along the street by three reluctant accessories.

'I went upstairs and I took an eiderdown off Blonde Carol's bed and we put Jack in that, and wrapped him up. There was blood everywhere, but I got a bucket and sponge and started to clean it up. I had a bucket full of blood when Blonde Carol came in.'

Carol asked Chris what he was doing and he said there had been a bit of an argument. There needed to be some tidying up. He suggested she should go off to bed and everything would be sorted by the morning when she came down. Unknown to Chris, there were two babies asleep in a bedroom upstairs, oblivious to the dramatic events involving the twins and Jack 'The Hat'.

Blonde Carol went to check on her kids, Chris emptied

the bucket of blood down the loo and he double-checked all of his cleaning. It was a good, thorough job. It was such a polished performance that Great Train Robber Bruce Reynolds, hearing about it all later, said he wished Chris had been working on his firm.

Chris, Ronnie and Tony lurched across the street from Blonde Carol's flat to McVitie's Zodiac and placed the body on the back seat, covered by the eiderdown.

It would never have gone in the boot, although the blood-soaked carpet fitted in there. Chris slipped back to the Regency and picked up his car, available to drive off now that other parked cars had moved.

'Then there was an argument about who was going to drive the car with Jack's body. We came to the conclusion that we should put it over the other side of the water on Richardson territory, so if it all came undone it would go on them people.'

Ronnie Bender said that there was no way he was going to drive. Apart from the large amount of drugs and alcohol he had consumed, more serious matters would have interested the Old Bill. Eventually Tony agreed to drive the Zodiac, a gesture which Chris thought was 'very brave'.

Tony's offer was a valiant gesture for other reasons: the car had a different coloured wing, only one windscreen wiper working and a broken headlight.

Chris was driving his own car, with Ronnie Bender in the passenger seat. The highly illegal convoy, Chris with his gun and Tony transporting the body, headed south over the water.

'When we went along by Mare Street in Hackney, a police car fell in behind Tony. It came that close to being a Harry Roberts scenario, when three police officers were shot dead. I couldn't let them get Tony with a body so I would have used that gun. Now can you understand the fatalities that could have happened from the time that the Krays lost control.'

The police following Tony probably didn't see the broken headlight, or possibly just opted for a quiet morning. Whatever the reason, they indicated and continued their patrol along a side street.

'Sometimes a comedy of errors can lead to a tragedy of errors. It just cascaded down. Policemen could have died; other people could have got involved. We drove over the water. What we didn't realise was that we were heading for Freddie Foreman's patch.'

McVitie's Zodiac ran out of petrol outside a church. A wedding had taken place, and there was confetti on the ground. The confused trio had no choice but to leave the body in the car outside the church.

Tony Lambrianou, in interviews later, said: 'The car was running out of petrol. It was an old Zodiac, a two-tone Mark 2. One light wasn't working, and there I was driving a body along at one o'clock in the morning with two people minding me.'

Tony said that anyone who stopped him would go the

same way as McVitie. 'That's how it had to be. I'm not proud to say that. I was in the thick of it. We were all implicated.'

Chris recalled: 'Tony and I discussed what was going to happen. We wanted to safeguard ourselves. We dropped Ronnie Bender off back at Charlie Kray's flat. Ronnie told Charlie what had happened and he went mad. And then the twins got involved. They went mad as well because they'd wanted the body put over the railway bridge.

'After that, Freddie Foreman and Charlie became involved because the body had to be moved. Well, that's what they were accused of. What really happened I don't know, because Jack's body was never found. It was all just crazy. Crazy.'

Freddie Foreman's memories of Jack 'The Hat': 'He was a nuisance if ever there was one. He was a drunkard and taking pills. He had some sort of scam going on. He used to have 5,000 pills in a can. He was weeding them out of a pharmaceutical company or something.

'It was a good coup for him because he was making money with these "poppers." You opened your mouth and they just popped.

'Girls used to love the pills because they helped with slimming. They never used to eat anything. They all lost weight with them. Everyone was on "poppers" in the sixties.

'If you went out for a drink, they were being popped in

your mouth whether you wanted one or not, you know? And if you had any musicians, they were taking them. They got more money to play after twelve o'clock in the clubs. And they'd be banging away and playing all night. But it was part of the culture then, you know?'

Former crime correspondent Duncan Campbell's view of Jack 'The Hat': 'He was a strange character, Jack. He'd upset the Krays by going along to one of their clubs wearing Bermuda shorts, carrying a machete, wearing a hat, and I think showing disrespect.

'And then he was hauled along to meet Ronnie and Reggie. I don't think he realised at the time that he was going to be killed, and then he was killed in a very messy way. They got their henchmen in to clean it up, to do what they used to call a wet and dry cleaning job on all the blood and everything.

'I think they assumed that they would get away with that as well, and he was just another minor criminal that the police would wash their hands of and ignore. And so it was in a way strange that Cornell and McVitie, both members of the underworld, were to finish the Krays.'

Their fate was also sealed by an innocent young lady whose bravery won the day for law and order . . .

Chapter 3

The Voice of an Angel

Nipper's large, multi-drawered and neatly tidied wooden desk was laden with paperwork. File after file about the Krays' background had to be scrutinised. The twins and all main associates had been charged and remanded to Brixton and Wandsworth. Nipper's main targets were Reg and Ron – although their henchmen were also locked up and charged with different levels of involvement, mainly in the McVitie case.

Now Nipper had to find a way of convincing judge and jury that guilty men stood before them. There could be no failures this time around. Months of waiting lay ahead while prosecution and defence prepared their cases; it would be a long, slow and drawn-out process.

There were few luxuries for the Krays and co. at Brixton, the former Surrey House of Correction. Conditions had improved substantially since 1823 when Harty Henry was charged with stealing a hat and two umbrellas from the Nag's Head in Southwark. Harty's sentence: twelve months' hard labour, followed by seven years' transportation for stealing more umbrellas. Despite the more humane conditions in the sixties, Ron and Reg still looked out on the world from small barred windows with only a basic table, hard bed and slopping-out bucket for company.

Other associates languished in Wandsworth, another former House of Correction dating back to the 1850s. The national collection of birch and cat o' nine tails was stored there; other dubious claims to fame included the disused execution chamber known as the 'cold meat shed' and the fact that it had been the location of the escape of Great Train Robber Ronnie Biggs in 1965.

A long succession of hangmen carried out their duties there. William Marwood presided over four executions between 1878 and 1882. Henry Pierrepoint hanged six men at Wandsworth, his brother Tom twenty-seven, with his busy son Albert taking care of proceedings forty-eight times.

New gallows were built between 'E' wing and 'F' wing in 1911, beside the cell of the condemned inmate. Many spies were hanged there. They included John Amery, who was hanged for treason after the Second World War and William Joyce, the notorious Lord Haw-Haw who mocked Britain on the radio with Nazi propaganda. Murderer Hendrick Neimasz, forty-nine, was to take his last breath on 8 September 1961. He was the last person to be hanged at Wandsworth.

There were other hangings at different jails in the

sixties: a close call for Ron, Reg and other members of the Firm who were facing the same charge after executions were suspended in the UK in 1965. While he was a child, Aunt Rose said Ron 'was born to hang'. It was a common saying of the time; in reality he and Reg were born to be locked up.

Crowds gaped at the enormous, complex police operation, destined to last for thirty-nine days, as they prepared for the trial. The reputation of the Krays' brutal network meant that nothing – absolutely nothing – could be left to chance.

Chris Lambrianou hated every second: 'We'd been that long on remand it was almost a relief when the trial started. We were all in one van, and it would go from Brixton to Wandsworth or Wandsworth to Brixton and then to the Old Bailey. There were motorcycle outriders, police cars back and front and even helicopters.'

The van, with 'POLICE – SPECIAL PATROL GROUP' emblazoned on the side, provided a regular spectacle for sightseers as it crossed Waterloo Bridge, heavily guarded, backwards and forwards to the Old Bailey. Officers with walkie-talkies were everywhere.

Freddie Foreman, accused of disposing of McVitie's body, thought it was well over the top: 'They used to try and beat the record of getting from Brixton to the Old Bailey. The motorcycles just tore up and down and never stopped for any traffic lights. There were sirens going, and all of London knew we were heading to the court. People were selling tickets to get into the public gallery. There were queues to buy them!

'The police used to change the route every day. They thought there might be an ambush on the way to court or something like that, so they took ridiculous routes.

'The Old Bill were posing with guns in the street. They used to time it, just when the jury was coming in, and they would block off the whole street at the Old Bailey. They were in doorways on their knees with rifles, holding about twenty or thirty people back on the pavement just as the van was arriving. It fitted in with the helicopters overhead. The whole thing was intimidating for everybody.'

Freddie said the police motorcyclists overtook the van, skidding with sparks coming up. One of them crashed, and was injured. The accused in the van found out that he wasn't badly hurt.

On their way into the court, the twins encountered Bobby Cummines, soon to be known as 'the baddest man in Britain' for his string of armed robberies. Bobby, who was later awarded the OBE for turning his life around and helping ex-offenders, was only just starting his criminal career. He was escorted into the court with a prison officer on either side of him. Bobby was a distinctive prisoner, standing at five foot six, with a shock of blond hair and blue eyes.

'I saw two men strutting along, looking like a million dollars, dressed in smart suits and immaculately groomed. I didn't know who they were at first.'

Bobby recalled the one with the round face asking: 'What are you doing here?'

'I'm up for possession of a firearm and armed robbery. It was a sawn-off shotgun.'

Ronnie was taken aback: 'You cheeky bastard. You've got some front. I'll give you ten out of ten for that. What age are you?'

'Sixteen.'

'We'll be seeing a lot of you,' Ronnie grinned.

'You probably will,' Bobby agreed.

'Do you know who you were talking to there?' a prison officer whispered, turning to Bobby. 'You might not have seen them before, but you'll have heard of them.'

'They're obviously villains. Who are they?'

'That was Ronnie and Reggie Kray – they call them the kings of the East End.'

Looking back at the Krays' court case, Professor Dick Hobbs, raised in East London and a respected expert on criminology, recalled: 'It was a great stage for them. The one thing people underestimate about both Ron and Reg Kray was: they were geniuses at public relations. They were good at presenting themselves in court as gangsters. That was what they were – and proud of it.

'They'd watched all the Warner Brothers movies of the thirties and forties with James Cagney, Edward G. Robinson, Humphrey Bogart and particularly George Raft who they adored, and got to know quite closely later on.

'And they were interested in the image. They were

interested in how they looked. They had a fresh shirt every day with silk tie and beautiful suits. When these guys were out and about they wore handmade cashmere overcoats. This was Hollywood, and it had come to London.'

The twins were fascinated by the way the Mafia operated. They shared the same hatred of so-called 'rats', who would do anything to save their own skin. They were intrigued by the way members were treated like royalty, with waiters finding them tables from nowhere and shopkeepers discovering that they had ample supplies of luxury goods, just for the privileged few. The film *Goodfellas* would have met the twins' aspirations with protection rackets, hijackings and those who fell out of line being 'whacked'. And, like the Krays, the people who suffered were 'their own kind'; they were fellow gangsters.

It was a period when crime began to take centre stage. The underworld was packed with villains who bordered on being celebrities, posing a threat to the establishment. In the post-war years, it was seen as important to have a sense of pride in the criminal justice system. The very heart of that system was under threat from criminals, and strong action was the agreed remedy.

Characters such as the Krays and the Richardsons were constantly in the news; their stories became part of the daily chat. The appetite for crime drama was served up with a new feast of real-life characters, committing heinous crimes and, in some cases, getting away with murder.

The gangster of the sixties was a masculine role model. He could never be told what to do, and he attracted a loyal following by breaking the rules and laughing at his accusers. While the legitimate economy grew, so did the criminal empires. Their businesses – protection rackets, fraudulent companies and illegal gambling dens – were thriving until the long arm of the law reached out with a vengeance.

The late enforcer Frankie Fraser was a staunch supporter of the twins and described them as 'absolute gentlemen'. He explained how, as far back as the war years, gangs built up their power in different areas of the city. The effects were then felt in the Krays' era.

'South London was always South London, and the part called Angel was always Angel, and the East End was always the East End. So officially you never intruded on any of them, and they would never intrude on us. That's how it was, very strict and all.

'If anybody did get up to any trouble in South London, if they came from East London, that caused a war – a very bitter war. That's how it was then. Not everybody had cars because of petrol rationing and all that during the war, and all the rest of it, so people couldn't travel as much as they can today. But of course you could always nick one and put false number plates on it.

'Those early days taught me more about thieving than anything, because everyone then was into crime, even the most honest people. Everybody was trying to get a little bit of something for nothing, because everything was rationed. So it was a thieves' paradise, there's no doubt about it. I'll never forgive Hitler for surrendering.'

As the Krays' trial began in early 1969, Maureen Flanagan remembered watching events unfold from the public gallery: 'As they came up I thought, "Oh my God, you are still thinking you're on show." They always liked to be playing to an audience: "Hey look at me." They were on trial at the Old Bailey, but they still thought they were going to get off with it.'

Even Freddie Foreman, contemplating his fate in the dock, thought: 'The twins saw themselves as invincible. They really believed that's what they were. Big mistake.'

Members of the jury, prison officers, people in the public gallery and lawyers were astonished to see another well-known face appearing for proceedings. One of the most recognisable celebrities in the world took a seat in the public gallery. It was hardly a scene from the set of *Ben-Hur*, but the actor would have graced any surroundings. The handsome, immaculately dressed newcomer proved to be none other than Charlton Heston.

'Is he a witness?' a confused voice asked.

'Don't be daft. He's just come for a look on his day off,' another hushed voice scoffed.

During the coming days, a stunning variety of celebrities could be seen going in and out of court, along with a lord or two. Famous or infamous, take your pick, the Krays made headline news in and out of court and intrigued all sections of society.

Chris Lambrianou was taken aback: 'In the public gallery you had people who were stars at the time, like Richard Greene who played Robin Hood. You had other people there like Lita Roza, who was a top singer at the time. All these different characters came in, and there were even MPs although I didn't know their names.

'The public gallery was always full. Not only that, the gallery upstairs was always full too.'

Wilf Pine, Ronnie's business manager: 'There was an unbelievable reaction to the trial. It must have sold more newspapers than Winston Churchill's funeral. The press played it up for all it was worth. Some people were telling the truth. And you had all the rats going in, some saying rubbish so they could get off on another charge.'

Commentators at the time viewed the trial as a social event. Everybody knew it was coming sooner or later. The Krays were society figures. They'd been on the BBC talking about their activities in London's nightlife. All during the 1960s, their names appeared in headlines as they escaped justice and flirted with the rich and famous.

Professor Hobbs found it interesting that, as with other gangsters, the twins made money from their reputations outside their local territory. The obvious place for the Krays to go was the West End of London . . . the great honey pot.

'That's where there was gambling, prostitution, and drink. That's where people went to spend their hard-earned leisure money. When they were young men coming through they were spotted by the gangsters of the day, Jack Spot Comer and Billy Hill. Both of these guys courted the Krays.

'The twins chose Billy Hill, wisely as it happened, because he was something of a criminal genius. And for years Hill had managed to establish himself in the West End of London, in gambling clubs. He knew how gambling worked. He knew all about the security. In the fifties everybody knew that gambling was about to be made legal, and there would be a boom in the West End.

'Billy Hill brought the Krays on. He mentored them, taught them the business and when gambling became legalised in the 1960s, the Krays were able to move into the West End and start to make serious money. They were introduced to the glamour, and the glamour was what they liked.'

Violet's love for the twins shone through, all during the trial. Every day, she arrived at the court with clean, ironed shirts. Every day, she appeared with roast dinners, in pots from her kitchen. There was always a little pot on the side, containing the gravy.

She headed straight for prison officers or anyone in authority: 'You'll heat the gravy for my boys? They always have hot gravy on their dinners. Tell me you'll heat it up?'

Violet's routine continued, unabated. It was as if the twins and Charlie were at home, enjoying the benefits of her domestic skills. Their unexpected move to the Old

Bailey, with trips to and from Brixton, meant an inconvenient disruption to her routine; nonetheless, she would continue to treat her boys like princes.

Violet, constantly on the case with solicitors, hoped for a sentence of perhaps twenty years, so that her heroes would be out in twelve or fourteen. Eldest brother Charlie, for his alleged 'after the fact' activities with the body of Jack 'The Hat', might get a very short sentence, she prayed. After all, Violet reckoned, Charlie was no villain and the judge could have some sympathies there.

Reflecting, many years later, Maureen thought that a massive sentence had to be a strong possibility.

'The press had a field day with the trial. People were saying to us not to hold our breath. They were saying to Violet not to get her hopes up. Not long before the trial I remember the Richardson gang in South London went down for a long time. Charlie Richardson got twenty-five years. So I thought, now it's the East End. Now it's our turn.'

Instead of the two murders being tried separately, the charges were put together – which meant Court One had ten defendants in the dock. The Krays protested, saying that anything detrimental in one trial would rub off on the other case.

The Krays' barrister, John Platts-Mills QC, made his feelings known about that arrangement: 'It was quite obvious that they should have been tried separately. I took the case to the Court of Appeal. But they refused. Back-room talk with the judges' clerks told me that the government were behind this, and the Court of Appeal wasn't going to interfere.'

Only Ronnie Kray and John 'Ian' Barrie were charged with the Cornell murder. The eight others, including Chris Lambrianou, faced charges relating to the killing of McVitie.

Chris recounted this most unusual scenario: 'The judge, Mr Justice Melford Stevenson, told the jury that people sitting in the dock who were charged in connection with the McVitie murder had nothing to do with the Cornell murder. Likewise with the Cornell murder, it was nothing to do with the McVitie murder.'

The only alleged connection with these two separate deaths was Ronnie Kray.

The accused were all aggrieved to be told to wear numbered cards around their necks. Ron swore loudly when he saw that they had to wear them. He was really angry at the judge, especially as he had the tag 'Number One'. The numbering system reminded some onlookers of *The Prisoner*, a TV series at the time starring Patrick McGoohan. Patrick was 'Number Six' and monitored in the Village by 'Number Two'. Ron detested the numbers game.

Ronnie felt as if he was public enemy number one. He wrote 'get stuffed' on a slip of paper and asked an usher to hand it to the judge. After a brief legal discussion, the numbers plan was abandoned and the accuseds' names were used by all parties.

Nipper Read sat quietly in the courtroom, keeping a low profile. He had worked day and night, long night after long day, preparing his case. Nipper had an advantage over other police officers who tried to nail the Krays. He had grown up in poverty, in similar surroundings. Like the Krays, he had been an amateur boxing champion. He had their lives and crimes mapped out, because he knew the territory. He knew what made them tick. Nipper also had an ace up his sleeve . . .

She wore a short skirt, sixties style. She climbed into the dock in her white high heels. This young lady had innocent, wide open eyes. Her hair dangled around her face and earrings. From somewhere, she had discovered bravery. From somewhere, she had become fearless. And she spoke with the voice of an angel.

Gasps and awkward coughs could be heard echoing around the polished wooden panels of Court One. What did this beautiful young woman have to say? One of the most publicised, important trials in British legal history was about to be turned on its head. The scales of justice were soon to weigh heavily against a pair of evil, ruthless killers who showed no mercy to their victims – and yet demanded clemency in large doses from judge and jury.

Dozens of staring eyes, belonging to both sides of the law, greeted the arrival of the humble, pretty young barmaid who held the key to the Krays' future. She may as well have turned that key and slammed the cell doors shut – with escape impossible and parole a distant hope on an unwelcoming horizon.

Two cold-blooded killers, still seen as 'Robin Hood' figures in the capital, were fighting for their freedom.

Ms X, skilfully prepared by the prosecution for her day in court, knew that this would be her final public appearance. The full force of the law would entail protection, a new identity and a life sentence away from her home in the East End. There was no other way. Nipper knew there was no other way.

Ms X looked the jury foreman in the eye. She glanced over at the crimson-faced judge, who pursed his lips as she spoke, ever so softly. Her words flowed in a gentle, unwavering voice.

'That's him,' she pointed. 'That's the man who did it. That's Ronnie Kray.'

The barmaid had seen everything in the Blind Beggar pub. She had witnessed the execution of George Cornell. Ronnie entered the pub with another gunman, Ian Barrie, and aimed his 9mm Luger. Cornell was shot in the forehead above his right eye.

Ronnie and Ian Barrie were driven there by Scotch Jack Dickson. Barrie fired a few warning shots into the ceiling, no doubt to warn of the consequences of grassing. Scotch Jack said Ronnie came back into the car, laughing his head off about shooting the 'bastard Cornell'.

The enforcer for the Richardsons died in hospital in the early hours the next morning.

Accounts of the killing at the time mentioned the record, playing on the juke box, 'The Sun Ain't Gonna Shine (Any More)'. The needle actually became stuck, repeating the ill-fated lyrics by the Walker Brothers. Cornell would never see another sunrise.

As soon as Ms X spoke, Reggie and Ronnie knew the game was up. The jury could see she was speaking the truth; the judge could tell that her testimony was honest and true; the entire courtroom fell into an eerie silence as the young barmaid told how Ronnie Kray had shot George Cornell without hesitation, in cold blood. Suggestions that Cornell had called Ronnie a 'fat poof' could never be considered as mitigating circumstances.

Also looking on in horror: Charlie Kray, Ian Barrie, Chris and Tony Lambrianou, Ronald Bender, Regency Club owner Anthony Barry, Freddie Foreman and Cornelius Whitehead.

Chris Lambrianou summed up the decisive moment: 'This young woman spoke like an angel, and you could not fail to listen and be moved by the things she said. From the moment she got in the dock we were finished.'

Chris said the McVitie case involved wasters, people involved in serious offences including murders, and steeped in crime history. But with the two trials heard together, the barmaid's words had the power to ensnare defendants in both cases.

'We were hoping that we were going to walk, that we were going to get a not guilty, but when the barmaid gave her evidence there was a slow, sinking feeling that kind of goes through you.'

Maureen Flanagan realised straight away that the barmaid's appearance spelled disaster for the brothers.

'I looked over at Reggie and Ronnie. They were shocked. They never dreamed that the barmaid, after all this time, and in fear of her life, would ever come forward. But Nipper Read used her as his trump card.'

Maureen watched, intrigued, as the defence team questioned this tricky new arrival. How did she know Ronnie Kray? How did she know he was the killer? Had he used the pub before?

It was well known that Ronnie hated the Blind Beggar. The pub was frequented by Richardson gang members. Ronnie didn't go in, apart from that one night . . .

'I know it's Ronnie Kray because I saw him walk in and shoot Mr Cornell.'

Maureen could sense a glimmer of hope for Ronnie; the defence team pointed out that the barmaid had previously told police she was down in the cellar.

'I had to say that, because I was told to. I was in fear of my life and my family's lives.'

Later, Ron made it known that the barmaid was lucky. He maintained she was a 'very silly girl' and could have been marked for life. One phone call would have been enough. However, as the Krays said they didn't hurt women and children, no action was taken.

Apparently they had tried to stop the barmaid talking,

via the manager at the Blind Beggar. Perhaps they wished they had taken more severe action to ensure she kept quiet.

Details emerged about the killing of Jack 'The Hat' McVitie. Ronnie Kray held Jack down while Reggie stabbed him repeatedly.

It was all true. Every word.

The tight, seemingly unbreakable East End community was shattered to see former associates giving evidence. Albert Donoghue, once an enforcer, told all. The Teale brothers, Bobby, Alfred and David, had been trusted confidantes of the twins; now they were sealing the Krays' fate.

A muffled voice: 'He's done skulduggery, Donoghue. Look, he's going into the witness box. What's he doing? He's saying what he knows about two murders. This is all going horribly wrong.'

Some of the Krays' associates gave evidence against Ron and Reg because they were being asked to take the blame for major crimes.

Ronnie Kray wanted Scotch Jack to accept responsibility for the Cornell murder; the Krays' cousin Ronnie Hart was asked to take the rap for Jack 'The Hat'; and Albert Donoghue was told to say he murdered Frank Mitchell, a former associate of the Krays who was also known as 'The Mad Axeman'.

Ronnie Hart was having none of it and became a main prosecution witness.

'I wasn't having that, no way,' Albert had decided after only a few seconds, with Scotch Jack making the same decision.

Even when he was on trial back in the sixties, Freddie Foreman knew that the Krays' plan, making lesser members of the Firm take responsibility, would never work.

'The twins were going to settle for fraud cases and expect others to take the rap for serious crimes. That was a ridiculous thing to do. They thought they could manipulate people and get them to give up their lives and go to prison for things they hadn't done.'

The Crown Prosecutor, Kenneth Jones, was an eloquent lawyer who painted a grim picture of the McVitie murder: 'Terrified and bathed in sweat, like a caged animal he tried to escape by throwing himself at a window and smashing it.

'Reggie Kray picked up the knife and stabbed McVitie in the face. Then he punched him over the heart and plunged the knife repeatedly into McVitie's body while his twin brother Ronnie shouted over and over again: "Kill him, Reg." It is a terrible thought that murders were committed as a matter of business, not for profit or gain, but as a businessman might buy a new car or move to a new office as a matter of prestige.'

Ron had his run-ins with Jones, who asked about the alleged murderer's nickname, 'The Colonel'.

Ron retorted, homing in on his adversary's Welsh roots: 'Your name is Taffy Jones to all the prison officers. They say you ought to be a miner instead of a prosecutor, then you might do some good. My name is better than yours.'

The jury deliberated for six hours and fifty-five minutes before returning unanimous verdicts on Reggie and Ronnie for the murder of Jack McVitie. The foreman of the jury repeated one word: 'Guilty.'

Nipper Read was looking down. He couldn't look up.

'My eyes were full of tears. I was overwhelmed. All the work that we'd done was justified.'

Chris and Tony Lambrianou and Ronald Bender were also found guilty of murder, staying loyal to the end despite the dire consequences.

Ronnie Kray and his right-hand man Ian Barrie were convicted of murdering George Cornell.

Anthony Barry was found not guilty and discharged. Albert Donoghue pleaded guilty to being an accessory to murder and was given a shorter sentence at a separate hearing.

The Krays' brother, Charlie, Freddie Foreman and Cornelius Whitehead were all found guilty of being accessories to McVitie's murder.

The Krays, Chris and the others in the dock were shown no mercy.

Mr Justice Melford Stevenson, widely regarded as a heavyweight in his field, stared unflinchingly at Reggie and Ronnie Kray. He peered through his thick rimmed glasses. He'd served as Deputy Judge Advocate during the war, presiding over courts martial, and proudly wore an array of polished medals on his courtroom gown. He was a stickler for law and order, and even named his country home 'Truncheons'.

Several years earlier, in the same court, he had defended Ruth Ellis, the last woman to be executed for murder in the United Kingdom. He was deeply distressed because that crime of passion – Ellis shot her lover in the street – led to death on the gallows.

Now, with the evil twins at his mercy, he was short of one option – the death penalty. In 1965, capital punishment was suspended for a trial period, and abolished later during the year of the twins' dramatic fall from grace.

Maureen Flanagan's earlier recollection was correct. In 1967, the Krays' arch rival, Charlie Richardson, was jailed for twenty-five years for fraud, extortion and assault. Mr Justice Melford Stevenson, now with even more infamous gangsters in the dock, kept his comments to the point.

'I am not going to waste words on you. In my view, society has earned a rest from your activities. I sentence you to life imprisonment which I recommend should be not less than thirty years.'

Later, in a light-hearted comment, he said that the Krays had only told the truth twice during their trial: Reggie referred to the well-built Crown Prosecutor, later to become Sir Kenneth Jones, as 'a fat slob' and Ronnie accused the judge of being biased.

Ian Barrie was jailed for twenty years; Ronnie Bender

twenty years; the Lambrianou brothers fifteen years each; Charlie Kray ten years; Freddie Foreman ten years; and Cornelius Whitehead seven years.

Professor Hobbs, with an in-depth knowledge of the underworld, analysed the significance of the Kray associates giving evidence for the Crown.

'It was enormously important for the police to have the cooperation of those who ran the Firm. The twins had assumed for many years that they had a real hard core of very loyal people working around them – and that was proved not to be the case.'

Duncan Campbell agreed: 'The fact that the police were persuading people that they would either give evidence, or go down themselves, was crucial. At that particular time it was unthinkable for criminals to give evidence against other gang members, and it was the beginning of the end for the Krays.

'In the 1970s it became established that, if you didn't want to go away for a long time, you could give evidence against your comrades. But before that, and certainly at the time of the Great Train Robbery in 1963, no one gave evidence against anybody else. Breaking that taboo finished the twins.'

Ronnie had had a premonition about Nipper Read pursuing him relentlessly. Well before the Krays' trial he went to Harrods and bought two snakes. Ronnie just walked into the reptile section, had a look at two pythons and said he would have them.

'You are going to be called Nipper and you are Read,' Ronnie is said to have told the snakes.

Other sources close to the snakes suggest that one was called Nipper and the other Gerrard, after a Chief Inspector Fred Gerrard who had been pursuing the twins with equal vigour.

The thought of Nipper and Read or Gerrard, both several feet long and slithering around their cages, put Maureen off visiting Violet. She had to receive assurances that the slippery reptiles would be hidden from sight, under lock and key, before visiting Braithwaite House again.

The conviction proved to be a massive result for Nipper Read and his team. At the same time, police corruption was being exposed. Gangsters found it impossible to operate without the help of bent coppers. The rival Richardson gang had more success than the Krays in gaining allies from inside the ranks of the police. Nonetheless, the Krays had their pet officers, receiving pay-offs for years, and Nipper was breaking through that barrier. Now the corrupt officers had no influence, couldn't drop charges, were unable to turn a blind eye and were forced to watch helplessly as Nipper tightened the noose.

If things had turned out differently the twins could have been killed or seriously wounded.

Confirmation from Freddie Foreman: 'If you throw stones, you're going to get them thrown back. It's people in glass houses, isn't it? I know they would not have lasted very long if the police hadn't stepped in. It was only going to be a matter of months before the pair of them were found on a pavement somewhere. And I mean that.'

Wilf Pine, Ron's former business manager, concurred: 'They would have been killed, you know that already? They had got a little bit too far out of hand. And then we wouldn't be sat here doing this interview.'

Maureen Flanagan had the same opinion: 'I have heard it was the best thing to happen to them. One of the twins, maybe both of them, would have been killed – or they would have killed somebody else.'

Professor Hobbs' recollection was that the general public didn't feel any relief once the Krays had been removed from the streets.

'The Krays didn't live amongst the general public. They lived in an underworld – where other gangsters lived. They inhabited pubs, clubs and casinos. That was their world. The people they operated with, and operated against, were of that world. So the general public didn't feel affected at all.

'People had a fascination for the Krays, which of course has grown over the years. Many members of the general public locally – in and around Bethnal Green – were people who were quite full of praise for the Krays. The twins gave money to charities, helped old people, put money into boxing clubs and gestures like those.

'They were quite astute in generating good public relations with the general public. But the twins lived in a world that was hermetically sealed.'

The crimes that the Krays were found guilty of were not the typical crimes of gangsters. They weren't earning money out of them. It wasn't as if they were profiting from the killings or taking on gangland competitors. They were murdering people who had insulted them. They were targeting people who they didn't like and didn't want around.

'They were quite unnecessary killings,' Professor Hobbs stressed. 'From the people I've spoken to in the years since, it was inevitable that Reg and Ron had to be locked away. The Krays were stepping away from being gangsters and they were turning into something else.'

The twins' sentence of a minimum of thirty years each stunned Violet. She sat, as close as she could get to the dock, head in hands. She wept. She cried and cried. The worst possible thoughts filled her head. The twins were only thirty-five; they would be locked up until they were sixty-five. They would be old-age pensioners. In her lifetime, she would never see them enjoying freedom.

'Charlie got ten years, Maureen,' she gasped, still trying to comprehend a sentence of three decades for her beloved twins.

'I know Vi, but he won't be in there for ten years,' Maureen whispered gently, trying to reassure her. 'You'll have one son out soon.'

Professor Hobbs and other criminologists, analysing the case, believed that the establishment was sending out a message to other would-be gangsters. The state wanted to clamp down once and for all. The Krays were being held up as an example of what would happen to career criminals in the future.

Maureen did feel sorry for the Lambrianou brothers, especially Chris. They were paying for their loyalty in the McVitie case.

'Chris wasn't even in the room when it happened. Tony was, and he paid for that, but then Tony always wanted to be a gangster. He loved being with the twins and the glamour of it all. He loved the violence, he did, with the twins.

'But Chris was a little bit different. He went along for the ride, as they say. To be standing there and know you're going to suffer the same fate as your brother . . . and he did, with those fifteen years. They didn't commit any murder but they did as they were told, as per usual, by Ron and Reg – or they weren't with the Firm.'

Shortly after the trial Ron, Reg and co. were in court again. It concerned the disappearance of Frank Mitchell, who had escaped from prison with a little help from the Krays. Ron and Reg had come across Frank during previous prison sentences. He received his nickname, 'The Mad Axeman', after holding a couple hostage while he held an axe at the same time. Frank became frustrated at not having a date for his release and he wrote to Ron, saying something had to be done.

Frank Mitchell was one of the most powerfully built men to stalk the streets of the East End. He was enormous.

During his time in prison he had received the birch, the dreaded cat o' nine tails and was even placed in a straitjacket.

The Krays had picked up Mitchell after he slipped away from a prison working party on Dartmoor, and in no time he was holed up at a flat in Barking. A nightclub hostess was kidnapped to keep him company and help to keep his moods in check. She feared for her life and even contemplated suicide before eventually being allowed to go.

Mitchell was becoming a liability, and of no use to the Krays during Britain's biggest ever manhunt, so he had to be killed. Was he lured out to a van, where bullets were pumped into him, and then the body weighed down and taken out to sea? Was it another gang, and another location?

How much did the twins pay?

Albert Donoghue, urged by the twins to confess to the killing, refused and he became a crown witness – testifying against the twins. Ron, Reg, Charlie Kray and Freddie Foreman were all found not guilty of Mitchell's murder; there was a lack of evidence and the jury were not sure whether to believe Donoghue.

Reg Kray was found guilty of helping Mitchell to escape from Dartmoor. He received a five-year jail term to run concurrently with his other sentences. Donoghuc and Scotch Jack Dickson were jailed for eighteen and nine months after admitting harbouring Mitchell.

Whatever the truth, Frank Mitchell's body has never been found, and the 'gentle giant' of the underworld will never rest in peace.

The Voice of an Angel

And so the prison years began. The calm, assured voice of an angel had spoken to condemn two devils. As far as the truthful young barmaid was concerned, the Krays had carried out Satan's work and spread evil here, there and everywhere.

Ron and Reg were about to endure what most right-thinking people believed they deserved: the Prison Years.

Chapter 4

A Mother in Despair

Alone in her flat, Violet tossed and turned in the night. All she had left: faint black and white photos, bunches of flowers from Reg and Ron, and contact telephone numbers for prisons throughout the country. Her boys could be moved anywhere at any time.

A flashback in the night. A clear image in Violet's dream took her back to 24 October 1933. Memories of the early family home in Stean Street, Hoxton where the twins were born. A robust cry from Reggie. Ten minutes later, after the sheer agony of extra labour, the appearance of identical Ronnie. A forceful cry from Ronnie, too. Her twins were to make an impact on Hoxton, the East End, the West End – and, indeed, the entire country.

These early years were worrying times for Violet. The twins caught diphtheria when they were three years old. It was a common ailment in those days, and Reg recovered well. However, Ron became quite unwell and doctors were concerned for his welfare. Violet became concerned that the hospital wasn't doing Ron any good, so she took matters into her own hands.

Maureen Flanagan knew the whole story: 'Ron was probably going to die, because it was a very serious illness. He pined for Reg. Ron wasn't getting any better and was actually getting worse with sweats, fever and high temperatures – no matter what the doctors and nurses did for him.

'Violet went to the hospital with her sister, took him out of the bed, wrapped him up and took him back to be with Reg, against doctor's orders. She just told them the twins were very close, and it was what Ron needed. Within seven days, Ron was better – all because he was with Reg. The doctors couldn't believe it.'

Times were hard during the Great Depression. Money was in short supply, decent food was hard to come by, and families went hungry. Those years before and during the war were hard for the Krays and thousands of other families in the East End. Violet was reduced to pawning her jewellery to make sure the family could eat.

Father Charlie was a proud parent too, but proved difficult to pin down. He went 'on the knocker', buying and selling anything he could get his hands on. His chosen role as a 'pesterer' took him to a myriad of locations. He appeared with money from time to time, helping to ease the strain on the pressurised Violet.

Violet's mind, in slumber, drifted to the next family home, 178 Vallance Road in Bethnal Green, a terraced house a short distance from Stean Street. It was a typical two-up-two-down dwelling from the Victorian era. There was an outside toilet; a tin bath also hung outside, and it was the only dedicated cleansing method for the inhabitants.

In 1939, father Charlie had other ideas when the call to arms came. He was supposed to report to the Tower of London, to help in the fight against Nazi Germany, but instead he made himself scarce.

In Violet's dream, mirroring real events, two burly policemen hammered at the wooden door in the early hours of the morning. In they came, searching all the rooms, getting the twins and Charlie junior out of bed while they searched. On this occasion their dad was in the coal cupboard, fortunate that it hadn't been searched thoroughly.

Sometimes, he also hid in the tiny outside toilet. On another day, the police visited while the family were having their tea. Old Charlie hid under the kitchen table, covered by a tablecloth, while Ron and Reg munched away quite happily. Again, the officers left disappointed.

If the Old Bill came too close, Charlie senior did have an escape route. There was a back wall, so he could climb over that. Violet's sisters, Rose and May, lived in the same street, providing options for hiding with the aunties.

Those thoughts merged into images of her twins at war with the Army. They also evaded the troops, going on the run after yet another run-in with authority. Like their father before them, they ended up battling with the men in uniforms. Ron and Reg had told Violet all about their exploits and the people they met during their adventures.

To start with, their future in the armed forces had looked promising. They were called up to the Tower of London to join the Royal Fusiliers. That was in 1952. All fit men between the ages of seventeen and twenty-one had to join up for eighteen months, later extended to two years. After that they remained on the reserve list for four years.

And the twins were fit. Fighting fit. Their idea was to become physical training instructors and take part in boxing tournaments. With Charlie proving his worth in the ring while serving in the Navy, they saw no reason why they couldn't follow in his footsteps.

Their plan went horribly wrong shortly after they arrived, suited and booted, at the Tower. The twins fell out with a corporal who said they would have to do what they were told. No one was guaranteeing positions as physical training instructors.

Their intention of returning to Vallance Road was not a good idea, the corporal announced firmly.

Whack! Ron punched the soldier as hard as he could, and the unfortunate corporal collapsed in a crumpled heap on the floor.

The next morning, as expected, an Army truck arrived in Vallance Road. There was no point in going into hiding, as their father had done; perhaps there was still a chance of becoming physical training instructors? No, the chances of that happening were nil.

'You are charged with being absent without leave and striking the corporal,' the commanding officer snarled when they arrived back at the Tower.

A regular case of mistaken identity prevailed because no one could be sure which twin had punched the corporal. Reg denied it and Ron pleaded innocence, so the only course of action was seven days' detention in the guardroom for the protesting brothers.

The only consolation was a visit from an 'uncle'. It turned out to be Charlie senior. Their dad was still on the run from the Army, but managed to pay them a visit in the guardroom.

After their detention, Ron and Reg slipped away at the earliest opportunity. They spent the next few months ducking and diving in the East End, hiding in friends' houses.

The CO and his men kept searching high and low for the elusive duo until, at last, a breakthrough. A postcard arrived, in the twins' erratic handwriting, addressed to the Royal Fusiliers supremo.

The CO, however, was no closer to snaring the Krays. They had acquired a motor, enjoyed a day out in Southend, and even had the temerity to send a card with the traditional message: 'Wish you were here.'

But there were only so many hiding places in the East End. A police officer, on the beat in the area, recognised

them in a cafe in Mile End Road, and the game was up –
temporarily.

Back into the custody of the Army, then, followed by
several weeks' detention at Colchester Barracks.

After that enforced loss of liberty they disappeared
again, only to be spotted once more by the same vigilant
policeman. Ron's response was a well-aimed jab in the
officer's face. The response from the forces of law and
order was another stretch behind bars, this time in
Wormwood Scrubs.

Into 1953 and the early 'prison years' were far from
over. They were sent to Canterbury Barracks, but found a
ladder and escaped again. Their inevitable recapture was
followed by nine long boring months in the military prison
at Shepton Mallet in Somerset.

The large, soulless, stone building at Shepton Mallet
was an intimidating place. Conditions were harsh and
punishments severe. It was known as the 'glasshouse', a
common term in the Army. The name originally came
from the glazed roof at the military prison in Aldershot.

The brutal history of Shepton Mallet dated back to
1625, when it opened as a House of Correction. One saving
grace for the twins: a large treadwheel, for those sentenced
to hard labour, was no longer in use. The evil contraption
caused hernias, with forty men pounding the boards at the
same time. They were powering a grain mill outside the
prison wall; this punishment was used until 1890.

So many deaths and executions had occurred that

prisoners felt an eeriness about the place. The Americans executed eighteen servicemen there during World War Two; sixteen were hanged and two were shot for murder and rape.

The twins were in good company. They spotted Johnny Nash, one of the Nash brothers from the infamous Islington firm. They owned clubs in the East End, so there was plenty to talk about.

'I think I know who that is over there,' Ron told Reg. 'Do you know who that feller is?'

'I heard he was pushing for a dishonourable discharge as well. One of the fellers says it's Charlie Richardson?'

'It is me,' Charlie grinned, overhearing and striding across the exercise yard. 'I know who you are from the boxing photos.'

'How is business?' Reg asked, knowing that Charlie, still only nineteen, operated scrapyards and had a few business interests on the south side of the Thames. Charlie was clean shaven, well groomed, and sized up the twins with his steely blue eyes.

'Well, I was turning over several grand a week until they tried to get me to sign the Official Secrets Act, and they offered me £1 a week or whatever they pay people. I told them to fuck off a few times. I legged it back home but they caught up with me, and here I am.'

'It's boring here,' Reggie said. 'Fancy a laugh?'

The trio of young rogues looked over at a tank, full of excrement and urine. The prisoners emptied their waste into it every day. The sight and smell of the container was horrific.

Charlie could guess straight away what Reg was suggesting. The two of them picked up the disgusting container and charged at a cell wall. The tank collided with the bars, spilling its unfortunate contents all over several guards, who tore into the pair after the incident. They both agreed that some rough treatment was worth enduring, just to see the look on the guards' faces.

Images from her boys' accounts, then recollections of earlier, happier times, filled Violet's head. Her husband was home for Christmas. Neighbours sang carols in the street, presents were wrapped and the coal fire burned brightly. Violet knew that the presents were only small gifts, like pieces of fruit, but these were luxuries in the thirties and forties.

As she continued to toss and turn, she relived the sound of explosions rocking Vallance Road. The Kray house shook and the penetrating beam of searchlights lit up the night sky. Violet, planning to celebrate the twins' seventh birthdays in October 1940, ran upstairs to the boys' room. Young Charlie was comforting Reg and Ron as the house vibrated violently. Violet grabbed the three children and led them into the street.

To her horror, the railway arch in Vallance Road had become a smouldering ruin. A block of flats crumbled into a pile of rubble. Mothers wept, children screamed, fire crews pulled at the brickwork with their bare hands, and bombs continued to fall. A flash of light illuminated Vallance Road, and then a thunderous explosion lit up in the sky. A German bomber, ablaze, plunged towards the docks. Air raid sirens blared as the searchlights continued to scour overhead. Crowds streamed into an air raid shelter, sweeping along Violet, who was clutching the hands of Reg, Ron and Charlie all at once.

The twins were thrilled to find pieces of shrapnel, bits of bombs and even chunks of metal from aircraft, friend and foe.

'Mum, look at this. Is it worth anything?'

'Mum, look what I've found.'

Inside the shelter, the terrified inhabitants of the Vallance Road area were entertained by performers on a small wooden stage. The main attraction was her own father, 'Cannonball' John Lee. His party trick was to lick a white-hot poker. He used to be safe as long as the poker was white-hot. A red-hot poker would have removed his tongue, Cannonball told onlookers.

Cannonball was also a formidable street fighter. John became known as the Southpaw Cannonball, because of the power in his left hand. He could demolish most opponents with that weapon during the street scraps, as crowds surged forward and illegal bookies were besieged for winnings.

Violet's memories of the war years included vivid scenes of the beautiful Suffolk countryside. In 1940, the bombing in the capital became more intense. During the

Blitz, London was pounded for virtually fifty nights in a row, and so there were mass evacuations to the countryside. The twins and their brother Charlie ended up at Hadleigh in Suffolk. They stayed at East House Lodge, with a Mrs Styles, and even attended a local school.

Living an almost parallel life, Charlie Richardson was also moved to safety with brother Eddie. He wrote: 'During the Blitz, when the bombing became intensive night after night, the Evacuation Scheme kicked in. It was called Operation Pied Piper or something like that. I was reluctant to follow any bloody piper, or anyone for that matter, out of Camberwell. However, I had no choice. Mum told me that, when Eddie and I were sent off to the countryside, she cried for days.

'All became clear in deepest Dorset. I saw a sign for Piddletrenthide, then another for Piddlehinton. We drove alongside the River Piddle, and I saw signs with more piddling variations. Eddie and I had a good laugh, and then settled back down for the journey as we tried to imagine what lay in store. There was some light relief from all the piddling jokes when Puddletown came into view. The bus driver, though, said it used to be called Piddletown. To keep the theme going, our bus skirted Piddles Wood on its journey.'

Violet remembered her own three boys sledging down a slope in Suffolk called Constitution Hill. Violet, Charlie, Reg and Ron adored the tranquillity of the place. It was so quiet, with pure air filling their lungs and the unspoilt countryside providing a feast for their eyes.

The twins went apple scrumping, nicking piles of fruit from orchards, and their favourite game was cowboys and Indians. There was a foretaste of what was to come in the real world when Ron shot one of his new young pals in the eye with a slug gun. On that occasion, unlike the Cornell debacle, it was an accident.

After a couple of years, when the bombing eased in the city, Violet and her young family headed back to Vallance Road. The downside of their absence was that they really missed Aunt May, Aunt Rose and everyone else in the family. Plus, of course, they were worried sick about what the continual bombing was doing to their neighbourhood back home.

The return meant more humane man-to-man combat . . . in the boxing ring. Boxing ran in the family. Cannonball taught young Charlie a few tricks, and set up a makeshift gym in an upstairs bedroom. He soon had Ron and Reg sitting on his knees, telling them about the great boxers from the East End. In the back yard, Cannonball used to punch a mattress over a clothes line, even as an old man. In the Navy, Charlie junior became a welterweight champion and took his young brothers to a local gym.

Violet woke up and cried. Now young Charlie was in prison, too, after the nightmare of the Old Bailey.

Still half asleep and sifting through pairs of old boxing gloves, Violet found the programme from a unique event at the Royal Albert Hall. All three of her sons fought that evening on 11 December 1951. Charlie Kray took on Lew

Lazar, Reg was up against Bobby Manito and Ron challenged Bill Sliney.

Reggie won, Charlie lost and Ronnie fell foul of the referee. He was disqualified for using his head.

So many memories for Violet, and yet the foreboding prison walls tainted everything. She imagined cell doors slamming shut; a single lightbulb glowing without the comfort of a shade. She shivered in the night as she envisaged heavy boots marching along corridors and strong, muscly arms pummelling her boys into submission. A blur of images cascaded through her waking dream, from the arrest, through the court case, to her current desperate existence.

Professor Dick Hobbs saw Violet, in many ways, as a typical East End matriarch.

'She was the boss, she was the guv'nor and they were her boys. And she ran the family because dad Charlie wasn't around much, so it was important for Violet to fill that gap. And the other person who was important was another very strong woman – Violet's sister, Aunt Rose. She lived just adjacent to the twins in Vallance Road and had a big influence on them as well.

'Rose seemed to have an understanding of the twins, and she was the one who suggested that, one day, Ron would hang.

'But that made no difference at all. People talked like that in those days. And they would say that sort of thing: "One day you'll hang, one day you'll go to prison, I'll call a policeman if you . . ." These were normal comments made in the East End at the time. It was just part of the background.'

Maureen Flanagan became friendly with Violet after meeting in a hairdressing salon. Maureen attended to clients at home, but her first introduction came at a salon in Bethnal Green.

In her book, *One of the Family: 40 Years with the Krays*, Maureen says Violet was a round, fair, good-looking woman of about fifty when she first met her. The hairdresser had been primed that the mother of the Kray twins was looking for someone to go round for home appointments.

'Violet Kray looked up at me with a friendly smile that made me feel instantly at ease. You could tell what type of woman she was. I'd been in the hairdressing business long enough to spot the Moaners and the Complainers straight away. Usually they were around Violet's age, discontented with their lot in life, endlessly reminding us youngsters what they'd lived through in the Second World War, sometimes widowed early or abandoned.

'Violet definitely wasn't a moaner. She oozed kindness. She had quite thick spun-gold hair, light blue eyes and a handsome face. Quite immaculate in her floral print dress and cardi, a thin gold chain around her neck, a small diamond ring on her right hand. There was something about this woman. Perhaps my instinct told me that she was a woman who loved her kids and lived for her family.

Just like my dear mother. In fact, Violet reminded me a lot of her.'

Maureen had heard about Ronnie and Reggie. She grew up in Islington, North London – and wasn't an East End girl. Maureen had no concerns about the Krays' reputation for street fights, protection rackets and the like. She had married into a family with a similar reputation.

The deeds of Violet's sons, though, made it difficult for the mum to go out. She was asked non-stop about how they were getting on. Some people who were in a spot of bother even asked Violet if the twins could sort out their problem!

Violet had a hard time at the hands of her husband, Charlie senior. He gave her 'a few wallops'. However, the father was caught out one day when he had Violet pinned against the wall. The reason was pathetic; he was going to have to wait for his dinner to warm up.

Charlie senior had no idea that Ron was upstairs, listening. The infuriated twin ran downstairs as the old man set about Violet, delivering punishing blows.

Ron pulled Charlie senior away, grabbed him by the scruff of the neck and warned: 'If you ever touch our mother again, I'll kill you.'

Violet defended her husband to the hilt. She said he was a good worker, provided for the family and made sure there was food on the table.

She revealed to Maureen that she had lost a baby girl during pregnancy. It happened when young Charlie was about four and she was six months pregnant. She had had a little girl. One afternoon, she was upstairs on her own when she had the miscarriage. The baby only lived for a couple of hours. Violet opened up even more after Maureen said that she had also miscarried after about six weeks of pregnancy. Together they consoled each other.

Maureen listened, sad beyond words, as Violet – full of emotion – described how the baby was so beautiful with big dark eyes and dark hair. Her dreadful experience explained why the twins, when very young, were dressed more like girls. They looked feminine, like little dolls in their pram. Violet still longed for her baby girl and was showering her love onto the twins – as if they were taking the place of the child she had lost.

The first time Maureen met the twins' brother, Charlie, he said she should become a model. All she wanted to do at that time was hairdressing, and Violet enjoyed having Maureen round for a 'hairdo' after that first meeting in the salon.

'At that time we were all like Twiggy and really skinny. I had long blonde hair. Charlie was handsome, tall and blond. He reminded me of Burt Lancaster. Charlie was friendly and warm and said I should give up being a hairdresser. He was the first person who put that into my mind. Before he said that, all I thought about was hairdressing. I told him I might try modelling later on.'

Maureen continued to go round to Vallance Road fairly regularly, without meeting the twins. Then, one evening at about six o'clock, in came Ronnie. She had no idea who he was. He came in on his own, very sombre and with staring eyes.

'I noticed apart from those eyes that he had beautiful, nicely manicured hands. He was also immaculately dressed with a navy blue suit and matching shirt and tie. Violet poured out her love and affection as soon as he walked in the door.'

Two weeks later, Maureen was doing Violet's hair, when in walked a familiar-looking person.

'Oh, hello again, Ronnie.'

'That's not Ronnie, that's Reggie,' Violet laughed with her head still in a lather in the kitchen sink.

Maureen told Violet not to be silly, because she had talked to Ronnie a few times during the hairdressing appointments. But it was, in fact, Reggie.

Reg was a touch more handsome, slightly on the slimmer side, but with the same facial features and mannerisms. 'Violet, how do you tell them apart? How can anyone tell them apart?'

In the early years, the only difference was a mole on Ron's neck. Maureen wasn't the only one who had trouble identifying them. The twins started to play tricks because of their identical appearance. If Reg got into trouble at school, he would say he was Ron, and had no idea where Reg was. Ron did the same, leaving the teachers in a state of confusion about who was who.

Violet, whether in slumber or wide awake, could always

tell her sons apart. In her eyes, they could do no wrong. Inside the house they were perfect gentlemen, and on the outside they wouldn't even swear in front of a woman.

She had happy days with them, proud days with her boys, but in the end her world collapsed.

'How could they murder anybody? Who would they have to murder? Ronnie had his dark moods. He'd have a fight and it would be all over. But Ronnie and Reggie would never murder anybody.'

Violet repeated those words again and again. The devastated mum could never comprehend the magnitude of the twins' crimes. She could never accept what had happened. They were still her innocent little boys and she worshipped them. She could never, ever, face up to the truth.

Violet was a mother in despair.

Chapter 5

The Krays Behind Bars

One ex-hitman who served time with Reggie Kray in several prisons knew exactly how Reggie felt with decades of 'bird' in front of him.

'When you're first given it, it's just numbers. And it don't hit you the first night – you're just banged up. Then, as time goes by, you think . . . you've got this for ten years, fifteen years . . . thirty years. You end up in a concrete tomb.'

Considered memories from Chris Lambrianou: 'After you're sentenced, you're looking at maybe fifteen years. You're not looking at a remand in custody for two weeks. You're looking at endless years, and you can't even begin to see the end of it. If you have an indeterminate sentence they won't take into account the time you spent on remand. Your sentence is forever.

'And then you think: where do my loyalties lie? What am I going to say to my daughter when she comes of age? Will I even know her? Will she know me? What am I going to say to my wife? What am I going to say to my family? You're totally cast adrift on a sea of emptiness and maybe you're never going to reach your final destination.

'And you don't think about a final destination. You think about one day at a time in a very dangerous world where life has no value. It's a world of nothing. It's a world of lies and deceit and deception. It's a world of heartbreak, of children without a father. It's a wife without a husband. It's a mother with a son in jail.'

The twins were kept as far apart as possible; in fact, they could hardly have been further apart. Ronnie was sent north to Durham Prison along with key members of the Firm. Reggie was destined for Parkhurst: a grim, foreboding place on the Isle of Wight where, for many, all hope was lost. Charlie Kray went to Chelmsford, and Freddie Foreman ended up at Leicester.

Reggie was taken from court to Brixton and prepared for the high security trip to Parkhurst. The police Jaguar ticked over in the prison yard, while the handcuffed Reg was led to the waiting motor. He resisted an attempt to put a blanket over his head and preferred to sit normally, in view of everyone. A convoy headed out of London, lights flashing and sirens wailing front and back. Reggie could never have imagined what lay in front of him.

The graceful Jag lurched aboard a ramp and into the hold of a ferry at Southampton. After an hour's ride atop the choppy waters of the Solent, Reg prepared himself for his new home. He was used to the crowded, smoky streets of East London; ahead lay a barbaric fortress on a pretty island. The Isle of Wight was a magnet for tourists; Parkhurst was the last place they would want to see.

No escape. No hope. No future. Hell on an island. A dark, evil place where killers lurked in the shadows. A stinking cesspit where all hope was sucked from the body.

Reg had been told all about 'Britain's Alcatraz'. Ex-inmates said Parkhurst resembled a gruesome vision in a bad dream; it represented the darkest of dark nightmares to anyone setting foot on the Isle of Wight. He knew that this ugly blot on the landscape would be laced with menace.

As he peeked through the car's side windows, Reg was enveloped with a feeling of hopelessness. This place was the gloomiest sight he had ever come across. As the vehicles passed through an enormous wooden gate, set in a featureless concrete block, he feared the worst.

The building reeked of a cruel history. Parkhurst began life in 1778 as a military hospital and children's asylum. It became a prison for children in 1838. Boys as young as nine, awaiting deportation to Australia, were kept in leg irons. Their offences included stealing handkerchiefs and thimbles. To prepare them for a new life they were trained in trades such as carpentry, iron and stonework.

Around 1,500 boys were sent to Australia, New Zealand, Tasmania and Norfolk Island in the Pacific. They spent five months at sea aboard ships such as *Simon Taylor*, *Shepherd* and *Cumberland*. The 431-ton *Simon Taylor*, for example, was a barque (a sailing ship with three or more masts) under the command of master Thomas Brown. Distraught parents, struggling to survive, had to wave farewell to young children who stole to feed the family.

Parliament was kept informed about the conditions on convict ships, moored in the River Medina and sailing from the Isle of Wight: 'When hatchways were opened under which people were stowed the steam rose and the stench was like that from a pen of pigs. The few beds they had were in a dreadful state, for the straw, once wet from the sea water, soon rotted.'

Reggie's predecessors at Parkhurst had committed minor offences to help their family survive. One, John Lynch, stole toys and sold them for 2d. He was well behaved in prison, and only ticked off for laughing in the chapel. At the age of nine, he was transported to Australia in 1844.

The need for labour in Western Australia meant that the boys were quickly put to work, many as farm labourers. In New Zealand, the boys received a grim welcome; settlers were trying to make ends meet with few jobs and a dire economy. Many of the young newcomers were befriended by the Maori and established their roots in that indigenous community. New Zealand's justice system was far from appealing. Two local children, six and eight, were whipped for theft. Some of the Parkhurst boys found ways of moving to Australia or Tahiti.

In 1847, more building work was carried out at Parkhurst by the prisoners themselves. They dug the clay and baked the bricks. In 1863, Parkhurst became a female prison. Six years later it was converted to a male prison, and stayed that way.

Reggie could have been sent to Albany, a short distance away. It was a high-tech prison, much more modern and nothing like the antiquated buildings of Parkhurst. Albany was a rectangular building, giving the impression that it consisted of offices. The truth was that, inside, inmates were surrounded by barbed wire, cameras and formidable fences. The cell doors were not opened by warders with keys; a control room opened them remotely, and the prisoner even had an intercom on his cell wall to say if he needed to go to the toilet.

The British Army used Albany Barracks until 1960, with mainly infantry regiments based there. Albany was a Category 'C' training prison, on the same site, in the early sixties. Shortly afterwards the prison was upgraded to Category 'B' and became part of the dispersal system in the 1970s. Albany was closed for more than a year after major disturbances in 1972.

Category 'A' prisoners like Reg moved around from time to time under the dispersal system. This was developed after the Mountbatten Inquiry when offenders were categorised from 'A', the most dangerous, to 'D', the least dangerous. Lord Mountbatten was asked to conduct the inquiry into prison security after George Blake's escape from Wormwood Scrubs on 22 October 1966.

Blake was a British spy who also worked as a double agent

for the Soviet Union. He managed to flee to the USSR, causing consternation that such a high-profile prisoner should have been able to make a successful bid for freedom. Mountbatten, in addition to categorising prisoners, recommended tough new security measures in jails as well as dog patrols, CCTV and a host of other measures. Parkhurst, Leicester, Chelmsford and Durham had, in effect, prisons within prisons to nullify any chance of escape.

Also on the Isle of Wight at the time of Reg's arrival: HMP Camp Hill. This jail was built in 1912 by prisoners from Parkhurst. The opening ceremony was performed by Winston Churchill. Camp Hill was a lower security Category 'C' prison where training was carried out and prisoners learned trades such as welding, painting and decorating.

Reggie, still thinking about the bleak, sinister shape of Parkhurst on a holiday island, was strip searched and taken for a supervised shower.

To start with, he was detained in the Special Security Block along with people like the Great Train Robbers and Eddie Richardson, brother of Charlie. The Great Train Robbers stole £2.6 million from a Royal Mail train travelling between Glasgow and London on 8 August 1963. The unit opened in 1966 and catered for the highest possible security rating; IRA prisoners received that status.

Each prisoner had a table, a bed, a chair and a corner area to keep cutlery, teapot and crockery. The window was heavily barred. There was still a 'peep hole' to ensure that warders could check on prisoners.

The recreation area boasted a pool table and dartboard. The exercise yards were constantly scanned by cameras. The walls of the yards were white, making sure that anyone trying to get out would show up.

Reg described Parkhurst as a living hell, like living in a jungle, with a constant battle for sanity and survival.

In 1969, Frankie Fraser organised the riots at Parkhurst while Reg was encased in the Special Security Block. Frank claimed that prisoners were beaten up while in segregation and arranged a sit-down protest. Prison officers overwhelmed the protesters and there was a violent confrontation.

Frankie was constantly in and out of prison. He first appeared in court at the age of thirteen for stealing 40 cigarettes. That led to a spell in an approved school. In later life, he specialised in smash-and-grab raids and wages snatches. By 1956, with fifteen convictions to his name, he had been certified insane on two occasions. Frankie was also jailed for seven years after cutting gangster Jack Spot on the orders of Billy Hill.

And he had a reputation as an amateur dentist, pulling out rivals' teeth with pliers, which he always denied. His brutal actions for the Richardson gang earned him a ten-year sentence in 1967 at the so-called torture trial. He was moved between various prisons more than 100 times because of his rebellious behaviour.

Frankie spent six weeks in hospital recovering from his injuries after the Parkhurst riots. He was given an extra five years for his role in the disturbance, as he described shortly before his death to *The Prison Years* researchers.

'I liked it when I led the riot at Parkhurst and this prison officer said I cut one of his ears off. They said they couldn't find it. Well, of course they couldn't. I said I put it down the toilet and flushed the chain. It's floating somewhere off the Isle of Wight. And for the rest of his career he was known as "Ear Ear" Harry.

'Anyway I was serving fifteen years already. The judge asked if I had anything to say. I said, "Yes, my lord, I realise you have to increase my sentence, but could you please make it up into even numbers as I hate odd numbers." He had a smile on his face so I thought . . . ooh I've cracked it here. He'll only give me a year and make it sixteen, or add three and make it eighteen.'

Frankie quoted the judge: 'I am taking into consideration your dislike of odd numbers. I will have to increase your sentence, but I will make it up into even numbers.'

A short-lived grin from Frankie, who thought he might have got one over on the judge.

'I will give you another five years, to run consecutively, so that will make it twenty years in even numbers.'

'You dirty . . .' Frankie yelled out, losing any hope of remission with his outburst.

While all of this was going on, Reg, in the tightest possible security and kept well away from the protests, was suffering from a chronic and painful ear infection.

In March 1970, after the Parkhurst riots, there was a

general reorganisation and Reg was moved to Leicester Prison.

HMP Leicester looks like a medieval fortress. That was the idea; the county surveyor in the early 1800s had a budget of £20,000 – a fortune in those days – and a brief to design a daunting building, resembling a castle.

It's about half a mile from the city centre in a residential and commercial district. The oldest part is the Gatehouse, dating back to 1825, with more building work taking place in 1874. The new visiting and administration block was added in 1990 beside the Gatehouse.

There was an old Borough Jail in Leicester, dating back to around 1297. Through the centuries prisoners endured intolerable conditions there, with one stating on record that it was 'Hell upon Earth'.

The only positive entry in a history of repression appears to be the fate of a thief, Matthew, who came from the village of Enderby, to the south west of Leicester. He was hanged and taken to a local graveyard, all ready for burial. But it seemed the hangman had failed with his rope work. Matthew lay perfectly still beside his intended burial plot, then suddenly spluttered back to life. Researchers assume he was allowed to complete his sentence without another abortive attempt on the gallows . . .

Reg discovered that Leicester had a smaller security block than Parkhurst, with fewer cells and inmates. The prisoners shared a kitchen, made from a small cell.

Exercise took place in a concrete yard. There was so much conflict with constant disputes. Reg had a violent fight with an armed robber called Pete Hurley over a doughnut.

In February 1971, Reg was transferred back to Parkhurst, although he knew he could be shifted anywhere in the country at short notice.

Ronnie Kray, meanwhile, arrived at a jail with a barbaric past. Even his brutal crimes could not rival what had happened within the cold, unforgiving walls of HMP Durham. The prison was built in 1810 and comprised 600 grim cells. Miner William Jobling was executed in 1832 for the murder of a local magistrate. The thirty-year-old was hanged, dipped in tar, placed in a steel cage and put on public display. Unlike Ronnie, it now appears that the unfortunate William was innocent after all.

That atmosphere of a dark past and a bleak present haunted Ronnie. He detested the Victorian surroundings and wanted out as soon as possible. The only friend, the only person he could talk to, the only hope for the future, was a senior prison officer called Bunker.

Ronnie made it known that, shortly after he arrived there, he was beaten up by prison officers. He said they wound him up until he retaliated, then steamed in with fierce kicks aimed at his body.

Punishment meant lengthy spells in the punishment block, with up to twenty-three hours a day of solitary confinement, and a single light glowing in his cell. Ron hated that light; he hated the cell; he hated the rock-hard bed; he hated his dreams; he hated his nightmares; and he really hated Durham.

All he had to look forward to was an hour of exercise in those twenty-four hours, walking round a small yard. That was his lot. That was his life.

After his punishment Ron returned to the normal high security prison system, when he said he was wound up, taken to the solitary block and back out again.

According to Ron, the senior prison officer, Bunker, caught sight of a good hiding being handed out. He intervened and called a halt to the kicking and punching. The beatings stopped. Bunker kept watch over Ron and some normality returned to his life.

'I've done some bad things, and now some really bad things are happening to me,' he used to tell visitors. 'They're laying into me too much. They don't need to do all of this.'

Ronnie could hardly believe the difference between Durham and other prisons he had stayed in during his criminal career. For example, he had spent time at Camp Hill in 1957. He'd been transferred from Wandsworth after being found guilty of a serious assault. Durham was a different environment; some days he felt that he had entered the gates of Hell.

Chris Lambrianou's recollection of Durham: 'They thought we were so dangerous we could get hold of a Chieftain tank to go through the wall and get us out, so we were confined to a wing with about ten cells. I remember being with Ronnie Kray, Bruce Reynolds, the Great Train Robber, my brother Tony and Ronnie Bender. That's how it was for six or seven months. If you went on exercise you were kept in a cage. They felt that was the only way they could control us.

'I just felt ordinary. What did I have to prove to Ronnie Kray or anybody? I didn't feel dangerous. On the outside I would be somebody who went to the shop to buy a packet of cigarettes, or bread or milk. I didn't feel dangerous at all.'

Violet could see that Ron was suffering, mentally and physically, from his ordeal at Durham. She started a campaign for Ron to move to Parkhurst, a more regular location for Reggie. The beleaguered mother wrote to the Home Office, her MP, the press and anyone she thought might be able to help. Ron eventually arrived in Parkhurst, meeting up with his twin early in 1971 after Reg's stint at Leicester.

All of the moving around was complicated for visitors. Maureen Flanagan recalled that Violet had to travel all over the country to see her boys.

'They kept being moved to different prisons. She went up north, she went to Parkhurst, Chelmsford and Lewes and other places, too. Sometimes she got a lift and other times she went by train.'

Ron attacked another inmate, Bernie Beattie, in the Parkhurst Special Security Block. Ron hit Bernie over the head with a bottle, and was moved from the SSB to the hospital for more tests.

Twice a week, Reg visited Ron in the prison hospital. Violet and the elusive father Charlie senior also travelled to see how Ron was getting on. But how would Ron react if he was sent back to the SSB?

More fireworks. Ron did arrive back in the 'prison within a prison', although not without incident. He struck a prison officer and received fifty-six days' solitary confinement.

Later, Reg and Ron were moved to 'C' wing, the newly opened psychiatric unit. Some of the country's worst psychopaths were kept there, many of them sex offenders. Heavy medication was the order of the day.

Reg was prescribed Librium and Stelazine to help with anxiety and depression. His medical log from the seventies stated: 'Over the past three or four months he has become increasingly depressed and anxious. He is obviously under some stress from his brother who has become infatuated with another prisoner and behaving in a very demanding manner, making intolerable demands.

'Admitted to hospital for observation. Librium 10mgs tds [meaning three times a day]. He was anxious to come into hospital and, since his arrival, I have noticed a remarkable change in his attitude. He seems relaxed and less depressed.'

There were various ups and downs; one report stated that Reg 'cannot stand people around him'; another assessment reported 'no evidence of paranoid ideas'. Also, to add to the variety, it was recorded that Reg proved to be a good influence on Ron. In 1977, Reg appeared to be depressed again, with Ron in a dominating role.

Ronnie hated the conditions at Parkhurst. It had taken Violet years to get them back into one jail together. And, of course, they then bickered and argued all the time.

Wilf Pine explained: 'Their relationship was horrendous, if I'm gonna be honest. Together they would die for each other, but they used to get into the most violent fights with each other, one trying to impose his will, and the other one trying to impose his. And it was unbelievable. But if anybody got in there to try and separate them, they'd turn on them, you know, it's as simple as that. It was always a volatile relationship. But they loved each other. That's just how it was.'

The Krays had a tough time on the Isle of Wight as Pine outlined: 'Because it was the twins there were always a few people who were a bit lively, and who fancied themselves. And they were doing a lot of damage.'

One man with a unique insight into the Krays' prison years is Norman Parker, who spent time with the twins at Parkhurst. Norman went on to write *The Parkhurst Tales*, based on his true experiences on the Isle of Wight.

Norman served six years for manslaughter after reacting because he thought he was going to be shot by his Nazi girlfriend. He pleaded self-defence. Then he argued with a violent robber and killed him. Norman was convicted of murder at the age of twenty-four and served nearly a quarter of a century behind bars.

He went through 'a particularly troublesome phase' and was moved around from prison to prison. After becoming involved in riots, escape attempts and acts of violence, he was thrown out of Wormwood Scrubs and ended up at Parkhurst with Ron and Reg. He said that, to serve long sentences, prisoners needed amazing strength, determination and tenacity. Parkhurst was a test for even the strongest of personalities.

When Norman arrived the twins were in 'C' wing, the special psychiatric unit.

'Nowhere in the prison system was there such a concentration of violent men, and that made for a very heavy atmosphere. The same twelve mentally disordered prisoners would see each other every day and they would see the same warders.'

Ronnie and Reggie complained long and hard that they couldn't have a sensible conversation with anyone in the unit. Dr Cooper, the head of psychiatric services who ran 'C' wing, tried to give the twins some leeway. The only way they could mix with other prisoners would be to join in an activity, such as an event on the sports field. Norman knew everything that was going on.

'Reggie said to Dr Cooper that they could then meet London "Faces" – or well-known criminals from their area. Reg asked if they could be let out onto the sports field once a week, and that's how I actually met the twins.'

The meetings on the sports field lasted a couple of hours, featuring all the latest news and how everyone saw the present prison system. More and more people were attracted to the field including Eddie Richardson, brother of Charlie and one-time rival of the Krays on the outside.

'I spoke mostly to Ron, because he was quite a fascinating man really. But you wouldn't find out too much from Ronnie and Reggie themselves – although you would from their Firm. There were certain things they did that weren't proper . . . they took liberties.

'A lot of people didn't like what was done to Frank Mitchell. Jack "The Hat" was a violent man, and when he got killed people said it went with the territory. George Cornell was another very violent man, and again it went with the territory.

'But a lot of people thought the murder of Frank Mitchell was a liberty. Frank was "The Hulk" before he was invented. This was a massive guy, slightly childish and always fighting with the warders. When the warders jumped on you, they did it seven- or eight-handed. You stood no chance. But Frank would shake them off like a dog shaking rats off. And if a warder was having a go at another prisoner, he would join in to help.

'Ronnie and Reggie got Frank out of Dartmoor to put pressure on the Home Office because he was doing a life sentence and he hadn't killed anyone.'

But later, Norman said, Mitchell supposedly made threats against the Krays' family, and they killed him like a dog.

'He went to get in the back of a van and he was shot in

the back of the head. By all accounts, a phone call was made that the dog was dead.'

Norman additionally accused the twins of robbing their own people – a big no-no in the underworld. If Ronnie and Reggie heard that a lorry had been hi-jacked or something else taken, they would get hold of the people, torture them and take the money or goods.

'So they took some liberties. Now nobody would say anything to Ron or Reg about it, for obvious reasons – but they would say it to people in the Firm, because some were no more than hangers-on. The Firm were always ready to tell you little rumours . . . this, that and the other . . . so that's why I knew so much about the twins.'

Norman recalled that Ronnie was the most polite man anyone could hope to meet. Ronnie believed in politeness, and he insisted that a man had a duty to behave in a certain way.

'He talked in a little bit of a high voice: "Hello boy, how are you, how's your mum, if you need anything, let us know and me and Reg will get it for you . . ." You'd look at this man, and you'd know that, behind that very polite facade, was a very violent guy.

'If someone upset Ron he would just go over to Reg and say a c*** had said something, and they couldn't have that. So Ron would be the dominating force, saying action had to be taken, and the two of them would sort it out.'

When the twins spent time in the Special Security Block at Parkhurst, the inmates included IRA terrorists and child killers. No one spoke to the child killers. And there were people who were just very violent, like Ron and Reg.

'When you got Reggie on his own he was pretty much like all the rest of the London criminals – very much down to earth, without the heavy duty mental illness that was so obvious in Ronnie.'

Norman started to get to know the twins well; he could spot their strengths and weaknesses. Ronnie confided to him that he had been doing some painting. He offered to give one of his works of art to Norman. The recipient knew it would be prudent to make a kind comment, whatever the state of the artwork. There was no way he would want to upset Ron. He decided to be constructive, not critical, when Ron appeared with his painting on the sports field.

Norman remembered what could happen if Ron took offence. In one of their West End clubs a punter exchanged pleasantries with Ron – but the clubber overstepped the mark. The conversation went like this:

'Hello, George, how are you?'

'I'm OK, Ron. You're putting on a bit of weight, mate.'

'Reg, that slag, you know what he said? We can't have him taking the piss. We've got to do something about it.'

Ron and Reg gradually emptied the club. The unsuspecting visitor was standing at the bar having a drink. Members of the Firm grabbed him and Ronnie produced a cutthroat razor. As deliberately as a surgeon would hold a scalpel, Ron sliced him down both cheeks. Afterwards, the victim was called 'Tramlines' because the wound had been inflicted so exactly. With this in mind, Norman vowed to be careful in his assessment of the picture, brought to the sports field by Ron.

Ron arrived on the field clutching his pride and joy; it looked like the work of a three-year-old. The painting itself was about a foot tall by six inches wide, showing little square houses with yellow lit windows and red roofs. Norman was so surprised that he decided not to say anything. He had to bear in mind that Ronnie had a serious mental illness, and could react in an ugly fashion, as in the 'tramlines' incident.

In many ways, Norman realised that Reggie was a victim of Ronnie. The mentally ill twin would kick things off, dragging Reggie in. Dr Cooper tried to keep them together as long as he possibly could, but even he had to concede to the inevitable.

Dr Cooper knew it. The warders knew it. Fellow cons knew it. Reggie knew it. Ronnie Kray was insane.

Norman described how the twins reacted when they felt threatened in any way.

'One day, a new prisoner was brought on the wing called Roy Grantham. He was a thug from Liverpool – pure and simple. Grantham was doing ten years, and then he showered a warder with porridge and got more time on top. Later, he hit a Scotsman with a hammer, and they put him in a high security wing.'

Norman recalled: 'Ronnie was a very proper person who believes a man has certain duties. So he collected some biscuits, jam, sugar and tobacco and got the warder to open Grantham's door. "Here you are, mate – some goodies for you." So that was the gesture from Ron.'

Norman said Grantham was extremely grateful. Ronnie continued his acts of kindness by chatting through the new arrival's cell door. This happened every day for three or four weeks, helping Grantham through the numbing isolation of solitary confinement.

Then Ronnie felt depressed and lay in his cell with the light out for three days, wanting to be left alone. The warders wouldn't go near him. The only ones he allowed in were Reggie and another prisoner, Joe Martin. So the last thing he wanted was Grantham making any unwelcome appearance. However, the Liverpudlian thought that, with solitary over, he could mix with whoever he liked. To avoid any misunderstandings, Ronnie wrote a polite note, saying he would be obliged if he could have some peace. Ron left the note on Grantham's table and thought that was the end of the matter.

Norman takes up the story: 'Ronnie and Reg were sitting there having a cup of tea and suddenly the cell door flew open. It was Grantham, who said they were c***s, he didn't want to fucking speak to them anyway, and they could stick their note. He threw the paper at Ronnie and stormed out. He didn't realise it, but he'd just made a very serious mistake.

'The following morning Grantham was lying in bed, because he didn't get up for breakfast. The only weapons Reggie and Ronnie could find were two tomato sauce bottles. So they emptied the sauce out, wrapped the bottles in a towel and broke them. That left the bottle tops with very jagged shards.

'Suddenly the door crashed open. It was Ronnie. He sat on Grantham's chest and started slashing away at his face with the broken glass. Reggie, right behind him, sat on the guy's legs and started slashing at his stomach. A hanger-on called Neil appeared. He came running in with a sort of spear. He had a broomstick with a bit of glass taped to the end. While Reggie and Ronnie were slashing away, Neil was stabbing and stabbing with the spear.'

Startled prisoners tried to find out what was going on. Screams and shouts filled the air. Joe Martin ran in, and he could see that all three had completely 'lost it'. Ronnie was acting like a raving lunatic, as Norman recalled.

'Joe grabbed hold of Neil and threw him bodily out the cell, then got hold of Reg. Joe told him that Ronnie was going to kill Grantham. They got hold of Ronnie and calmed him down. Grantham looked like butcher's meat but the wounds were superficial because it was broken bottles and not knives.'

It has to be said that Reg had a particularly dim view of Grantham, who had the reputation of being a bully and troublemaker. Reg told his friends that Grantham would follow him to the toilet, looking over the door and talking a load of rubbish while ablutions were underway. On several occasions Reg complained because Grantham, who had appeared from Gartree, went into his cell and took food off his plate.

Grantham used other tormenting techniques to wind Reg up; the pest fancied himself as a hard man, boasting more than six feet of muscle. He could be seen shadow boxing everywhere with a towel over his head.

He wasn't the only one to go posing around the cells, throwing imaginary punches. Bill the Bomb, a former professional boxer, looked like a gorilla. He said he was taken to America by promoter Angelo Dundee, and claimed he sparred with Muhammad Ali. Bill the Bomb got involved with drugs, and built up quite a criminal record with violence and serious driving offences.

Bill the Bomb was controlled, though, compared to Grantham.

Reg told friends that, one morning, Grantham burst into his cell, waving a knife around. He was saying that Reg had insulted him by taking his name in vain. Reg picked his exact moment, using all of his boxing experience, landing a fierce punch and knocking Grantham out. Reg earned fifty-six days' punishment for thumping Grantham. The newcomer's problems were many and varied; eventually he committed suicide.

Ronnie made it known that he was fed up of all the aggravation at Parkhurst. Despite a promising start, meeting old friends, he desperately wanted out.

One of Ron's main complaints involved the death of a fellow con's mother, who died from cancer. Reg and Ron were always looking after old girls and mums, so Ron decided to send a wreath to the funeral of his friend's mother. He stated his intentions on the usual application form, but said he was stunned to receive the reply: permission refused.

Ron marched up to the governor's office and demanded to be seen. After calling the governor a 'fucking c***', Ron was taken to the chokey, the inmates' name for the punishment cells.

At Parkhurst the chokey was attached to 'B' wing. There were twenty cells with a slops sink, shower and a toilet. Ron spent several weeks in solitary, after a series of assaults. There were about twenty attacks on a cross-section of prison personnel, including a charge of GBH. He would hit anyone through frustration, and even gave his cell a good going over.

With Ron in unpredictable form, they sometimes locked him in a room called the strongbox. It was a small, dark, claustrophobic place made entirely from concrete. A stone slab, covered by a blanket, comprised the sleeping accommodation. He spent twenty-three hours a day in there, with occasional exercise in a small pen. The warders watched him like a hawk all the time.

And yet, in the middle of this hellhole, compassion found a niche. It came from Dr Cooper, whose work and treatment of Ron was admired by other prisoners.

Dr Cooper was concerned about Ron's long, long days with no company in his tiny cell. So he gave him a radio, which thrilled Ron no end. He could listen to favourite singers such as Judy Garland who'd performed at his clubs – and he could keep a track of the news on the outside.

It wasn't the first time Ron's mental problems had been identified. As far back as 1958, alarm bells had rung. That year, he had been jailed on a charge of grievous bodily harm. Ron became depressed and paranoid and was taken to the psychiatric wing of Winchester Prison to be checked over. The conclusion? Ron was insane. After that, a visit to Long Grove mental hospital in Surrey, where he thought that one of the other patients was a dog.

While at Long Grove, Ron was worried that he would never be a free man, so he hatched a plan that relied on misidentification. Reg went along for a visit to Long Grove and announced that he needed to go to the toilet. A short while later Ron said that he wanted to pay a visit, too. Inside the cubicle, Reg put on Ron's pyjamas and Ron donned Reg's smart clothes. It worked a treat. Ron pretended to be the visitor and, when the time came to go, he simply walked out to freedom.

Half an hour later, Reg went up to one of the staff and said it was time for him to leave. He wanted to go home. After a long debate and questioning by the police they had to let him go. He showed his driving licence and the scam became clear. Reg just told the officers he had felt tired and, when he woke up, Ron was gone.

Norman believed Ron's move from Parkhurst was unavoidable: 'Dr Cooper tried to keep them together as long as he possibly could, but even he had to admit the inevitable with Ron.'

Old friend Frankie Fraser, a veteran of the psychiatric hospital, advised at the time: 'Broadmoor's fine. If you get yourself nutted off and go to Broadmoor, you can wear your own clothes. And you can have as much sex as you like.'

Even the wise old owl Frankie could never have predicted that Ronnie would end up with his own room, fine furnishings including velvet curtains, plus an eager butler or two.

Ronnie took Frankie's advice and 'really played up' to get himself out of Parkhurst. He was under control while taking his pills; but then he stopped taking medication. That was when the paranoia and schizophrenia kicked in again.

Ronnie's own words: 'Every time I thought I could have a fight with somebody, I'd have a fight with somebody. Every time I thought I could have a go at a screw, I'd have a go at a screw. Thankfully, in time, they said I was uncontrollable and they nutted me off.'

There was nowhere else for Ron. It had to be Broadmoor.

Chapter 6

Welcome to Broadmoor

Ron's arrival at Broadmoor, in July 1979, prompted the same questions for him as for any other patient. He had heard this was a hospital. Would it look like a hospital? Would the wards be filled with nurses, and patients sprawled out on the beds?

There was no chance of escape from the prison van. Ron was handcuffed to a warder in the back, while a driver and passenger, both guards, occupied the front. A sign for Crowthorne. A winding road. A car park. A massive wall. Welcome to Broadmoor.

The large, sprawling site was observed from high above by a gigantic circular clock, several feet in diameter. There were windows everywhere, covered by bars. The size and length of the wall almost took Ron's breath away. Not only that, he could see a multitude of cameras, fenced-off areas and no sign of a warm welcome. He remained handcuffed to a guard as he entered the building. They stood by a door until a red light changed to green. The door unlocked and he was led to an admission ward. Handcuffs were removed and Ron stood by a cell while paperwork was checked.

'You need to strip now,' one of the guards said.

Ron would soon learn that the main block consisted of Somerset 1 (admissions ward), Somerset 2 and Somerset 3. Somerset 3 was a ward of mixed ages, while Somerset 2 was a ward specifically for juvenile patients in their twenties. Most of the juveniles were incredibly childlike and immature but, nonetheless, extremely dangerous. Most of them suffered from sexual disorders of a violent disposition.

Dr R, who worked at Broadmoor and was a prominent figure in his field in the eighties, said treatment was overseen by a multi-disciplinary team. Typically, this would comprise psychiatrists, psychologists and nursing staff. There would also be occupational therapists, and perhaps teachers.

The approach to treatment or therapy was coordinated. All the teams met at regular intervals to review progress. Treatment would depend on the nature of the mental disorder. Ron was in need of specialised treatment.

'Patients with mental illnesses, such as schizophrenia which is a common and severe mental condition, are treated with medication. Psychological therapies often relate to what we call their index offence, or what they did before they came in. They need to come to terms with that and acknowledge what they've done. That can mean looking back on childhood histories which might include really terrible neglect, abuse and deprivation. And it could have left them very damaged.'

The idea, he explained, was to look back gradually and try to repair some of that damage. This, hopefully, would make them 'more whole' and better functioning as personalities with the hope of moving on at some point.

Ron, with his severe mental illness, was going nowhere. He stared at a basic bed, attached to the wall, covered with a couple of blankets and a pair of white cotton sheets.

In he went, naked, as so many before him, with no clothing or accessories to inflict harm. There was nothing to do apart from take his medication and go to sleep. This was his new life.

The next morning, a nurse – a guard with medical training – appeared at Ron's cell, unlocked the door and led him to a bathroom. He put disinfectant in the water, allowed Ron to have his bath and provided a set of fresh hospital clothes. Ron put on clean grey flannels, a blue cotton shirt and a pair of slippers. He was surprised that everything fitted. He discovered that he could wear what he wanted as long as it didn't resemble any of the nurses' uniforms for security reasons.

On the admissions ward, inmates bathed or showered once a week. It was on a Thursday evening, when a call came from the charge nurses' office: 'One for a bath and two for a shower.' There was then a rush to be escorted to the bathroom for the clean-up. There were two shower cubicles and one bath.

Some patients never took a bath, as it meant sharing the water. You never knew what sort of person had gone in beforehand! Members of staff always supervised the bathing and showering sessions.

The guard led squeaky clean Ron to the admissions ward day room, where some of the patients were having their tea. Ron carefully moved a chair back from a table, sat down and prepared to eat. There were three other patients at the next table: one was well fed, short and bald with a large red nose; another appeared thin and weedy and covered with a mop of blond hair; and a third had a freckly white face and black hair with streaks.

Ron nodded, they all nodded back and the newly arrived gangster looked at the food on his plate. Ron realised he was mentally ill. He also knew that a lot of the other 'fellers' heard voices. Those voices told them to attack people.

'I'm Mike,' the plump, bald one said. 'I believe you're Ron Kray?'

'I am,' Ron answered, sizing up the assembled group.

'My name is Merv,' the weedy one said, holding out his hand.

'I'm Jamie,' the freckly patient told Ron, who smiled and continued to assess his dining companions.

'The food's OK then?' Ron asked no one in particular as he continued to survey his surroundings.

He was answered by three nodding heads.

'Who's that over there?' Ron asked, sounding irritated. 'The feller keeps looking at me.'

'That's Keith,' Merv said. 'He seems to just sit on his own. He doesn't say much. We invite him to join us but he never does. He knows who you are. He knows who everyone is. He finds out very quickly, when you think that we're on the admissions ward. We'll get moved in a day or two.'

A day or two came and went, while Ron and his new acquaintances got to know each other. The moving process would be underway soon.

Ron was still unhappy about the patient who had been staring at him. All of a sudden, as the new patients sat down to lunch, Ron snapped. He jumped up and ran over to the table where Keith was sitting alone. The recent arrival seemed innocuous enough, sipping his water and rearranging his fish and chips.

'You know what you did?' Ron screamed as he stomped over to the table.

'You what?' Keith mumbled, his mouth full of orange-coloured batter.

Keith was totally unprepared for what happened next. He was an older patient, in his early sixties, with a lifetime of unpredictability behind him. His greasy grey hair had a parting roughly around the middle; his teeth had yellowed after years of baccy; his baggy trousers needed an iron; and his thick-framed glasses were steamed up.

SMACK! Ron punched his right knuckle into his own palm and stood over the intended victim. He bent round to the right, took aim and prepared to deliver a mighty blow. His technique, finely honed from his boxing days as a youngster, was perfect. Fortunately for Keith, Ron's thick glasses may have distorted the target. Keith ducked, and the fiercest right uppercut ever to be thrown in Broadmoor collided with nothing more than the smoky atmosphere of the dining room.

'You were flicking peas at me!' Ron raged. 'Never do that again, or . . .'

Two nurses rushed towards Ron and led him to an isolation room. They gave him a few minutes to calm down. After a few deeps breaths from Ronnie, Keith and the nurses, normality was restored.

Keith shrugged and held up his plate. He had baked beans, but no peas.

After his brief spell on the admissions ward, Ron was moved to Somerset 3. An aerial view would show, in a row, the day room, dining room, scullery, isolation room and medication room. Then a gallery, or corridor, led along the same line to the staff room, staff toilet and a washroom. At one end of the day room, patients played pool. At the other end they had the use of a TV and video recorder.

At right angles to those rooms was a row of cells and 'privileged side rooms'. That was really another name for a more luxurious cell. One of those better rooms, in the same row as the charge nurses' office, was used by Ron. He was four cells away from a bath and shower. This arrangement continued when he was behaving, earning the right to his room with associated privileges. He could have furniture, a TV and the permission to have a patient visiting in his cell. He could also go in there during the day.

Ron soon became used to the routine. A normal day began just before seven o'clock when staff came round and unlocked the rooms, as many patients preferred to call them. The next twenty minutes were spent visiting washrooms, washing and dressing and getting ready for the day ahead.

When Ron had a partner at Broadmoor, he found a way of having a sexual liaison in the washroom near the charge nurses' office. They had a lookout and chose times when other patients were at work, and things were more relaxed with no dramas going on. Ron chose a period when the staff wouldn't be walking around the ward checking on everyone.

The lookout, Andrew, was always in and out of the washroom with his electric shaver. He would turn it on and off a few times, giving signals to Ron and his partner further inside the washroom. The shaver went off and on to a predetermined code, depending on the level of nurses' activity. Andrew's shaving also drowned out any grunting noises which could have drifted out into the ward.

After the various ablutions, it was time for a cup of tea in the day room. That lasted until eight o'clock, when patients headed for breakfast in the dining room. That took around half an hour, followed by a return to the day room for any medication. In Ron's case there were daily doses.

Between 9 a.m. and 11.45 a.m., patients set off for the

work areas where the occupation officers taught carpentry, arts and crafts and other skills. Ron showed no inclination for making furry toys; he was happy to clean out the staff toilets every so often. The Yorkshire Ripper was left alone, and not included in any work party. There was too much animosity towards Peter Sutcliffe for inclusion in any activity.

After the morning's work, the group returned to the wards. They moved to the dining room for the meal at midday, with the usual three to a table and Ron avoiding the Ripper at all costs. The morning or afternoon could also entail a visit to the dentist, chiropodist, optician or other practitioner visiting from the outside.

More medication for Ron was provided after lunch, then some recreation in the day and rest rooms. Ron enjoyed a cup of tea with Mike, Merv, Jamie and a few others while they watched television or listened to the radio. Books could be read and letters written; the small library in the school block was a popular venue.

It was back to the occupation areas after lunch. At the end of the sessions, near to four o'clock, the occupation officers checked that all tools had been returned and were present and correct.

Tea followed, then more medication as required, and time for a rest. The late afternoon also provided an opportunity to wash clothes, using the washing machines and tumble dryers in the wards.

In the early evening, nursing staff escorted patients into the garden for some fresh air. There were facilities for tennis and football, while green-fingered patients could undertake some gardening.

The roll call took place in the ward after seven o'clock, followed by supper for any extra-hungry patients in the ward. Indoor recreation continued after this to include table tennis and snooker, all under staff supervision.

Bed clothes and dressing gowns were donned at half past eight, followed by sedation in the clinical room. At Broadmoor, Ron's moods were generally controlled by his drugs. His nerves were kept in check by Stemetil capsules four times a day. He said that the drug had side effects, mainly shaking legs, as visitors were to discover. The cure for that was another drug called Disipal.

In addition, Ron's schizophrenia was managed every two weeks by an injection of a drug called Modecate. It helped to fight depression, too.

Ron acknowledged that he needed the drugs to keep him calm. If he didn't take them he imagined people plotting against him. In the day room, if he saw a couple of patients chatting in the corner he would automatically think they were talking about him. He felt he had to hit out, fight back against their chatter and make sure the gossips suffered. His anger built up and all control was lost.

At nine o'clock, the patients' rooms were locked, and another day came to an end.

Highly educated Patient P, who lived in Somerset 3 at the same time as Ron, said all of the inmates had to be on guard all of the time. Potential death lurked around every corner.

'I will not say that I had the mentality of kill or be killed, but I knew that the nutters in Broadmoor were murderers, so I had to understand the need to adapt. While I pride myself on being a man who walks as a man of peace, I understood the meaning of the phrase, *needs must when the Devil drives*.

'My mindset had to be to prepare to be killed, or to show off an ability to defend myself in a fight. I haven't mentioned that for theatre; it was the reality.

'Unfortunately, in the company of animals, one has no choice but to show a mask of fierce aggression as a shield, as animals can be trusted to attack, and the animals in Broadmoor were always looking for what weaknesses they could find in one's armour. One should not try to practise diplomacy with an animal unless one is a madman or a fool.

'As human beings we are at the top of the chain in the animal kingdom, and it is said that we are separated from being mere beasts by our ability to reason. However, Broadmoor had animals that couldn't rationalise and didn't understand reason – it was a lonely hell.

'If I hadn't had some training in self-defence, I would have died or been seriously injured on three separate occasions in that hellhole.'

In January 1981, Reg was a full-time member of the dispersal system and found the whole arrangement confusing. One day he was at Parkhurst settling into the routine on the Isle of Wight, with the restrictions of a high security wing. Then he was moved to Long Lartin, in Worcestershire, where he found a prison in which inmates mixed more freely. There were relaxed open association periods, and the sudden change made Reg withdraw to his cell.

With Ron at Broadmoor, Reg was allowed to visit; after the visits, though, Reg felt frustrated and vulnerable as past, present and future dominated their lives in a bleak haze. They never knew when they would see each other again.

The governor of Long Lartin accepted that Reg no longer needed his Category 'A' status but, because of his notoriety, downgrading would be difficult. Another report recognised that Reg was unlikely to make any escape attempt, but noted that plans to write a book and produce a film would make any downgrading difficult.

In the autumn of 1981, Reg was reported to be distressed while still at Long Lartin. Reg was worried about correspondence he had received from a woman; he was concerned that this friend of the family might commit suicide. A prison officer, after trying to contact the woman and Reg's mum, got hold of brother Charlie. Despite reassurances, Reg was concerned about the woman's state of mind and wanted the police to check on her.

Ron wrote to the Long Lartin medical officer, saying that he was concerned about Reg's mental health. Ron said Reg believed his cell was bugged and his food had been poisoned.

'He has lost a lot of weight. I, as you no doubt know, have had mental illness all my life. I can tell by my brother's letters that he is now mentally ill.'

The reply to the Broadmoor Medical Superintendent stated that Reg was in excellent health, and this fact was to be relayed to Ron.

Reg believed another prisoner at Long Lartin was plotting against him and confronted the inmate. Both men were sent to the Segregation Unit, in solitary confinement. Reg was later found with blood coming from his wrists. He had used the glass from his spectacles to cause the injuries and stitches were required, especially to his left wrist.

After the two men left solitary, Reg attacked the same prisoner and was confined to the Segregation Unit once more. The next morning he was found with wounds to his wrist again, this time caused by a razor blade. More stitches were required to repair that damage.

Reg was prescribed the antidepressant drug Imipramine. That didn't stop him setting fire to toilet paper on his bed. He went back on the wing, then back to the Segregation Unit and confusion reigned.

Although he was banned from having matches, he got hold of a box from a priest who innocently believed they were for lighting cigarettes. And he ignited his bed once more. Another factor worrying Reg was talk of a possible transfer to Rampton or Broadmoor.

In the spring of 1982, Reg was transferred back to Parkhurst where the paranoia continued. Dr Cooper was still in charge of patients with mental issues. Reg was moved to the F2 observation landing of the hospital. Shortly after arriving he cut himself on the arm again with a shard of glass. After more bandaging and doses of valium and chlorpromazine, an antipsychotic drug, Reg returned to his cell under constant supervision.

Reg's mental state and general health improved after reading a book about how never to give up, whatever the odds. He washed and shaved, after a relapse in those departments, and started to write letters. His normal letter-writing activity had suffered during his disturbed period.

Reg was happier when he was in the normal prison system in the high security 'B' wing at Parkhurst.

The ground floor was called the ones; the first floor was known as the twos, and the second floor as the threes. Violent, unpredictable prisoners were normally housed on the middle floor, where they couldn't go through the roof or dig their way out.

Reg's white-painted cell, around thirteen feet by six, contained an iron bed with a foam mattress and a bucket for his toilet needs. There was also a cupboard with six compartments. The cupboard was about three feet across, with just enough space for his clothes. He packed in a couple of shirts, trousers, shoes, socks and underpants.

Reg treasured his radio, and he was allowed that as well as a record player. The radio was battery powered and received one waveband only.

His window was small, only a few inches across, covered by a panel that could be slid open for fresh air. The old iron cell door looked as ancient as Parkhurst itself.

If he looked out on the landing he could see brown floorboards with white painted railings. The walls were also a neutral creamy colour. Nets separated the floors to catch any jumpers.

Reggie soon became used to the routine. The cells were unlocked at 8 a.m., and an hour later everyone prepared for the day ahead. Some prisoners tackled metalwork and tailoring. Reg was allocated cleaning duties on the landings, although that was done by the young boys who acted as his protectors. The work lasted for nearly two hours, and then the prisoners were allowed to go into the exercise yard for a walk around.

Reg and his fellow cons were 'banged up' after lunch, with more work in the afternoons. After tea, at six o'clock, evening association began. Inmates could go to TV rooms, play table tennis or visit the gym.

At 9 p.m. it was time to retire for the night. Reg's favourite radio programme was *Friday Night Is Music Night*, bringing back memories of clubland. During other evenings Reg listened to his record player or wrote letters. Out of his prison wage, £2.50 a week, he had little change left after paying for all of his writing pads, envelopes and stamps.

Maureen Flanagan was a regular recipient: 'Reggie wrote non-stop. He would be up in the middle of the night, writing. At the top of the letter it would say 3 a.m. and I used to think, "What is he up at 3 a.m. for, writing letters?" It was because he had to write at least twenty letters at a time. They were a scribble. It was terrible writing, veering to the left and veering to the right. It was difficult to understand. You had to really study it.'

Reg hated the nights. He suffered from nightmares, and felt as if he were trapped in a tunnel with no way out. There was no light at the end of his tunnel; the darkness went on and on. When he woke up from the nightmare, sweating, he stripped to the waist and walked around the cell, trying to calm down.

And he was watching his back, just to stay alive . . .

Chapter 7

A New World for Reg

Reg was immersed in a world of violence where death lurked around every corner. Any minute, a prisoner could be beaten up, stabbed, tortured, intimidated or poisoned. Every second of every day he had to be on his guard. On the outside, he was a marked man, with countless enemies and a determined selection of young pretenders to his throne. While he did receive massive respect on the inside, the threat of death or serious injury kept Reg's senses finely honed and constantly on alert.

Bobby Cummines, jailed for thirteen armed robberies, met Reg at Parkhurst several years after their first encounter in the Old Bailey. He spent the next few years watching Reg come and go, building up a friendship and looking out for the criminal legend.

'There was quite a change in him. For a start he was eleven or twelve years older. When I first saw him he was immaculately suited and booted on his way into court.

Now his hair was going grey. He was wearing black shorts, a white vest and a shiny pair of new trainers.

'Reg explained that it could get hot on the island and prisoners tended to wear casual gear. I tended to wear a shirt and trousers, because that's what I wore when I was doing business and I felt underdressed wearing anything else. When I looked around I could see people wearing all sorts of things, like headbands.

'Reggie's cell was on "B" wing, for high security prisoners, and he was at the extreme end. I was three cells away from him. Amazingly, I was also only a few cells away from Charlie Richardson, head of the other big firm!'

Reg got on OK with Charlie Richardson, although Ronnie bore grudges and hated their firm. Reg was also prepared to be friendly to Bobby, the new arrival, and invited him in for a cup of tea.

Reggie had a group of young followers who attended to his every need. One of them had already gone into the cell and brewed the tea. Sugar and milk had been placed on his small basic table. Reggie picked up the teapot and began to pour. He told Bobby that prisoners had quite a bit of freedom if they behaved themselves. They could walk around the landings, visit the TV rooms, exercise yard or use the small gym. Reggie, still keeping himself as fit as possible, told Bobby the gym had a punch bag.

Reggie thought that, one day, he could write a book about exercise in a confined space. He imagined working out a Jane Fonda-style exercise routine for prisoners and anyone who had little room to work with.

Reggie's followers had made a good job of making the cell comfortable. There were burgundy curtains and a matching bedspread. He even had a home-made settee, formed from a mattress and a chair. The bits and bobs were brought in by people 'on the outside'.

Reg was surrounded by pictures of Judy Garland, Barbara Windsor, Al Capone, George Raft and Shirley Bassey. He said he was looking forward to a visit by Barbara Windsor, and showed Bobby a pile of letters from stars of stage and screen as well as famous boxers.

The main picture in his cell was one of the Queen, carefully placed in the middle of the white painted wall. She was wearing her crown and jewels. Reg also had a picture of the Queen Mother. He said he always had pictures of royalty in his cell, and he was proud of the Queen Mother and King George for visiting the East End during the Blitz.

'A couple of young boys came into the cell and cleared up the tea things,' Bobby recalled. 'I'd say they were in their late teens. They even wore the same type of trainers as Reg. I went on to have regular chats with both Reggie and Charlie Richardson over the next few years and really got to know them.'

Bobby became the prison fixer and banker. He could arrange loans – not that Reg was ever short of cash – or acquire items for self-protection.

Reggie regularly clutched a rusty old blade. This half a pair of garden shears had the potential to be a lethal weapon, and needed to be kept well hidden.

Normally Reggie stored his weapons in a false hole beside the showers, down on the ground floor. After receiving warnings about genuine threats from other inmates, Reggie thought it would be prudent to have his protection closer to hand. He slipped the blade inside a false bottom on his mattress.

Reggie received the blade from armed robber Bobby, who had obtained the shears for a tenner from a gardener in a working party. It turned out to be a good deal for Bobby, because Reg paid a tenner for just the one blade.

'Don't go down to the showers alone,' Bobby warned Reg. 'Take one of your people, or I'll go with you.'

Bobby was becoming concerned about Reggie's safety, despite the number of young protectors running around.

'A couple of people were cut last night,' Bobby told him. 'The geezer who did it had a pillow over his head with just eyeholes. He even had his feet covered up so he couldn't be recognised. He struck from behind while the guy was vulnerable. So what I do is hand the blade to my pal. He sits outside the shower, then I go and wash and all that. When I come out, he gives me the blade and I wait for him. It's the only way.'

Reg and Ron – from earlier incarcerations at Parkhurst – were also familiar with other methods of inflicting pain. Reg knew that the IRA used a particularly nasty technique involving garlic. A blade was run through a bulb of garlic before an attack. When someone was cut, the wound puffed up and failed to react well to stitches.

Another IRA speciality was a poisoned six-inch nail. This would be steeped in human excrement for more than a week and then used for stabbing. At first the puncture wound looked minor, until blood poisoning kicked in with the potential to be fatal.

Reg's protectors were always on the lookout for anyone carrying a sock. Filled with a billiards ball or chunky PP9 batteries, these could inflict serious injuries. One of the worst punishments involved boiling milk and sugar. The mixture was poured over a victim's face, sticking to the skin and causing disfigurement. Even the urn used for the tea was always on standby to be tipped over someone.

Reg – and Ron in his early Parkhurst days – was also aware of a lethal technique used to cause an inferno in a cell. People on painting courses could easily collect the necessary ingredients to make a petrol bomb. The cells had flags on the outside, allowing a prisoner to attract attention by pressing a button. However, cotton could be used to tie the flag up from the outside. It would then fail to drop down, meaning that if a small inflammable package were slipped inside the cell, there would be no alert for the warders and no hope for the fried inmate.

Even mealtimes could prove hazardous. Anyone putting a spoonful of sugar into a cup of tea had to be on the lookout for small pieces of glass, ground down very finely. These were hardly noticeable until the pain kicked in as internal organs were torn to shreds.

Reg was familiar with another technique although, fortunately, he never became the recipient. A tube would be inserted up a wrongdoer's backside, and then barbed wire pushed inside. The tube would be taken away, and the barbed wire ripped out.

The queue at the hot plate for breakfast seemed an unlikely place for loss of life. Normally it was an orderly affair with everyone exchanging pleasantries and preparing for the day ahead. However . . .

'Grab the knife. Get it from him. Grab it now!'

'I can't. He's too strong. Stop the blood. Stop the blood.'

'Get the screws. Get more screws.'

Pandemonium. Screams. Shouting. Yelling. Snarls of hate. Cries of pain. All in the queue for breakfast at Parkhurst.

Reggie gaped at the bizarre scene developing in front of his eyes. On the outside, he'd been used to a life of violence, with people being cut and shot. Now, in a place where law and order was supposed to rule, a savage murder unfolded before his eyes.

A stream of blood spewed over the queue as John Paton stabbed and stabbed, with his filed-down length of steel glinting eerily in the light around the hot plate. Francis McGee, his target, began to slump forward as a clutch of hands tried to offer protection from Paton's thrusts. A prisoner, risking his own life, grabbed Paton in an improvised bear hug as McGee struggled for breath and warders appeared from everywhere on the wing.

Basic attempts at first aid were being provided by Nizamodeen Hosein or 'Nez', who provided more information during the fracas: 'He's done it before.'

Nez had plenty of form himself. He and his brother demanded £1 million in ransom money after they kidnapped a woman who, they believed, was the wife of Rupert Murdoch. They didn't realise they had captured Muriel McKay, the wife of Murdoch's deputy chairman. The money was not paid, and so Mrs McKay was consumed by a herd of pigs at a Hertfordshire farm. The unfortunate lady's fate meant that anyone enjoying bacon was indulging in a piece of Muriel; it was part of the dark humour in the breakfast queue.

Behind Reggie in the line: Charlie Richardson, his one-time adversary and Fat Fred Sewell, who had killed a police chief superintendent during an armed robbery. Charlie's close friends, Bobby Cummines and blond-haired, blue-eyed armed robber Gary Wilson, were also stunned by the ferocity of the attack. The entire group of Category 'A' prisoners could only watch as the scrum developed and warders tried desperately to save McGee's life.

'I think he's dead,' Charlie Richardson muttered as the racket subsided. He confirmed Nez's comment. 'Paton's done it before. Killed someone with a table leg.'

Charlie and Nez were correct. At Wakefield, Paton

attacked Robert Houston, twenty-three. It was over a row about home-made hooch. Paton was an expert at making the dodgy home brew from fruit and potato peelings. He suspected Robert of helping himself to some of the precious liquid and launched into an attack. That resulted in a life sentence for Paton, but there he was in Parkhurst, claiming the life of another inmate.

'Did you know it was about a game of chess?' Nez asked, receiving no response. 'McGee cheated, apparently, and Paton never forgave him. Someone made a joke about it. Paton went back to his cell and got the weapon. Look what he's done.'

Nez cradled McGee's head in his lap: 'It was over absolutely nothing, you know. Paton didn't forgive him for cheating. That's what it was all about. There was a joke about the chess game. The guy went back to his cell and got the weapon. There's no hope.'

A group of warders took over, trying desperately to stop the blood spurting out of McGee. It was spraying everywhere. Nez was right. McGee could never be saved.

'Some of the geezers are just stepping over the body!' a voice whispered from the queue.

'I got on OK with Paton,' Reggie told Charlie as the warders removed the limp body from the scene. 'What could have got into him? Just shows you. We're at risk here, twenty-four hours a day. It's safer on the outside.'

The bizarre set of events had a rather dubious finale. Fat Fred Sewell was concerned about the state of his breakfast: 'Look, there's blood all over my cornflakes! He's taking a liberty there!'

Charlie and Reg looked at each other in disbelief.

'You can have mine,' Charlie offered. 'I can't be bothered with breakfast after seeing that.'

The warders moved everyone back to their cells while order was restored, and Fat Fred was on the prowl at Charlie's cell door: 'Is it still OK to take your cornflakes?'

'There are too many murders in prison,' Reg muttered ruefully. 'I remember that feller Terry Peake who used to cut my hair. I was over in "C" wing when Dougie Wakefield beat him with a cosh. Strangled him, too. No idea what that was about. He was a decent feller, Terry. He was good at paintings.'

Reggie chose the wrong place at the wrong time, yet again, when another life was snuffed out in the kitchen.

'That was over something trivial as well,' Reg told his protectors over more cups of tea in his cell. 'It wasn't a game of chess this time. It was a row about an onion.'

'A fucking onion?' one of the young boys asked, looking incredulous and shaking his head. 'Was it Rocky? Didn't know it was about an onion.'

'Yeah, he was making spag bol and borrowed an onion from Harry the Cook. Well, Harry reckoned he nicked the onion and Rocky wouldn't give it back. Harry was using a knife under supervision, so he used it against Rocky. Really gave it to him, he did. Rocky was only forty-one. What a waste.'

Reg almost became the victim of an attack himself. He was saved by his best friend at Parkhurst, Pete Gillett. Pete was in the cell next door; Pete was in number thirteen, and Reg in fourteen. The names and numbers were written on the door.

Pete was a talented musician and, had the pair not been incarcerated, a business link would have formed in the entertainment industry.

Reg went to watch Pete playing on the football pitch – a tarmac area beside a basketball court. It was a bizarre scene with players, young and old, running around furiously. No one seemed to know which side they were on.

As Reg watched the entertainment, six inmates started to move in on him. One of the group was related to George Cornell, which could hardly have been a coincidence. Pete, spotting the danger, raced over to intervene. He was in his twenties, much younger than Reg, and more than capable of holding his own. Before Reg could be targeted, other allies piled in, too, and emerged victorious. After that incident, Reg's young protectors stepped up their patrols.

Reg Kray, the prisoner with the highest profile in Parkhurst, had no intention of being clumped, cut or whacked. He was living in a dangerous world, where predators were commonplace and life was cheap. He was never going to slip up. His young army of protectors ensured that would never happen.

Reg encountered a variety of prison officers. There was Foxy, the principal officer on 'B' wing, an older warder with silver hair and glasses. He was a familiar sight, walking round the landings with a sackful of Isle of Wight apples. He handed them out to warders and prisoners. He also taught the inmates a few local words: 'grockle' meant tourist, 'overnor' was a settler from the mainland, and 'caulkhead' was someone born on the island.

Reg also got on well with John, a landing screw with a fair beard and hair to match. He looked like Captain Birdseye from the old TV adverts. When the weather closed in, John said it was 'blowin' a hoolie'.

There was another John, although he was called Johnny, a laid-back SO or senior officer. He organised the rotas and enjoyed football chats with Reg and his pals.

Gold Top was a warder who just didn't understand the system or the prisoners' needs. He used to be a milkman, hence his name, and he suffered excessive goading.

The problem with Gold Top was that he liked to boss people about. The category 'A' prisoners at Parkhurst, with nothing to lose, refused to be bossed about by anyone. A major issue for Gold Top was that he couldn't count very well, so they gave him a clicker device to count inmates in and out when they went to the exercise yard and back.

All went well to start with. He clicked for one man, then two when the next appeared and so on. However, the two would go back out and in again, joining another group. People in the group went in and out, leaving the bemused Gold Top clicking away with not a clue as to how many prisoners were really coming and going.

Another warder during Reg's time made a complete hash of a medical problem. A prisoner had a really bad headache after smoking too much weed.

Instead of calling a medical officer, the warder found some tablets and gave them to the unwell prisoner. Unfortunately, the pills were purification tablets for the swimming pool. That meant a painful spell in hospital for the inmate, and a black mark on an unsuccessful career for the careless pill provider.

As Reg survived in a jungle full of predators, a person very close to him on the mainland was feeling the pain – and struggling to get through every day.

For one resident of the East End, in particular, the confinement of the twins was a living nightmare. Her suffering continued through every long day and night.

Violet Kray was heartbroken.

Chapter 8

Violet Is Dead

Maureen Flanagan has vivid memories of the day she visited the twins' doting mum – and could tell that something was wrong with Vi, late in 1981.

'All of the visiting took its toll on Violet. I remember going to see her at Christmas. I bought her a lovely little cardigan that I knew she'd like, and I thought she looked dreadful.'

Maureen recalled voicing her concern: 'Is there anything wrong with you? Are you ill?'

'No, no, I've had a bad visit. I'm just upset, that's all.'

Violet endured years of drained emotions, seeing Reggie caged in Parkhurst and Ronnie trapped – albeit in more comfortable surroundings with velvet curtains and upgraded meals – in Broadmoor. Several times a week she travelled the length and breadth of the country, visiting Reg, Ron and Charlie. Even when her health began to deteriorate, she saw both of the twins once a week via road, rail and ferry.

'Little did we know – because she didn't tell any of us,

especially the twins – she had cancer. Their brother Charlie told me. He said, "Mummy's got cancer," and it was such a shock.'

Maureen remembered weeping and asking: 'Oh, Charlie. Ronnie and Reggie don't know, do they?'

Maureen thought that the twins might do something terrible to themselves because they'd be so upset.

'They have no idea,' Charlie assured her. 'She is going to go in to see them as long as she can still stand.'

And she did just that, despite the intense pain and supreme effort to put on a cheery face. Maureen was full of admiration for the mother's supreme effort.

'It was only in the last few weeks, about the beginning of March, that she couldn't go any more. She was too weak. The next thing I heard, she was in hospital. I took a friend of mine along, who knew Violet well, and we sat at either side of the bed.'

During that poignant day in hospital, Violet had looked at Maureen with an unflinching gaze. 'Would you promise me something?'

'Of course,' Maureen answered gently. 'What can I do?'

'I want you to promise me that, when I die . . .'

'Oh, don't talk about dying, Violet. You've got something to live for. The boys will be coming home!'

'No,' Violet said firmly, knowing that the boys would not be coming home and that she was, indeed, seeing out her final days. 'When I die, promise me that you'll continue to visit Ronnie and Reggie.'

'Of course I will,' a tearful Maureen replied. 'I'll visit them wherever they are.'

'Promise me that you'll continue to visit Reggie?'

Maureen was puzzled; Ronnie had always been Violet's favourite, and yet she had chosen to single out his twin for extra attention.

The hairdresser and future model knew that Violet's major achievement was having the twins reunited at Parkhurst, with Ronnie arriving after a difficult time at Durham. That made visiting easier, although Ronnie's mental state soon led to a permanent home at Broadmoor.

'Why do you say to visit Reggie? I'll see the two of them of course, but you surprise me saying about Reggie.'

Violet was still lucid, despite the searing pain and the strength draining from her frail body: 'You must understand this. Ronnie can have as many visits as he likes — men, women, film stars, pop stars and boxers. Everybody goes to see Ronnie. But Reggie can only have seven visits a month. You have to take my place.'

Violet referred to the twins as 'my lovely boys' and constantly showered them with love and affection.

Maureen recalled: 'So I was with Violet that day. The day before she died. I made the promise and I kept it by doing all the visits. The visiting all over the country took its toll on her, and I always say that it caused the cancer.

'And Ronnie even said to me, with people at the table in Broadmoor, "We killed our mother," although we used to maintain that anyone, even young kids, could get cancer. He said, "No, no, she was lively and she'd have gone on forever," and he was convinced. Ronnie blamed the travelling, the anxiety, all the worry they'd given her, and all the upsets she'd had.'

After his mother's death, Reg wrote to Broadmoor asking if Ron could return to Parkhurst. Ron also felt they should be together, and wrote a letter to Parkhurst asking if he could go back. The request was denied. Reg even asked if he could go to Broadmoor to be with Ron, but he was not certifiable, so that could not happen. All avenues were firmly closed.

Reggie Kray cried. Ronnie Kray wept uncontrollably. The news, filtering through to Parkhurst and Broadmoor on 4 August 1982, was devastating.

Their beloved mother, Violet, was dead. It seemed that everyone in the East End knew Violet. She had been born in Vallance Road in 1910, of Jewish and Irish descent.

Violet was a typical mother figure in the East End, nurturing her family, catering for their every need and seeing no wrong in anything they did. One man who had a great regard for Violet was Father Richard Hetherington, who conducted the funeral service.

He had great regard, respect and affection for Mrs Kray. In the East End, everyone kept insisting that loyalty was the byword; Violet had that in abundance, especially to her family, which she displayed until her final days.

The late Billie Whitelaw, who played Violet in the 1990

film *The Krays*, said the caring mum was the most important part of their lives.

'Violet was just as well known as the twins, but for different reasons. She was a classic East End mother figure.

'The three boys were besotted with her. They all loved her. In fact, everyone I've spoken to who knew Violet Kray loved her.'

The good, the bad, the shady and the even shadier emerged from the shadows to attend Violet's funeral, including the twins themselves, who were let out of prison for the day under heavy guard. For miles around, it was as if the Queen had died. For the twins, the funeral of their beloved mother was a day filled with heartbreak.

More than 500 friends and family converged on the old church at Chingford on 11 August 1982. There were roses, chrysanthemums, and a variety of blooms sent from the Great Train Robbers, film stars, pop stars and a legion of admirers in the East End. A display of carnations and lilies arrived 'from the boys at Parkhurst'.

The twins sent floral crosses. Ron's cross had the heartfelt message: 'Mum, the most beautiful woman in the world. Love, Ron.'

Reg also made his feelings known in verse: 'Remembering so many things that you have said and done; remembering the times we shared . . . the laughter and the fun.'

Friends and neighbours, looking on as the funeral procession passed by, were full of praise for Violet.

One neighbour said: 'She always asked after my son and grandchildren and she didn't even know them. She was a very fine woman.'

They all agreed that Violet had so much energy, running around doing chores, unlike many people of the day. She was recognised as 'a fantastic woman'.

Duncan Campbell stressed the significance of the occasion: 'It was very important to the twins, because they were so close to their mother. It was also important for the general public because it was open – anyone could go along to the funeral.'

Duncan said one of the main talking points was the physical size of the guards: 'The Krays weren't very tall, but they sent them out with the tallest prison officers they could find. The shortest officer was probably six foot four. Reggie complained that they were trying to make the brothers look like dwarfs.'

Fred Dinenage, who contributed to *The Krays: The Prison Years* for Discovery Channel, reflected: 'The twins absolutely idolised their mother – there's no question about that. Violet was a huge influence on their lives.

'I agree that Reggie was furious about the funeral because they handcuffed him to a huge prison officer – making him look small next to the big guy.'

Reggie had told Fred: 'There was no need for them to do that. Where was I going to run away to?'

Maureen arrived at the church and waited outside with a group of old friends from the East End while a sedate procession of black limousines surrounded the historic building. Her recollection backed up Reggie's complaint.

'Ronnie arrived first. They'd handcuffed him to a guy who was much taller. Ronnie waved to me and he waved to the crowds. It was as if he was royalty. People were shouting out, "Ronnie, it's me. Ronnie, it's me." And then he was taken into the church.

'Reggie had come a lot further, over the Solent from the Isle of Wight, and he arrived in a police van. His left hand was also handcuffed to a giant officer.'

Reggie's friend, Bobby Cummines, was more than angry: 'How would you feel if you went out, shackled like an animal, when you're burying your mother? They call us gangsters. They call us torturers – that sort of thing. We don't parade people, in a moment of terrible grief, and say, "Oh, come and have a look at this wild animal we've got – this exotic animal." That's what I keep saying about the brutality of the system.'

Fred remembered that Ronnie was visibly upset during the day; he struggled to accept that his mum was dead, and he was emotional about being with Reggie and surrounded by their old friends.

Maureen continued to relive the day's events: 'We all went into the church and sat down. I was two rows behind Diana Dors. Some people were screaming. They thought they could run forward and take pictures and get autographs.

'That's what the public are like, aren't they, when they

see a star? Diana had become very friendly with Mrs Kray.'

Maureen described how Reggie and Ronnie, although highly emotional, managed to hold back the tears. She knew that they had broken down when they were alone. 'They both told me that.'

The twins were allowed to hug and quickly share memories with friends and relatives. Stories about Violet, caring for her boys over so many years, were condensed into a few priceless minutes.

'I remember that there was a helicopter above us. I was surprised to see that. I was very, very sad that day. There was a pub that certain people were going back to in the East End, but I didn't want to go.

'I had lost a real friend. I'd got used to her the same as any other woman in my family. Violet was like a sort of a second mother.

'When I had my baby I went to see Violet. She said she was going to give me a present. I thought she was going to give me something for the baby, but she handed me a necklace and said not to tell Ronnie.

'It was a diamond necklace on a white gold chain. I asked why I couldn't tell Ron, and she said that he had bought it for her one night when they were going to a club. She said she didn't like the necklace, and it suited me. I never told Ron that I had it.'

The twins had lost the one person they believed in. They both swore she was the main driving force in their lives. They trusted each other implicitly and they trusted their mother. Ronnie and Reggie Kray bowed their heads, with memories of their mother flooding back.

The twins spotted Billy Hill at the funeral service. They saw many people from the past, although it was difficult to meet and greet them among the security, crowds and general mayhem of the day.

Also present was the twins' father, who was in poor health. He had never been close to Ron and Reg; there had been no bonding in the early years, and that lack of contact continued. Old Charlie had been on the run for two decades after refusing to fight in the war. The twins did not attend their father's funeral when he died a year later.

The emotional day soon ended for the prisoners. Reg and Ron continued to hug whoever they could. There were tears. More hugs. Final farewells. A return under high security to Parkhurst for Reg. A return under heavy guard to Broadmoor for Ron.

They weren't allowed to attend the graveside service, next to where Reggie's wife, Frances, was buried. Terry Downes, world middleweight boxing champion in 1961, stood solemnly at the graveside. Two of the Nash brothers, the East End club owners, also mixed with mourners.

Ron reflected after the funeral that it had been the saddest day of his life. He was also upset that the day had been turned into a carnival. He and Reg had been hoping for a private affair with a simple and solemn service.

Many years later, when Ron discussed the funeral with Fred Dinenage, he handed over some words to express how he felt. He wrote about his mother's silver hair; how he wished he didn't have to say 'hello' and 'goodbye' all the time; how the years seemed to fly past; how Violet had been a rainbow in a dark sky; and how he hoped that, one day, there would be a 'hello' without the need to say 'goodbye' ever again.

All of their memories came flooding back. Violet had cared for them night and day during their early years. She had taken them away from the dangers of the wartime bombing. She had supported them during their boxing careers. She had backed them to the hilt, even when the long arms of the law kept reaching out for them. She ensured that the business meetings at the house, known in the underworld as Fort Vallance, were interspersed with drinks and snacks. She travelled all over the country, despite failing health, to see them in various prisons and institutions.

Ron and Reg were left with nothing more than memories of their mother. Just memories.

Chapter 9

Sexual Encounters of the Kray Kind

Alan's first sight of Ronnie Kray, close up, was in a toilet at Broadmoor in 1983. Alan, incarcerated after a manslaughter case, went into the loo at the hospital shortly after his arrival. He was followed by another eager resident on Somerset Ward 3.

The keen follower obviously found Alan attractive. With a full head of black hair neatly parted, Alan was a slim figure, clean shaven and standing at five foot eight tall.

The urinals were situated in an open area, allowing four people to stand and do their business. As Alan was finishing, Ron burst in and occupied the space to his right.

'Take this and put it in your pocket,' Ronnie urged.

Alan finished and examined the parcel. He had been given a two-ounce pouch of tobacco, containing the expected ingredients as well as a note.

'Are you gay?' the scribbled scrap of paper read. 'I hope you are! I am! I would like to get to know you better! Please throw this note down the toilet when you've read it.'

Nowadays, such an offer of a sexual liaison would hardly cause a ripple of concern. But Alan felt extremely troubled. He'd recognised the unmistakable figure of Ron Kray from the newspapers. Also, the previous day, he'd spotted Ron in the distance walking around the exercise yard with his close friend Charlie Smith. Ron had been wearing a fifties-style donkey jacket during one of his rare appearances outside the main building.

Alan scrunched the note up and pushed it far out of sight under the toilet bowl, pulling the chain with all of his strength.

Peering around the wards, Alan emerged from the loo and bolted for the comparative safety of his cell.

The next morning he visited the urinals where Ron, with eyes bulging slightly, was waiting.

'I'm ever so sorry, but I'm not gay. I'm so sorry,' Alan ventured, trying not to look embarrassed.

'Pity!' Ron said.

'Do you want your tobacco back?' Alan asked nervously.

'No, you keep it. Don't tell the slags I gave it to you!'

Ron often used the word 'slag' when he was referring to people he regarded as trash. Sex offenders, in particular, incurred his wrath and the use of various derogatory terms.

It should be said that Ronnie spent his time in Broadmoor as an openly gay man. Undeterred by Alan's rebuttal, they became instant friends.

Alan's impression? 'When I met Ron Kray, he was a

shadow of his former self. I was used to seeing pictures in the papers of his days as a high-profile gangster where he had looked brutally frightening. He had lost some weight in Broadmoor, but he was well groomed, and he always wore a suit that was well fitted. Nonetheless the man looked frail in comparison to how he had looked in his past days in the East End of London, when he and his brother called all the shots.

'He didn't seem to mind that I had spurned his advances. But straight away he told me about his days as a gangster, and how he taught people a lesson with a "piece of action." He would offer someone a cigarette to put them off guard and then lash out. It was easier, Ron said, to break a slag's jaw if he had a cigarette in his trap. So we talked about that sort of thing rather than sex because he knew I wasn't interested.'

Ronnie Kray's late mother had accepted his homosexuality. She told Maureen Flanagan that Ron was homosexual. She had received the information from son Charlie.

Violet, though, had never talked to Ron about his sexual preferences. In the sixties, it was not an everyday occurrence to talk openly about sex. This was a new experience for Violet. As long as Ron was happy, though, there was no problem in her eyes. Charlie senior failed to take kindly to the idea, which did little to improve the fragile relationship between twins and father.

Ronnie told Alan that he couldn't change, and he'd always felt that way. He 'came out' in his mid-teens and fell in love with a younger boy called Willy. Willy, a card sharp, was terrified when a friend told him about Ronnie's feelings. He realised that Ronnie could be a frightening prospect.

Reggie was actually bisexual, although many believed him to be gay. Homosexuality was not approved of in the East End and it was a criminal offence until 1967. In their early years, the twins were worried that rivals would see their sexuality as a sign of weakness.

Author John Pearson has written extensively about the Krays. When he was interviewed about one of his books, he said they were brought up in a classic pattern with an indulgent mother, an ineffectual father and a surrounding cast of loving women. They had their Grandma Lee and two Aunts, May and Rose, fussing over them.

With the onset of adolescence, the twins discovered that they were both gay. In the future this would be a real asset and a source of valuable connections. For a long time they kept their sexual leanings to themselves. Mr Pearson said Ron revealed that they were so keen to keep their secret safe that they only had sex with each other.

Ronnie fell in love with a young Arab boy in the sixties. He met him during a trip to Tangier in North Africa. He loved dark, clean-cut boys with pristine white teeth.

Ronnie believed that the boy loved him, too. He showed childhood friend Laurie O'Leary a photo and a letter from the boy. It was a love letter, describing how the youngster wanted to live with Ronnie in England.

O'Leary said Ronnie lost interest in the Arab boy.

'When he was sentenced, he still had many boyfriends and would do anything he could to make them happy.'

Entertainer Jess Conrad told the press he played a private gig for Ronnie in Broadmoor, after receiving a call from Diana Dors.

'Ronnie told me he thought I had a great body and asked me if I went running. I told him I did, and asked him if he did. He told me he ran, and then I put my foot in it. I looked out the window at the grass and beyond, and said, "Around that grass?" and he said, "No, around this room."'

Before the gig, the entertainer's entire band was petrified. Bravely, Jess went out in front of seventy-five inmates in his catsuit and performed 'Johnny B. Goode'.

There was no response, until Ron went 'yeah' and everyone started clapping – he began the applause after every song. Afterwards, there was a standing ovation, £5,000, and a 'thank you' letter from Ronnie.

It wasn't just the celebrities who clamoured to be part of the Krays' circle. Inside prison, fellow inmates wanted to be associated with them too, despite the fact that it was openly known Ron was gay.

Duncan Campbell, former crime correspondent: 'What Ronnie used to say was, "I'm queer but I'm not a poof," and that was the kind of way he presented himself. In his early days it was very difficult for a criminal to be gay – first of all it was against the law. A lot of gay people in the fifties and early sixties, until it was legalised in 1967, were blackmailed. For Ronnie to be so open was quite a statement.'

In prison, the Kray name was a formidable weapon; it meant that many people were afraid to take advantage of the Krays, and the fear engendered by the twins overruled talk about sexuality.

'I think there was a fascination for younger prisoners with the Krays because of the glamour. The Krays liked it and there would be these nice-looking young men hanging around, looking after them.'

One young patient at Broadmoor caught Ron's eye. With Alan out of bounds, Ron turned his attention to an occasional visitor from Somerset 2. The young man, around twenty, came over occasionally for sports events.

'Look at him,' Ron gasped. 'He's like a porcelain doll. He's beautiful. Blond, blue eyes, look. What's he doing over here, Alan?'

'I know what's happening. There's going to be a table tennis tournament in the dining room. Haven't you heard about it? They're taking the chairs away now and they're going to put up a table. The boys are here from Somerset 2. They're just young lads, but they'll be up for it, so we have to be on form.'

Ron couldn't play table tennis. He couldn't even imagine his bat making contact with the ball. He said he would be happy just watching, although he was keen to know the young boy's name. Could Alan provide any more details? Was this a one-off visit?

'He's called Kev. I've seen him over here before. Don't know what he's in for. Says he was framed. He's very young to be in here.'

'And very beautiful,' Ron swooned, not caring who heard. 'He looks smashing in his T-shirt and shorts. Alan, can I ask you something?'

'Go ahead!'

'How does the tournament work? Who will Kev be playing? How long will he be here? Is there a draw?'

'Let's have a look. Well, he plays me in the first round. I think it's a knockout format. Not sure how good he is. I'll do my best . . .'

'No, no . . .' Ron cut in. 'I want him to beat you.'

'Beat me? But I'm playing for Somerset 3 against Somerset 2. I can't let him beat me!'

'It's just a game. We don't want him knocked out, do we? Let's keep him playing and get to the final or however it works. We can't have Kev being beaten. He needs to keep winning.'

As it happened, Kev was an ace player and he swept all aside, winning the tournament for Somerset 2 while Ron looked on, full of admiration. The staff kept a good eye out; there was no way Ron could make any advances, although he was quick to congratulate Kev on his triumph. Ron relished the company of sporty young males like Kev.

'I have a cleaner to clean my room,' Ronnie told a flabbergasted Maureen Flanagan when she visited shortly after the table tennis tournament.

'A cleaner? Who does your cleaning?'

'Oh, a young boy in here,' Ronnie answered proudly. 'He removes all the bedding, takes it to the laundry, then brings it back all washed and ironed and starched. He dusts all round and brings me my tea in the morning.'

Norman Parker, sharing prison memories, recalled that some years later he met someone who had been in the wrong bed at the wrong time with Ron. That was when the police arrested the twins back in 1968. Norman called the boy Michael – not his real name. He would have been a teenager when the Krays' door was smashed in by the police, with Nipper Read at the helm.

'I met him five years after that arrest, when he was doing fourteen years at Wormwood Scrubs. We were all sitting at the same table, about eight or nine of us, and I didn't know who he was.'

Norman explained that he became friendly with Michael, and they went to the gym together. Freddie Foreman let it slip that Michael was the boy who had been in bed with Ron at Braithwaite House.

'The strange thing was – Michael wasn't gay! We would have known if he was gay. He was very young when the police raided, and a straight kid.'

Norman recalled that, in the sixties and seventies, criminals had their own prejudices. Many people were racist. Others were homophobic. Another section could be described as 'Little Englanders' who believed in right-wing politics. In practice, though, hypocrisy was the order of the day.

'Some people in prisons did get involved in homosexuality. Sometimes if things went on in the gay community, that we saw the results of, then we would talk about it. But it wasn't a topic of conversation on a regular basis.

'There were certain young men – not Londoners – who would go to the prison church and send little notes over to Ronnie, and he'd send them back. And these young men had absolutely no standing whatsoever in the prison community. They were thought to be absolute idiots.

'Their credibility was zero, because they were attracting Ronnie's attention purely for shagging.

'Then we thought, what would happen on the wing if Ronnie had two or three of these people with him? What if the same happened to Reggie? What if all of a sudden their boyfriends, however you want to call them, started giving it large? That could have been a problem. What if they had started swaggering and throwing their weight around? We would never have stood for that.'

Ronnie's constant companion in Broadmoor was Charlie Smith, a double murderer. Charlie was about thirty-five, fifteen years or so younger than Ron. The two of them ate together, chatted together in the day room and spent as much time as they could with each other. Charlie was quite good-looking, well built with light brown hair and about five foot ten. His face had little pockmarks in places.

'I'm only gay when I'm in Broadmoor,' he would say. 'Unless you've tried it, you'll never know.'

Charlie wasn't someone who went berserk all the time,

but on occasion he would 'lose it'. A corridor – or gallery as they called it – ran alongside the scullery, isolation room, medication room, staff room, staff toilet and washroom. Charlie's job was to clean that corridor, and he put up signs to say what he was doing.

If someone walked on the floor before it dried, he would flip. He would kick out at an offender, bringing the nurses running over. They used to talk him out of it rather than restrain him, and then the cleaning could restart.

Charlie doubted whether he would ever be released. He was allowed out once, and killed again, so the signs were far from hopeful.

Charlie watched Alan's back under Ron's orders. If anyone stepped out of line and hassled Alan, or any of Ron's friends, then a word from Charlie would be enough. He didn't look the type of guy anyone would want to mess with.

Ron told Alan: 'If you have problems with any of the slags on the ward, just tell Charlie. He'll sort it out.'

While it was no secret that Ronnie Kray was homosexual, many rumours have circulated about Reggie's sexuality inside prison . . .

Fellow inmate Bobby Cummines: 'Ronnie was gay. Reggie – well, whether he was bisexual who knows, but he was definitely gay.

'Don't forget at the time, in the sixties, homosexuals were being bashed up. It was not a good time. In fact, one of the Mafia shot another Mafia guy 'cos they found out he was gay.

'So it wasn't accepted in them days. But, as we were in prison, who gave a monkeys? No one did. And Reggie was surrounded by guys in there, young guys, and maybe he was coming to terms. But at that time in their life, Ronnie was quite open about it.'

Patient P, in the same ward as Ron, was shown plenty of Ron's personal photos of family and friends from a burgeoning collection. However, photos were a form of contraband unless the resident medical officer had given approval.

'Ron knew the staff who would overlook his pictures and he had them brought in during visits, so he had many photos. I never saw pictures of him with a boyfriend, which I thought was strange, as he often talked of having many boys. I saw some pictures of him with his brother at their boxing club. He showed me a photo of his home in London, which was not very grand.

'Ron also showed me a picture of Lord Boothby. He mentioned that, when he had his affair with him, he was questioned as to whether he knew Russians or a foreign power, which he found funny. He did say that Lord Boothby adored him, and did him favours to keep the Special Branch away from his business. I was shown pictures of Ron and his brother in his clubs with celebrities like Judy Garland and Barbara Windsor.'

Former armed robber David Fraser, son of Parkhurst rioter Frankie, spent time in jail with Reggie.

'Young prisoners tried to follow him everywhere. When

we used to go out on exercise, I thought, "Please God, don't come and have a walk round with us, because . . ." But he made it known that he didn't want to have a walk round with them, so they would just stay away. But the minute he went back to the cell, they would have everything ready for him. They were stargazers.

'Good luck to him. He wasn't doing any harm to anyone and, if he was that way inclined, that was his business. That's how I looked at it, but it was quite funny with the young fellows and there were the rumours . . . but then in prison there are always rumours.'

Bradley Allardyce, who served nine years for armed robbery, spent three years in Maidstone Prison during Reg's time there. They were four cells apart.

Bradley opened a restaurant in Altea, Spain's Costa Blanca, shortly after his release. Bradley said Reggie trusted him implicitly and, just before he was freed, the Kray twin handed over a pile of old photos and letters.

Bradley told the BBC: 'I am openly admitting for the very first time that we had a sexual relationship.'

Later Bradley Allardyce was jailed for life after being found guilty of murder. It followed the killing of 26-year-old David Fairburn in Barking, Essex. On appeal, this was reduced to fourteen years and three months.

For Reg and Ron, that would have been a more reasonable sentence. They could see no way out. Would they be locked up for the rest of their lives?

Chapter 10

Ron, Hooch and the Yorkshire Ripper

With Reggie stagnating in Parkhurst and Ron hoping for a brighter future in Broadmoor, mealtimes brought a ray of sunshine. For Ron, now more of a guarded patient than a prisoner, the food moved up a notch or two in quality.

Breakfast, dinner or tea would be brought onto the ward in yellow plastic containers. Porters brought it all over from the kitchen. Inside the containers would be metal trays containing the main meals.

Four members of staff opened a hatch to a scullery, meaning that the meals could be served straight to patients in the dining room. A cupboard in the scullery contained the cutlery and serving utensils.

A trustee – a patient with a reliable record on the ward – asked patients what they wanted during the week, and then a list was drawn up and handed to a charge nurse. That meant the kitchen knew what to prepare and the exact dishes to serve every day. There was a vegetarian option for all meals.

Plates were placed on the hatch, ready and waiting for a unique gathering of diners to consume the variable fare of Broadmoor.

The dining room had two rows of five tables opposite each other, with another table in a corner. Three patients sat at each table. Ron, after the pea-flicking and attempted punching incident, had kept his emotions in check and chatted about his past life during meals. He was now a permanent fixture on Somerset 3; any previous altercations were firmly in the past.

Ron and his friends and enemies were not allowed into the dining room until the order was given. That area was strictly out of bounds outside of mealtimes. A trustee laid out the knives, spoons and forks as well as cups with saucers and metal pots of tea. Every item of cutlery had to be accounted for and the staff kept a constant watch. Tomato ketchup, HP Sauce, mustard and a bowl of sugar completed the offering.

'Dinner is almost ready,' a reluctant-sounding trustee said. 'We're about to serve.'

This particular trustee, Den, must have eaten very little of the food. He was five foot eight, with a straggly mop of ginger hair, a pale white face and dark eyes, set behind thick, unflattering lenses. The frames were the sturdy type that most people regarded as ugly.

Den walked with a stoop, although he was only in his thirties, and looked as if the world was about to end. He was painfully thin. It seemed that Den's call to the diners was his single task for the day; after that he just mooched around and looked gloomy.

Den called out the patients for their meals by shouting individual names for 'diet one'. When that had been served, he called for 'diet two'.

Ron was always hoping to be placed with sensible dining companions. The Yorkshire Ripper had to be avoided at all costs. Other slags who had killed women, children or the elderly were off his guest list too.

After the meal, all plates and cutlery were collected and washed and dried by the staff. They counted every single knife, fork and spoon. The count had to tally – or there would be a body search of patients.

One time in the dining room, Ron stepped in to tell staff about a case of mistaken identity. A patient called Glen had grabbed a meek and mild arsonist called Geoffrey. Alan came to Geoffrey's rescue, striding through the dining room to get hold of Glen. The staff saw Alan throwing Glen against the wall, and grabbing him by the throat.

'If you ever touch Geoffrey again, I'll smash you black and blue.'

The staff could see Alan's part in the disturbance, but had no idea about the earlier attack on Geoffrey. Alan was led to an isolation cell, protesting his innocence.

'You've got the wrong man, ya slags,' Ron yelled out. 'He was doing your job. He was helping Geoffrey.'

Ron became even more aggressive and started shouting. The staff, fearing that Glen would face another assault, put Ron in an isolation cell. Ronnie's constant companion, Charlie Smith, then started complaining about what had happened. In a short space of time, Alan, Ronnie, Charlie, Geoffrey and two others were in isolation.

The ward quietened down, a doctor saw the patients in their cells, and the truth came out. The protesting group were let out of isolation, to be replaced by Glen for the attack he had made on Geoffrey.

Early on in his sentence at Broadmoor, Alan joined Ron for breakfast on a day when the dining room was sparsely populated. Perhaps some people were enjoying a lie-in, or had been unimpressed with previous breakfasts. The bacon was normally of low quality, and the sausages had a synthetic taste. The scrambled eggs had a gooey texture. Some patients wondered if they were, in fact, real eggs or possibly made out of some type of dried egg powder.

It was always three to a table, and the staff chose the diners. You couldn't hop from one table to another. The third person at Ron's table was freckled Jamie. His head was buried in a racing newspaper, so Alan felt free to talk without interference. When they chatted, Alan listened closely to Ron's older style of English accent. It was soft; almost gentle. There was nothing harsh at all. It seemed far removed from the present day.

'Ron, I'd love to know . . . but please don't tell me if you don't want to. How did you get into crime in the first place?'

'I've got nothing to hide about that,' Ron answered,

prodding at his brown and grey, odd-looking sausage. 'We got into trouble back in our teens. Actually Reg was arrested when he was twelve.'

Alan guessed that Ron would have had a lot to hide in later years. 'Twelve? How could he be arrested at twelve?'

'Well, we were on a train coming back from Chingford. You know Chingford?'

Alan shook his head, never having heard of Chingford; he noticed that Ron's staring eyes were bulging a little as he recalled the story.

'We went there for a picnic. It's a village in Essex. Nice place. Well, Reg had an air gun – you know, a slug gun thing – and he fired it out of the train window. He never hit anyone, but the guard saw him and locked him in his cabin.'

'Oh, did he get a rollicking?'

'The feller gave Reg a right ticking off but it wasn't over, because he told the Old Bill and the case went to court. I don't know what could have happened to Reg because he was so young, but anyway the local vicar spoke up for him. He was called Hetherington. The vicar praised Reg to the hilt and all he got was a warning.'

Ron, neatly finding an exit point in his mouth for a lumpy section of sausage, explained that Father Hetherington ran a youth club and local boys did odd jobs for him. This was the clergyman who became an important figure in the family's lives and conducted the service at Violet's funeral.

'I'm not having the bacon any more,' Alan muttered,

prodding a greasy, heavily salted slice to the side of his plate.

'We had to call on the vicar's services again a few years later.'

'Oh, what was it this time?' Alan asked, screwing his face up as he sampled the scrambled egg.

'It was much more serious. We were still in our teens. What happened was, we got involved in a scrap with some other fellers outside a dance hall. There were chains, coshes and all that. We stood up for ourselves.'

Alan assumed that, as was usually the case, they escaped justice.

'It was a close-run thing. It went to the Old Bailey with charges of GBH, but true to form, the vicar appeared to say what good boys we were and we never meant to hurt anyone except if we were defending ourselves. Well, there wasn't enough evidence, and with his kind words we walked away. What are you in for?'

Alan explained that his girlfriend was murdered and he was accused of killing the killer. He denied everything, but was offered a shorter term in Broadmoor if he pleaded guilty to manslaughter on the grounds of diminished responsibility.

There was silence as Ron sized up his dining companion. He had been disappointed to learn that Alan was not gay. But no one had spotted the earlier advances or said any more about the incident in the loo. Jamie's head was still obscured by the newspaper; although he wasn't involved in the conversation, the two men chose their words carefully. Jamie was just drinking coffee and not eating.

Alan swirled his fork around runny sections of scrambled egg as he wondered what to say next.

Another patient had told him that, on the outside, Reg and Ron would go into a bar, have a drink and say nothing. They did not need to say anything. They just stood there at the bar, looking powerful.

The strong, silent type, Alan mused, must have had a definite effect in the East End, especially as the threat of violence came with it. Alan also realised that an outsider walking into one of those clubs might have thought that the pair of them looked ridiculous, all suited and booted with nothing to say. He imagined that scenario, at the same time asking Ron what he preferred from the lunch menu.

'I like the fish and chips on a Friday,' Ron said, looking around for some reason, perhaps because his medication made him edgy. 'I like the chicken on a Saturday because it comes with nice veg and those sautéed potatoes.'

'I haven't been here too long, as you know,' Alan said, pleased that the short silence had been broken. 'I had meat pie the other day and Sunday lunch was good. I had the trifle, but I see you can have rhubarb crumble and custard.'

'Yeah, Sunday is good,' Ron answered, settling down once again. 'I always have a roast like the beef or pork or the lamb and they do good roast potatoes. You can have cheese and biscuits if you don't fancy a sweet.'

Alan could see that Ron was polite and well mannered,

apart from his occasional outbursts and the side effects of his medication.

'Any more for any more?' the ginger trustee shouted, prompting a general sprint for the hatch.

Ron and Alan stayed put, full to the brim of the low-quality breakfast. Perhaps, they thought, a different chef cooked the breakfasts.

'I tell you who I don't see much down here,' Ron mumbled, looking around again. 'Where does the Yorkshire Ripper go? He should be starved to death, so maybe that is what they're doing. He should be slung out of a place like this and sent somewhere really horrible. I hope they're giving him some really bad treatment.'

'It's the exact opposite,' Alan answered, pleased that he could provide a valuable update. 'You're not going to like this. They're treating him like a lord.'

Ron had no intention of getting up from his chair. He wanted to know about the Ripper's special treatment.

He was up to speed with the background. Serial killer Peter Sutcliffe had begun his sentence at Parkhurst in May 1981. There, he was attacked by a Scottish prisoner, Jimmy Costello. Costello's weapon of choice was a broken coffee jar. He used it while Sutcliffe was totally unprepared, filling a plastic bowl with water away from the relative safety of his cell.

It took thirty stitches to repair the damage, with a deep cut running from the Ripper's mouth to his neck, and another wound from his left eye to his ear.

Jimmy was found guilty of wounding Peter Sutcliffe with intent to cause him grievous bodily harm, receiving five years on top of his sentence. He defended his actions: 'How can anyone use too much violence against the Ripper?'

Even Frankie Fraser, a regular visitor to Parkhurst, had commented: 'Jimmy Costello deserves a medal.'

Sutcliffe was diagnosed with paranoid schizophrenia in 1984 and transferred to Broadmoor.

'You're telling me they're treating the Ripper like a fucking lord?' Ron gasped.

'Well, I was talking to him the other day. Big mistake. He's getting stuff together for journalists to tell them about this place, how he's innocent and everything else. But they're up to something. The police or whoever are trying to trick him.'

'What do you mean?' Ron coughed, halfway through a chain of cigarettes.

'Well, you're not going to believe this.'

'Go on, try me.'

Alan remembered from first-hand experience that Ron couldn't read very well. Unless someone pointed out the exact story and explained it, he would miss the fine details.

'Well, the newspapers that came in the other day – there were stories about the Ripper in a few of the papers. I saw one about celebrities writing to the Queen to get Sutcliffe a pardon. There was also a story about masses of people signing a petition to get him released. I saw him reading the stories in his cell. They were manufactured, I guess, and slipped into the newspaper. It was done professionally, though. It did look like a real part of the paper. Maybe the publishers were in on it, I don't know.'

Ron assumed that Alan was having him on.

'Not at all. The other day a nurse brought him his dinner and asked whether his steak and mushrooms were cooked to his satisfaction. The nurse asked whether he wanted Hollandaise or Béarnaise Sauce with the evening meal.'

Again, Ron stared in disbelief. Surely Alan was kidding.

'No, he was even offered baked Alaska or lemon soufflé for dessert. The nurse apologised to him for being behind bars. I saw through it, but I think he's being taken in.'

'Are they madder than the Ripper?' Ron almost stammered.

'Well, I think the idea is to gain his trust and maybe find out about more crimes. It's all about making him seem like an iconic figure, praising him to the hilt and making him think he's going to be released.'

The Ripper had been found guilty of murdering thirteen women. Voices from a headstone in a graveyard told him to kill prostitutes. The headstone voices came from God.

Ron and the others did notice that the Ripper had his favourite shows recorded so that he could watch them during the day. He was allowed to have a portable black and white television in his cell. He was also informed,

Alan believed, that his mail wasn't being monitored and no one was allowed to read it – or they would be in serious trouble. The patients were confused because Sutcliffe didn't do any work, enjoyed gourmet meals, watched television and read newspapers featuring stories about his good nature.

'They're hoping he slips up,' Alan explained. 'He might say something about other crimes in a letter. Who knows what he might reveal?'

'Sounds a bit over the top,' Ron agreed, 'but you never know.'

'Oh, and there's something else.'

'Something else?' Ron asked.

'Well, yesterday I was in the day room and the Ripper was there, saying he was expecting a visitor. Now this woman went along the path in the gardens and I would swear it was Princess Diana. If not, it had to be her double: tall, slim, elegant, with that distinctive nose. The Ripper just waved and shouted out, "Hi Di!" and she didn't look back, but there was an astonishing resemblance. Maybe they told him she was coming to check on his progress, and they sent a lookalike along to be seen in the place.'

Although the patients discussed the lookalike theory, the attractive lady could actually have been Diana herself. She visited on several occasions.

Diana, Princess of Wales, officially opened the Richard Dadd Centre. Dadd was a talented young painter during Victorian times, who killed his father and was sent to '

162

Bethlem, the psychiatric hospital in London. The hospital was also nicknamed Bedlam.

Dadd was then sent to Broadmoor, where he was encouraged to continue painting. He died in 1886. Opening the centre, Diana gave a short speech.

'I always enjoy my visits to the hospital which give me an opportunity, as patron of Turning Point, to discuss a range of mental-health issues with staff and to meet many of the patients. I have always been impressed with the commitment of the staff who have a very difficult task in providing care to patients, some of whom are very seriously mentally disordered. I know that the centre with its academic unit and Phoenix Therapy Unit will further enhance the work of the hospital.'

Alan said the Ripper claimed, in his high-pitched squeaky voice, that he'd had a chat with Diana. It was too much for people to believe, and so the 'lookalike' theory persisted.

'What were you doing with the Ripper at the pool table the other day?' a bemused Ron asked Alan as they arrived in the day room to read some magazines.

'You probably saw I was staring, well maybe I looked vacant, out over the courtyard. The Ripper decided to occupy a space to my right. He said his friends would be flashing him from a great height. I ignored the bastard and went back to my cell.

'The next day he was back at the same spot, where I'd been standing beside the pool table. I went over for a look, and he was peering out of the window. He glanced at his watch, and then a helicopter – must have been a police one on an exercise – flew over the courtyard and I saw flashes from a camera.

'It could have been just coincidence. The Ripper was looking smug, and I reminded him he would never be allowed out. He said that's what I was supposed to think. He's been conned, but he doesn't realise it. They're just trying to gain his confidence and get more gen from him.'

'They probably won't let me out either,' Ron mumbled, burying his head in a couple of tabloids. There were no stories about the Ripper in the papers that day. 'Alan, can I ask you something?' he continued. 'Some days I don't mix much and I think I missed something yesterday. Something about the Ripper. Was there some sort of special meal?'

'For once I can't give you a 100 per cent answer. People have been talking about it. Again, I think it's to do with gaining his confidence and getting him to admit stuff. You were in your cell yesterday and I saw people having a meal in the day room. The Ripper was there. It might have been for his birthday. There was a three-course meal.'

Alan told Ron something else that baffled him. During a visit to the medical area at Broadmoor one of the pretty young assistants said the Ripper shouldn't be in Broadmoor because he had only killed prostitutes. Also, Sutcliffe appeared to enjoy a foot massage while Alan had to make do with a few basic rubs.

At the dentist, based beside the chiropodist on the ground floor, Alan said he had a basic examination while the Ripper had his teeth cleaned and polished. To be fair, when Alan had painful toothache, the dentist sorted out an abscess. The Ripper's extensive treatment confused him, though.

Ron was totally amazed and found it all hard to believe.

Alan, reflecting on his time at Broadmoor, recalled that Sutcliffe caused a scene when he ordered a kitchen knife as a wedding present for a family member. Other patients assumed that he had negotiated to be able to order the knife, because it arrived in the charge nurses' office. Knives and the Ripper are hardly the ideal combination, but in any event the potential weapon vanished from the office.

'There was a state of panic in the hospital. Sutcliffe screamed that a nurse had taken the wedding present, and the ward was put in a state of lockdown with cells searched. The privileged side rooms of Ronnie and Charlie [Smith] were given thorough inspections. Staff thought that Ronnie, in particular, posed a threat to the Ripper.

'The staff manoeuvred all the patients into the day room, and they were addressed by one of the head doctors. He said a nasty weapon had been hidden, and anyone who knew of its whereabouts would probably gain a favour from the Parole Board.'

There were no favours for anyone, and no carving knife for any loving young couple. The controversial wedding present was never found. As the search was scaled down, another dubious activity gained momentum. There was no way that the Ripper could be involved . . .

'Ron, could you help me make some hooch?'

'What do you want to make that stuff for? It stinks. You're better with this non-alcohol stuff I have here.'

The request for help came from Will, the hooch brewer, who said he disliked the taste of Ron's zero-alcohol beer. He thought it was tasteless; besides, he wanted to enjoy the kick of alcohol, even from a home-made concoction.

Ron was, as usual, in generous mood: 'Well, I get these yeast tablets with my medication. Good source of nutrients, they say. I've got plenty of them. I'll pretend to take the tablets next time and give them to you.'

So that's what he did. When the nurses came round to give Ron his medication, he kept the yeast tablets in his hand and collected a pile over a few days.

'Here you are, Will, do your worst with these.'

Will grinned. He was a portly man, balding, in his forties, with a slight beer gut. It had been a large beer gut at the start of his sentence five years ago, now shrunk by the lack of booze.

'Where do you make it then?' Ron asked, peeking over his glasses as Will reached under his mattress to assemble his ingredients. 'Here in your cell?'

'No, come with me,' Will gestured.

He led Ron to the scullery and a cupboard where there was a designated secret hooch-making area. One of the cupboards had a board covering the base, which hid more of his secret ingredients and brewing equipment.

'This is what I do,' the amateur brewer said as he produced some pears, adding the yeast tablets and mashing them with the back of a serving spoon.

Will quickly produced more items: sugar, raisins, more pears, water and a bag of his top-secret ingredients. Working feverishly, he poured the mixture into a selection of plastic bottles. Then he refitted the board to the base of the cupboard, completely concealing his potent brew.

'The trustees know it's here,' Will explained. 'They won't give the game away. I'll leave it in the cupboard for about three weeks.'

And so the time passed, no one became suspicious, the hooch bubbled away in the cupboard and Will carefully sprayed deodorant if he sensed any pungent aromas emerging from the scullery.

Eventually the day of reckoning came. In the afternoon, when all was quiet, Will knocked at the door of Alan, Jamie and other trusted pals. A collection of mugs, borrowed from the scullery, was arranged on Will's table and he poured out five or six measures.

'It's strong,' Will gulped, his red nose developing an extra tinge of crimson.

'Plenty of flavour,' Charlie said as he sampled a generous mouthful.

'Very nice indeed,' agreed Keith, kneeling in the corner on his own as usual.

'Tastes very much of pears,' added Jamie with the freckles.

'A bit like antifreeze,' Alan mumbled to himself, putting his hand over his cup to prevent any top-ups. It's great, Will, but I'm not really a hooch drinker.'

The next morning, confusion reigned. There was a flurry of activity among the inmates. One of the trustees was walking about, whispering that Will had wet the bed. Keith said he would change the sheets and Alan needed to find a fresh pair of underpants. The danger was that staff could suspect a hooch session if they realised the patients were hungover.

'That Robbie is a dirty slag,' Keith yelled. 'He's been ratting on us about the hooch.'

It seemed that a disorientated patient, Robbie, had been allowed some of the hooch to sample. He had let it be known that all the patients on the ward were going to get some – a direct route to disaster. Not only that, he knew where the hooch was brewed.

Robbie admitted that he had planned for one patient to bang a drum and another to blow a whistle while celebrating consumption of the highly illegal hooch. Will and the others concluded that Robbie had lost his marbles completely.

Somehow, Will and his friends had persuaded everyone to keep quiet about the hooch, and the brewing continued unabated. Fortunately, the nurses were kept out of the loop. As in Parkhurst, a life could be lost over absolutely nothing: an onion or a bottle of hooch. Ron had the last word: 'If that Robbie was outside, he would be dead by now.'

Chapter 11

Reg Kray: VIP

Very Important Prisoner. That was Reg Kray. Even the warders respected Reg. They were astonished at the amount of fan mail received by both twins, much of it from celebrities. The glamour of the London club scene, of which the twins were an integral part, had left a legacy of adulation behind bars.

Ron and Reg, separated by the seventy-five miles of water and roads between Parkhurst and Broadmoor, kept up with the news. The twins, from that close-knit East End community, liked to find out what was happening in their local area.

Reg, especially, took a keen interest. Soon enough, Fred Dinenage, who presented the south of England's ITV news programme *Coast to Coast*, attracted Reg's attention.

In July 1985, Fred was presenting as usual, although a certain section of his audience was paying more attention than normal.

'One evening we had a feature on a father from Gosport

whose daughter had had a lifesaving liver transplant. We explained how the father was trying to raise money for the hospital, because he was so grateful that his daughter's life had been saved. He wanted to buy the hospital specialised equipment that wasn't available on the NHS.'

A couple of days later, Fred looked in his mailbox at work. There was an interesting addition. He had received a letter, franked HMP Parkhurst. Fred was intrigued. His only link with the prison was delivering news reports on it from the mainland.

'I opened up the envelope. The letter was from a certain Reggie Kray. He said he'd watched the programme, and he'd been moved by the story. He said there were many talented artists at Parkhurst, and he would talk to the other "chaps" as the main respected prisoners were known. He said he would get people together, sort out a collection of paintings and arrange for them to be auctioned. He thought they would raise quite a bit of money for the father's campaign.'

Fred put Reggie in touch with the dad and, sure enough, thirteen paintings arrived at the TVS studios in Southampton. Twelve of them were really good. One of them was more child-like, showing two boxers in a ring. It was signed 'R. Kray'. That painting by Reggie made the most money.

'In fact a lot of money was made at the action. It was called "The Rogues' Gallery". We carried a report on the auction, and how much money had been made. It was thousands of pounds, actually. Then I received another letter from Reggie.'

Fred recalled the contents of the letter: 'Fred, next time you're on the Isle of Wight, why don't you come and see me in Parkhurst?'

It was an invitation that Fred simply could not refuse. He had read all about the Krays' court cases and now had the chance to meet one – possibly even both of the twins.

He remembered his first arduous trip to the grim destination.

'Parkhurst Prison – in Reggie Kray's time there – was a tough, violent, intimidating place. Visiting prisoners there was never a pleasure. For a start you had to get there. You had a ferry or hovercraft ride from Portsmouth to Ryde. Then a taxi or bus from Ryde to Newport in the centre of the Isle of Wight. After that, a walk down Clissold Road with that dark, grim, red-brick Victorian monstrosity towering over you.

'And then a not-too-friendly welcome from the prison officers in reception. Forms to sign – a body search for phones, cigarettes, cash, weapons and, of course, drugs. Your photo ID to show, and proof of your address. Little or no conversation. You were almost made to feel you were guilty of an offence yourself.

'Then a wait until, finally, you were marched down a series of corridors to a large visiting hall. There was yellowing paint on the walls, strip lights beating down even in the heart of summer, and very basic chairs alongside Formica tables.'

Fred Dinenage's first visit was with Charlie, the Kray twins' brother, and Wilf Pine, a close friend of the family. They sat at a table in the corner of the room 'reserved' for Reg. All was quiet. Suddenly, the calm was broken by sheer bedlam as the prisoners poured into the hall. They were all under heavy guard.

'Reg, as always, wore a grey tracksuit and white plimsolls. And, as always, he was accompanied by three tough-looking young guys. They all had fair hair. They all had blue eyes. And they would all have ripped your throat out if Reg gave them the nod.'

Fred noticed that Reg strained to hear what he was saying. He was turning his head to the side, concentrating hard. Reg was still suffering from otitis externa, that chronic ear infection. It was diagnosed in the late sixties, and the partial deafness stayed with him for the rest of his life.

Wilf explained to Fred that the young guys were Reg's bodyguards. His protectors.

Fred was left under no illusion by Wilf that this was serious business: 'Reg is a marked man. He's a target for any young punk who wants to make a name for himself. These boys make sure no one gets near to him.'

They were, apparently, all 'tooled up' with weapons – though, of course, you couldn't see what they were carrying.

Visiting times in Parkhurst lasted for just an hour. Conversation was never easy. The noise levels were high, causing problems for Reggie with his hearing issues. He tended to whisper. It was difficult to understand what he was saying.

But Fred listened intently to Reg: 'I've heard all about the auction. The feller must have plenty of readies now for the hospital. I saw you doing it on the news last night.'

Fred told Reg that the auction made thousands of pounds, and all of the money was going to the hospital. Ron also had kept across what was going on, from his Broadmoor base.

Fred reflected: 'Reggie and Ronnie were soft touches. People would write to them and say – often quite genuinely I'm sure – that their child was poorly, dying, and needed to go to Florida to swim with the dolphins. There might be another letter saying that a young boy needed plastic surgery or whatever, or a young girl needed something else.

'They would never say "no." They would never check it out. If someone needed £5,000 and said they were in need of special treatment they would just say "pay them". That happened quite a few times.'

Visitors noticed that Reg's eyes were constantly darting around the room, always looking for danger. Occasionally a fight would break out between two prisoners at adjoining tables – or between an inmate and his wife or partner. The prison officers pounced within seconds.

'It was ugly, it was violent, and it was intimidating. When you walked out of the murk of the prison it felt like a weight had been lifted off you. I always felt sympathy for

Reg and the other prisoners who would rarely feel the sunlight on their faces.'

Fred, reflecting on Parkhurst's dark history and the cruelty to children jailed there all those years ago, believed that the place should have been torn down.

Maureen Flanagan also detested the journey to Parkhurst. She understood why the barbaric-looking fortress had been nicknamed 'Britain's Alcatraz'. There was no escape and little hope for anyone incarcerated there.

'When you go to Parkhurst it's a terrible journey 'cos it's a train from Waterloo to Portsmouth Harbour. I used to do it every month, and I hate water. I'm terrified. I can't swim. So when I was told that you had to get a ferry over to the Isle of Wight I thought, "Oh my God."

'Most of the time I was on my own. When I was on the ferry I would go downstairs to the bar and sit there. I could never be up on the deck, watching all that water.

'Reggie got somebody to pick me up in Ryde. A local cab driver picked up his mother when she went, so eventually he picked me up. We would go into a little local pub and have a half of Guinness because we had to kill three quarters of an hour before the visit.'

When she first travelled to Parkhurst, Maureen thought it was the most dreadful, horrible place on Earth. Reggie hated it. He said Parkhurst was the worst prison he'd ever been to. When Ronnie was moved there in the early seventies, on the other hand, he thought at first it was marvellous meeting old friends. He met people from other firms; at times they had wanted to kill each other, and now they got on OK.

'Reggie was treated very badly after he was sentenced,' remembers Maureen. 'He was beaten up and his mother saw marks and bruises on him. They really did try to declare him insane. Reggie was actually quite sane.

'Ronnie, though, had been to Harley Street, he'd been everywhere, and been treated by the best. They said there was an abnormality about his brain.'

When Maureen arrived at Parkhurst she viewed the place as a terrible prison, like something you might see in Transylvania. There were dark, grey, haunting corridors and you had to go up a back staircase to a waiting room.

'Reggie appeared, bounding up in a blue and white prison shirt. He could wear trainers and a pair of jeans, but the jeans weren't to his liking as he'd never worn a pair in his life. Later tracksuits started to become popular, so Reg wore those.

'The visit was always upbeat. He would come out with pieces of paper and say what he wanted me to do and who he wanted me to phone. He might say he needed me to go and buy him a pair of trainers. So I asked, where was I going to get the money for that, and he would say it was already arranged. Somebody had dropped the money off at his mother's house, so I had to go and buy a pair of Reebok trainers.'

Maureen was aware that the Krays were not the only

notorious prisoners in Parkhurst at the time. In fact, the twins became close to one in particular.

Reg and Ron had first met Charlie Bronson, often referred to in the press as 'Britain's most violent prisoner', in 'C' wing at Parkhurst. Ron clicked with Bronson straight away and regularly gave him £20 to spend on tobacco. Charles and Reg enjoyed going to the gym together; Charles said that Reg was a joy to watch on the punchbag, moving well all the time and showing amazing punching power.

'C' wing was a volatile environment where anyone could snap at any time. It was a good idea to have the powerful Bronson on the side of the Krays.

One day, this notorious inmate received a welcome visitor. Bronson was being visited by his mother Eira, before Ron's transfer to Broadmoor.

'When we went to visit Charles he was sitting at a table in the visiting hall. I went in, and he said, "See those two over there, Mum. They're the Kray twins." Charles said he'd asked if it would be OK for me to meet them.'

Eira went over to their table and was greeted politely by the Krays.

Ron made it clear that Charles should be somewhere else: 'Do something now. Plead as though you're insane and get to Broadmoor because it's different there. It's a hospital.'

Ironically, in 1978, a year before Ronnie was sent to Broadmoor, Charles was declared insane and sent to the Berkshire high security hospital. He had committed 200 acts of violence in four years. There were no other options available.

When he arrived, he recorded his thoughts for his own bestseller: 'From the moment the gates opened I could smell the madness. The place was full of despair. It was full of souls that were lost. For the first time in my life I felt fear . . . a fear that I would never be free again.'

Eira was grateful to the twins for being good to her son. Ron had given good advice, but she was concerned about Charles's health when she visited him at Broadmoor.

She was worried about his general condition. He said he had been wired up and it made him jump off the bed. Whatever antipsychotic drugs he was given, she said they made him balloon up to nearly twenty stone.

The Krays' notoriety exerted an attraction on disparate characters outside prison as well as inside. Steve Wraith from Newcastle wrote to Reg, hoping that he could visit. Steve was only nineteen, a so-called straightgoer who was fascinated by the Krays. This ardent fan of the twins was disappointed to receive only standard replies, thanking people for their support.

In the meantime, Steve found out that Reg had a pen pal. He wrote to the friend, Brad, and decided to pay him a visit.

While he was there, the phone rang. Reg, knowing Steve was with his pen pal, wanted to speak to the tall Geordie.

''Is that you, Steve?''

'Yes, Reg. It's Steve from Newcastle.'

Reg said Newcastle was a long way away and he must have travelled some distance to see his pen pal, Steve said it was worth it.

'Good, good. Well, you look after Brad. He's a smashing kid. Be like a brother to him. I'll see you soon, OK? God bless.'

Reg had invited them both to see him at Gartree Prison in Leicestershire. Steve felt honoured.

Gartree, near the town of Market Harborough, is the largest lifer centre in Great Britain. The building opened as a Category 'C' training prison before coming under the high security system to cater for people like Reg. Gartree became a Category 'B' prison in 1992. Age Concern became involved in providing extra support there after it was revealed that hundreds of inmates were over fifty years old.

Steve and the pen pal waited in the reception area for Reg to arrive. When he appeared, the handshake from Reg was a vice-like grip.

Steve looked him up and down. Reg was much shorter than he expected. Steve, at six foot two inches, towered over his host. Reg wore Levi jeans and a denim shirt with buttons undone and a gold crucifix. A pair of branded white trainers completed his outfit.

'He was so athletic and well built. He was obviously still training. He held the bench press record at Parkhurst and then at Gartree. He was at a physical peak for someone in his late fifties.

'I discovered that Reg would always find a way of getting a drink. Someone must have brought in spirits in a medicine bottle. There were some glasses of orange on the table, and Reg started pouring from the bottle.'

Reg spent a lot of that visiting time shaking hands and chatting to other people in the room. However, Steve was able to tell him that he had a job as a sub-postmaster and edited a magazine for Newcastle United fans. And, when it was time to go, Reg gave Steve an almighty hug.

Fred Dinenage also visited Reg at Gartree; Reg could be anywhere at any time under the dispersal system.

'A young visitor, who resembled Reggie's protectors at Parkhurst, appeared to be innocent enough as he strolled across to the table. In actual fact he had a packet of drugs up his backside.

'Once in the visiting hall he went to the toilet. Reg followed minutes later and retrieved the packet from behind the cistern. I learned later that Reg inserted it in his own back passage and returned to the room.'

Reggie Kray wasn't into drugs in a big way, although Maureen Flanagan knew that he smoked dope. But all drugs were a valuable currency inside high security jails . . . however they were wrapped and stored.

There was a lighter moment at Gartree; lighter as far as the inmates were concerned, but a disaster for the security team.

As Christmas 1987 approached, an airborne visitor appeared from the bleak, grey December sky. The pale afternoon sun, with not even a hint of warmth, was preparing to set on the horizon. Reg and a group of friends were chatting in a field used for exercise.

A speck in the sky grew larger until the familiar shape of a helicopter appeared, hovering over the field. Was it an emergency landing? Had the pilot lost his bearings? Was it an unexpected visit by a VIP?

A man named Andrew Russell had booked a Bell LongRanger from Stansted Airport. Approaching Leicester, he produced a gun and gave the pilot his landing instructions.

Terrified, the flabbergasted pilot carefully descended onto the field. John Kendall, described at the time as a gangland boss serving eight years, ran towards the helicopter along with Sydney Draper who was jailed for life after the murder of a security guard during an armed robbery.

After the two criminals clambered on board, the pilot took off again and said he couldn't land at a golf course, where their getaway car was waiting, because of mist. He landed at an industrial estate and was handcuffed to the controls for his troubles.

The carefully planned operation dominated the news, with a statement made in the House of Commons by Home Secretary Douglas Hurd:

Two highly dangerous Category 'A' prisoners, Kendall and Draper, escaped by air from Gartree prison at about 3.15 p.m. on 10 December 1987. They were taken out in a helicopter whose pilot had been hijacked by an armed passenger. They disembarked a short distance from the prison and made good their escape by road. Police inquiries into the escape are continuing, but both men are still at large.

The escape was able to succeed mainly because, while Kendall and Draper were taking their normal exercise in a large open space under the supervision of prison staff, there was no physical barrier to stop the helicopter from landing in that part of the prison and no practical means of preventing it from leaving. The attempt was made easier because it came as a complete surprise to the staff and because those planning it had been able confidently to predict the time and place at which the escapers would be taking their outdoor exercise that day. The helicopter was on the ground for only 23 seconds and then in the air for less than five minutes before it landed again outside the prison. That was too short a period in which successfully to track it by radar in accordance with existing contingency plans, which have been further refined in the light of this incident.

Immediately after the escape an immediate and vigorous review of security measures was ordered and all establishments holding category 'A' prisoners were put in a heightened state of alert.

A number of practical steps were taken at once

within dispersal prisons to frustrate any similar or other possible method of escape.

It's believed that all sorts of deterrents were considered, including barrage balloons, nets and a variety of barriers. In the end, Reg noted that orange balls were stretched across the field. They looked very attractive, with the prison lights reflecting from them.

The prisoners at Gartree made the most of it.

Reg saw posters appearing on notice boards offering helicopter trips, with tickets available from the Chief Security Officer. Information was made available on the amount of luggage allowed on helicopters. Some personal items would have to be left behind on future helicopter trips, apparently.

One poster on a notice board tickled Reg: 'Helicopter trips all full for the season. Check vacancies at a later date.'

Kendall and Russell were recaptured shortly afterwards, but Draper remained on the run for more than a year.

Great Train Robber Ronnie Biggs had apparently thought about a helicopter escape in 1965. The prospects of police possibly firing at the escaping aircraft put him off; in the end he scaled a thirty-foot wall with three other prisoners.

With Reg being ghosted around the country, Leicester was one of the usual destinations because of the 'submarine' there. This was a special unit, like a prison within a prison.

There were four of these security wings in the sixties: at Parkhurst, Leicester, Chelmsford and Durham.

There were so many bars that daylight couldn't come through. Floors, ceilings, doors and fixtures and fittings were bombproof. To get to the exercise yard, prisoners went through a tunnel into a small cage.

There were regular hunger strikes in protest at the conditions and sleep deprivation. Reggie was furious because warders knocked at the door every fifteen minutes, checking he was inside the cell. The doors had so many locks and bolts on them that 'no one inside could believe it'.

As a protest Freddie Foreman ate nothing for twelve days at Leicester, and saw his own ribs for the first time since he was sixteen.

'The prisoners weren't allowed into the main prison. It was completely over the top, you know? We weren't going anywhere. Although it was a big prison, I never saw another prisoner apart from the ones in the security wing. I never saw a blade of grass, a leaf, a tree or a bird.'

Even the visits took place inside the 'submarine'. It was a distressing experience for families, he recalled, with a prison officer writing down everything that was said in an intimidating atmosphere.

Freddie, thinking back, said Reggie wasn't there that long before he was ghosted off again to Parkhurst or another security wing.

Freddie spent four and a half years in those conditions, with bolts being rattled all the time and locks checked, and no chance of any sleep. Prison officers would bang on the door with lights flashing on and off, he said.

'The walls were the highest in the prison system and on the other side it was all cobbled stones so if you went over and you dropped, you'd break your ankles and that. There was a no man's land which was all wired up with alarm systems.

'There was a hot water pipe but it was lukewarm, so there was no heat at all from it. You could put a jug of water beside it in the winter and it would become solid with ice. That's how cold it was. You had to put a sheet over your head to keep warm.'

Reggie, and Ronnie before him, experienced the same conditions as Freddie. If they were spending time in any of the security wings, then that was their lot.

Freddie's impression: 'We went from cage to cage. It was like being kept in a zoo.'

At Broadmoor, by contrast, Ron's visitors could hardly believe their eyes. He had entered a different world.

Chapter 12

Ron, the Butler and the Whistler

There was a stark message for anyone who wanted to visit Ronnie Kray during certain periods at Broadmoor: 'He's on very heavy medication.'

The warning, from the hospital's chief medical officer, was double-edged.

'You'll find that Mr Kray appears to be a perfectly amiable sort of man, but nonetheless he is a chronic paranoid schizophrenic.'

Fred Dinenage took on board the fact that Ron's leg might shake, meaning that a change of conversation was desirable; he also tried to come to terms with a stranger in a white Rolls Royce, blowing cigar smoke out of the blacked-out windows and issuing reminders about the power of Ron's friends.

Fred strode towards the unappealing black gates in the pale winter sunshine, still bemused by the mysterious man in the expensive limo. He realised that, whoever it was, there had been prior knowledge of the visit to Ron.

'I was met by senior staff and taken into the visiting hall. It was a bleak sort of place, like a factory canteen. It had a big stage on one side where they used to put on shows. There were several tables, some occupied, and I sat down at a vacant one.

'After a few minutes, down a stone corridor, I heard marching feet. I can still hear that sound now. *Thump. Thump.* It had to be Ronnie Kray. He never walked anywhere. He marched everywhere, which was why he was known at Broadmoor as the Colonel.'

There was another reason for the 'Colonel' name, as discovered by Maureen Flanagan. She found out, during a chat with Ron, that he was obsessed by leaders of men. He dressed as close as he could to the likes of Al Capone, but his real heroes were Gordon of Khartoum, Lawrence of Arabia and skilful commanders, prepared for battle.

In her book, Maureen says: 'It was a fantasy world, fuelled by what he'd read and images he'd seen. I believe fantasy is fine if the mind is balanced and sane. But Ron's illness, tragically, could blur the line between fantasy and reality – to disastrous effect.'

Fred stood up as the footsteps approached. Ron Kray strode into the room, like a high-ranking officer in the military. He was much smaller than Fred had expected, and smartly dressed. He wore a grey suit, silk tie and waistcoat as well as a polished pair of brogue shoes. His hair was slicked back, and there was definitely an aura about this criminal legend.

'As soon as he arrived at the table we shook hands and sat down. He summoned another inmate, a sort of personal butler, who asked me what I would like to drink. I said I would like coffee, and Ronnie ordered a pot for me. Shortly afterwards the butler returned with my coffee and several bottles of non-alcoholic lager for Ron. He drank the stuff like water.

'The butler also brought two packets of cigarettes. I watched as Ron lit one, and then another, and another, taking a few puffs from each one before stubbing it out. That was just his habit.'

Fred mentioned the unexpected figure in the Rolls, and Ron knew the identity: 'That would have been Joey Pyle. Great friend.'

Joey Pyle was a close associate of the Krays, and a feared professional criminal. His trade was the protection racket. Pubs and clubs would be offered security after a series of violent fights on the premises. It was never wise to turn down Joey's offer; club owners who wanted to stay in business found it prudent to pay a regular, tidy sum.

The police found it hard to nail Joey. He went on trial for the murder of a nightclub owner in the sixties. The first case collapsed after jurors were intimidated, and at the second he was acquitted. There were later disappointments for the forces of law and order when key witnesses in other cases refused to testify.

If Fred had known the true identity of the man in the Rolls, he would have thought twice about carrying on!

The conversation began with pleasantries. Ronnie asked about Reg. Fred said Reg was fine, well shielded by his protectors at Parkhurst and looking fit.

Fred feared that, even in the relatively comfortable surroundings of Broadmoor, Ronnie could still be prone to violent outbursts. He had not heard about the missed punch after the alleged pea-flicking incident.

Ron took a puff of his cigarette, stubbed it out in the ashtray and gulped down a large mouthful of his non-alcoholic lager. Fred recalled the conversation.

'You want to write our story?'

'Yes.'

'What do you want to put in it? What do you want to write about?'

'Well, it will be very much the material that's already been covered in the past. But I also want to go into other areas that haven't been covered before.'

'What sort of areas?'

'Well, for a start I would like to ask you what happened to Frank Mitchell. They called him "The Mad Axeman." You remember you released him from jail at Dartmoor and he disappeared?'

Fred realised he had pushed far enough. Ron's right leg started shaking violently, and Fred remembered the warning about Ronnie becoming irritated.

The wary TV man changed tack: 'The weather is beautiful for this time of year, don't you think? It's a clear blue sky. It's a nice area, this, with all the countryside.'

For the moment, he would have to steer well clear of any discussion about Frank Mitchell, the Mad Axeman. Fred thought he would move the conversation away from Ron and involve the butler. Perhaps the butler had had some sort of breakdown and wasn't really a danger to the public.

'My name is Tony,' the butler said, looking Fred up and down as he placed the coffee pot and cups back on the tray.

'Hello, Tony. What are you in for?'

'I'm here 'cos I stabbed a couple of people to death.'

'How did that happen?'

'I was at a railway station and these two people were looking at me. I didn't like the way they were staring at me, so I stabbed them both.'

After a silence of thirty seconds or so, with Fred absorbing the magnitude of the butler's crimes, Ron rejoined the conversation.

'Yes, you can write the book. You can write our story. I'll tell Reg you can do it.'

Fred's recollection: 'Our meetings for probably the first couple of years were in that visiting hall. Then the Broadmoor authorities began to trust me, and we were allowed to have a private room. I even managed to record some of our conversations on tape, which I'd never been allowed to do before.'

During the visits, Ron showed Fred more poems, to add to writings about his mother. He handed a collection to Fred, some neatly typed by his helpers. Ron was pleased with one entitled 'The King'. He'd heard a programme on the radio about polar bears, hunted in the wilderness. He felt that the animals, battling to survive against all odds, represented the twins.

The poem described cold winters, with a polar bear being king in his environment. He was always looking for the hunter and, if cornered, would smash his foe. The polar bear was the king and would always triumph.

They were certainly Ron's ideas, because Fred could see a bundle of earlier unfinished thoughts in unmistakable Kray handwriting.

Ron enjoyed writing about the world around him, as he told Fred: 'There was a full moon the other night. It was so beautiful. It didn't seem right, shining on this awful place.'

Ron described how the moon appeared to be pale blue, like a flowering bluebell in the sky, so far away and high. When people believed in God, Ron suggested, it was easy to understand why they devoted their lives to religion.

Fred was impressed: 'The relationship I managed to build with Ronnie and Broadmoor became so strong that I was even allowed to go and see his cell. When I first went there it was really grim. It really was an old Victorian cell with the iron bars and a narrow slit of a window with a bit of daylight coming through, an iron bed, and very basic washing facilities.

'But by the time my writing was complete after three

years, a lot of the modernisation of Broadmoor had started. In actual fact he'd got himself a very nice room with velvet curtains that he'd selected, and a nice double bed. So things had improved considerably for him.'

Ron's business manager, Wilf Pine, remembered the tricky assignment facing Fred Dinenage.

'The twins liked the cut of him and they liked the way he spoke. They loved the way he argued with politicians, when he had a chance to, on the news show.

'But the twins would tell him one thing and then they would change their minds. So Fred didn't have the easiest book in the world to write!'

When Wilf first visited Ron, he had no idea what to expect. Reg was having a hard time in the callous regime of Parkhurst, always having to watch his back and surviving in an ancient, soulless cell. Wilf saw that things had improved for Ron, who admitted that 'life ain't bad.'

'He was sitting there in a beautiful cashmere suit. I thought he owned the place. I didn't think he was a patient.

'He had a separate cell as most of them had in there. So he had just about everything he needed that could be allowed. And although this is quite a while back, you know, they still allowed them little luxuries of this and that, so he was happy enough. He also only had one relationship from the time he went in there to the time he died.'

Duncan Campbell also witnessed the marching gait of Ron Kray: 'I saw this military-type figure coming across the quadrangle to the meeting room and he looked like he could have been in charge of the hospital. He had a sort of valet with him, pouring his Barbican non-alcoholic lager and handing him his cigarettes.

'He had on a pinstripe suit, white shirt, tie, silver sixpence cufflinks, everything like that, and he was striding along. He was obviously given more leeway than in a prison. So he was treated very differently to Reggie, and probably felt he had an almost normal life.'

On the outside, Ronnie had employed a personal barber to ensure that he enjoyed the best of trims in the family home. He'd heard that was what the Mafia dons did. Even in Broadmoor, despite the lack of home comforts, Ronnie always managed to look immaculate – hair and all.

Steve Wraith, away up north in Newcastle, continued to be fascinated by the Krays. At the age of fifteen, he had been transfixed by John Pearson's book, with the stark David Bailey image of the twins on the front cover.

Steve was allowed to study the book for his GCSE English exam, and passed, mainly because of his avid interest. After his success in speaking to Reg, he wrote to Ron, at Broadmoor, but received a standard reply. Ron said he couldn't enter into communication, although signing the letter and thanking the wellwisher for his support. It reminded Steve of his earlier dealings with Reg.

However, Reg now trusted Steve. And he thought it would be a good idea for the inquisitive Geordie to visit his twin in Broadmoor.

'The actual trip from Crowthorne Station to Broadmoor was like something out of your worst nightmare; never-ending rows of trees leading, not to a horror house, but a massive, bleak monstrosity. Although modernisation was taking place, it was still very much that old Victorian blot on the landscape.'

There were a few gates and doors to go through but, once he was in the main building, Steve felt more relaxed. It looked like a hospital, with walkways and wards. He arrived at a big, bright room that doubled up as the entertainments area, containing a stage and curtains.

Looking around the room, Steve couldn't see any prison officers, but doctors and nurses hovered around in their white outfits. At the far end of the room there was a greenhouse that led out into a garden.

'I was more nervous about meeting Ron in this mental institution. He appeared and came straight to the table in the visiting room. He clicked his fingers and a nurse appeared, to light his cigarette. Ron was immaculately turned out with pinstripe suit, tie and shiny Gucci shoes. He was every inch stuck in a timewarp and holding court. I remember he spoke in a sort of soft, old-style London accent.'

Ron ordered a can of non-alcoholic lager and a pack of king-size cigarettes. As usual he smoked one, then the other, only part-way down, then stubbed them out in an ashtray.

'Steve, you don't mind that I'm bisexual, do you?'

'Well, as long as you keep yourself to yourself and have no designs on me!'

Ron peered over his glasses and said, 'Good, good . . .'

George Cornell even came up in the conversation. 'It was great,' said Ron. 'I can play the moment over and over again in my mind. I can smell the fear.'

Ron had a wicked sense of humour. He asked if Steve was hungry, and indeed he was, so Ron recommended the burgers. Sure enough, a burger and chips arrived on a tray and Steve polished the lot off.

'There's a really good chef here,' Ron told Steve.

'Oh yeah, who's that?'

'Graham Young. He makes some really tasty dishes with a bit of kick in them.'

Steve recognised the name and the horror that went with it. Graham Young, the ex-Parkhurst 'Teacup Poisoner', had been sent to Broadmoor after dosing family and friends with murderous mixtures. Steve assumed that burgers would be fair game for Young and his potions, although thankfully the poisoner was actually in Parkhurst with Reg and died there from a suspected heart attack in 1990. Steve looked at Ron with a desperate expression.

Ron smiled. It was obviously one of his jokes.

Then, on a lighter note: 'Steve, I'd like you to come with me on a cruise. I'd like you to go with me to the Bahamas.'

Steve didn't make any promises but, sure enough, after a couple of days, a dazzling brochure arrived through his letterbox. Was it a joke? Steve thought Ron might have been genuine.

Also, there was a note from Ron asking if Steve could post some pictures in his shorts, doing weight training and boxing. Steve had mentioned his fitness regime, and half expected some interest in that area.

During another of Steve's visits, Ron almost erupted when a patient squeezed past him in the visiting room.

Ron was sitting in the middle of the room, as usual, and Steve joined him. A click of the fingers, and a valet-type person disappeared to collect a consignment of Ron's non-alcoholic lagers plus a pot of coffee for Steve.

Steve's chair was nudged from behind as a patient moved towards one of the tables, where a visitor was waiting. There was no 'excuse me' although Steve didn't think too much of the incident.

Ron stared at the offender with a venomous look: 'He's a slag. A rat.'

'Calm down,' Steve said. 'It was nothing. He just brushed past. I'm not worried.'

It became obvious that it was the person, rather than the incident itself, that had aggrieved Ron. The stare continued, along with various mutterings of the 'slag' and 'rat' variety. So who was this invader of Ron's space? Steve recognised the man from somewhere, with his beard and curly hair, although the grey tinges were years on from early photographs.

'You know who that is? It's the fucking Yorkshire Ripper. Peter Sutcliffe. Slag and a rat.'

The Ripper had been attacked several times at Parkhurst and Broadmoor, so it came as no surprise to see Ron at boiling point. Like other figures in his world, Ron abhorred crimes against women and children and his volatility was clear for everyone to see in the visiting room. Ron pushed his chair back, stood up, and kept staring at Sutcliffe. Then, in an instant, his mood changed and he sat down again to talk about business. His illness provided those traits.

The actors Martin and Gary Kemp, who played the Krays in the 1990 film, also went to Broadmoor to meet Ronnie. They saw that he had a nice room, he had a TV and wore his own clothes.

Martin said they never wanted to do impersonations, but just capture a feeling and an atmosphere; impersonations would never have worked. Gary would never have felt comfortable taking on Ronnie's voice, which sounded high and camp. Meeting Ron meant that Martin didn't want to meet Reggie. He captured everything he needed from Ron.

Ron appeared dashing in a sky-blue suit and cufflinks with diamond-encrusted Rs. The white shirt Ronnie wore at Broadmoor was even copied for the film.

'You're not going to play me with that earring in?' Ronnie said as he stared at Gary. It was such an intense stare that Gary felt he had to return the look as long as it lasted.

At the end of the visit Ron said he was feeling dehydrated because of the medicine they gave him. A butler-type patient, who attended to Ron's needs during other visits, brought the bill from the prison canteen for the drinks the three had consumed. It was for £100.

Gary reminded the attentive server that they had only had a couple of non-alcoholic lagers. 'I hope you don't mind, but Ronnie put a few fags on there,' the attendant replied.

Sometimes Ron's bill didn't run into hundreds; it totalled thousands of pounds.

After one visit, Maureen Flanagan, with two of Ronnie's friends, was approached by a twitchy Broadmoor employee. He indicated that a large canteen bill had to be paid. One of the friends offered to help, producing a couple of £50 notes. That kind offer wouldn't have made a dent in the money owing. The total was £7,000.

The notes were handed over to make a slight impression on the bill. Later Ron revealed that he had been buying in pork pies from Harrods and holding weekly parties, with wine, in his room.

Also, Ron had the habit of ordering huge bouquets of flowers through the canteen. The recipients were often strangers, who were given the fragrant blooms to take home to their mums. Not only that, children of visitors received toys from Ron. Added to all of this: Ron could have visitors twice in one day, with his entertainment bill covering mini buffet lunches. In the end, Ron's visitors paid off his bill . . . bit by bit.

Ron received an unexpected visitor in the eighties. The name, Angela Tremble, didn't exactly have him shaking in his shoes. Of course, Angela Tremble could visit him. Of course, he would make the lady welcome as she had taken the trouble to write to him.

Perhaps she would enjoy a pot of coffee while he indulged in his booze-free lagers. Maybe, even, she would enjoy one of his king-size cigarettes.

When the visitor arrived, Ron was in a state of shock. Everyone else who saw her was in a state of shock, too. Straggly blonde hair. Fabulous figure. Sparkling green eyes. An entourage, lurking outside in the car park. It was Debbie Harry, whose real name was Angela Tremble – although that was never going to work as a stage name.

The normal visiting arrangements went ahead, with Ron enjoying his non-alcoholic lager and Debbie sipping ground coffee as they chatted about Ron's future and her string of number one hits. It took Ron a long time to recover from a visit by such an icon of the time.

Maureen Flanagan: 'When they were separated, with Ronnie in Broadmoor, Reggie did apply to see him. He was entitled to do that, maybe once or twice a year. They put them in a very small room with two guards. For God's sake, what were they going to do?

'We petitioned and I used to deal with Dr Tidmarsh, the consultant psychiatrist at Broadmoor. I asked why they had to listen to private conversations between two brothers when they were only going to see each other twice a year. I thought that was terrible, just to see each other so rarely, when they'd been together for so long.

'The visits between the twins became more private. They said they didn't want to talk to each other about their past. They only talked about the future, or who had visited them, and any old friends that had seen them. They talked about their mother, father and brother Charlie. Once Charlie was out after seven years he could visit them.'

Maureen remembered that Ron was always around fifteen minutes late in the visiting hall, to make an impression. He would appear in a Giorgio Armani suit, white silk shirt, silk tie and expensive polished shoes. Onlookers thought he was the psychiatrist, striding along with purpose. Ron wanted to appear the same on the inside as he did on the outside: immaculately groomed.

Dr R, who worked at Broadmoor during Ronnie's time, saw visiting as key; it was a crucial contact with the outside world and something patients needed desperately in their lives.

'The sad fact is that many patients, because of their history or what they did before going into the hospital, had damaged or even severed relations with their friends and families. During my period of working there, quite a number of patients had no visitors at all.'

The doctor said that at least escorted trips provided limited excursions away from Broadmoor.

'But that didn't happen very often. For most patients it was quite uncommon and would be very infrequent. For some patients, that would not happen at all – or they would have to wait several years to get out for the day.'

Dr R said the average length of stay back then was about eight years, and a number of patients stayed considerably longer than that. All of them were detained under the Mental Health Act.

'Some, including Ronnie Kray, would have been transferred from prison. Others would have been sent perhaps by the courts. So, instead of receiving a prison sentence for their crime they were, if you like, sentenced to hospital. For them, there was a kind of indeterminacy about the length of time that they might expect to stay.'

The people who received a prison sentence knew where they stood. They knew how long they were going to be inside and when they were going to come out. However, in Broadmoor and similar secure in-patient units, that wasn't the case because the length of stay was determined by a number of factors. Importantly, it was determined by the response they made to treatment and rehabilitation, the level of improvement achieved and a perceived reduction in the risk posed to the public.

'If people made an improvement and responded to treatment quickly, then they might expect to move on fairly rapidly. On the other hand if that didn't turn out to be the case and the mental disorder was resistant to treatment, people spent a very long time in Broadmoor.'

Chris Lambrianou was well aware of Ron's mental issues in his early crime days: 'If you go back to biblical times, you've got Moses with a staff. In hand it was in control. The minute he threw that staff on the floor, it turned into a snake. Out of hand it was out of control, and that was Ronnie Kray. He was without medication and proper support.'

Chris said that, far earlier, Ron should have been put somewhere to suit his needs and be looked after in the correct way. A lot of unfortunate events happened, involving Charlie and Reggie, because of Ronnie.

'And he had a steely, vice-like grip on Reggie's emotions and everything else.'

One unexpected visitor was the late Charlie Richardson, after his own release from prison in 1984.

'The Krays were all right. They were just ordinary people. They were no better and no worse than anybody else, you know? I didn't mind them. When I come out I went down to their snooker club and had a game. And I went to see Ron in Broadmoor along with Steven Berkoff. Good actor.'

Steven played the role of George Cornell in the film, *The Krays*, starring the Kemp brothers.

During one visit, Steve Wraith came across Ron's chilling side. The normal arrangements took place. Ron clicked his fingers, and a hand appeared from nowhere with a lighted cigarette. A valet-type figure arrived with several cans of non-alcoholic lager. The only difference on this visit: Ron had a furious expression.

'I want you to do something for me,' he hissed.

'Of course. What's that, then, Ron?'

'Reg is upset.'

'Oh?'

'Two people have upset him.'

'What do you want me to do about it?'

'I want them killed.'

Steve said nothing. He had never been placed in a situation even remotely like this before. Here he was, talking to the murderer of George Cornell. This was a throwback to the sixties. Ron thought he was still calling the shots in his Firm, giving orders to have someone taken out. For Steve's benefit he wasn't using language such as 'whacked' or 'clumped', but the message got through.

Ron named the two people, assumed his friend would make the necessary arrangements, and the visit ended. The usual 'other business' had been discussed, although Steve could hardly concentrate on commercial interests or anything else apart from the ordered killings. He had never even stolen a toffee from a sweet shop, let alone acted as a hitman!

Another visit was arranged, and Steve knew what would be on the agenda. Ron sipped his non-alcoholic lager, took a puff of his John Player Special cigarette and stared at Steve. 'Have you sorted it out?'

'No, I need more time.'

'Good, good.'

And the executions were never mentioned again. Ron's mood swings had led to the request, he had accepted the time extension, and then the matter was dropped. Out of all the hitmen in the underworld, he had approached innocent Steve! That incident proved to Steve that Ron could never be trusted on the outside, drugs or no drugs. The killer instinct remained.

Another patient appeared at Broadmoor with a track record that was totally opposed to Ron's beliefs. Kenneth Erskine, the Stockwell Strangler, was convicted of killing seven pensioners in January 1988 after a reign of terror that lasted for fifteen weeks. He strangled his victims in their homes in the Stockwell area of South London.

Erskine's murder convictions were downgraded to manslaughter on the grounds of diminished responsibility. He had a mental age of ten. His youngest victim was sixty-seven and the oldest ninety-four.

They were all strangled and some were sexually assaulted. Erskine was suffering from severe schizophrenia which would have diminished his responsibility to a 'massive degree', a leading psychiatrist told the court.

'Erskine was put on the antipsychotic drug Haloperidol,' fellow patient Alan recollected. 'I knew from experience this was a nasty drug. Erskine was just wandering around, looking bewildered and unsettled. He said to me, "I don't want to be on drugs," as if I could change his situation. I wanted him to suffer from taking drugs the same as I had done.'

Alan watched as the Stockwell Strangler pretended to take the liquid drug, and then spat it into a cup of water. The nurses were none the wiser, so Alan told them what had happened. They gave him the drug again and said they would be monitoring his medication. Alan had landed

Erskine in trouble, because of his brutal crimes involving elderly people. Ron, bizarrely, was far from amused, despite his admiration and respect for the elderly.

'Alan, can I speak to you?'

'Yes, Ron?'

'I heard what you did to Erskine. In here it's the screws versus the cons.'

'Erskine isn't a mate. Look at what he's done, killing those old people.'

'You were out of order there,' Ron insisted.

'But he murdered old people. They were mothers and fathers.'

'Still out of order. You don't grass up another con.'

Alan took that on board; he had another mission to complete, however. The Stockwell Strangler had an appalling BO problem. Alan believed that the stench at the scene of the crimes helped police to trace the killings back to Erskine.

There was a stumbling block facing fellow patients and staff who wanted Erskine to clean up his act. The niffy newcomer appeared to have a fear of washing or coming into contact with water. Ron took a back seat, watching as Alan looked for a solution.

The staff asked Alan, who was a trustee when Erskine arrived, to ensure that the strangler had a bath at least once a day, 'by hook or by crook'. Nurses actually provided a special tap, which fitted onto the bath, so that washing was strictly monitored.

'I don't want a bath. I don't want one,' Erskine would respond as Ron peered through his glasses and Alan took the initiative.

'The bath is run, could you get in?' Alan ordered.

Alan decided not to throw Erskine in and left staff to carry out the delicate operation. They were always on hand if anyone was having a bath because of the obvious dangers.

'That was very kind of you, Alan,' Ron said, praising the efforts to keep Erskine clean. 'Good for you, helping the feller.'

Not once did Ron mention the Stockwell Strangler's pong. Perhaps he thought it was too embarrassing to mention. He certainly kept abreast of the efforts to bathe Erskine and the subsequent cleansing by staff. And Ron remained calm as the washing episode unfolded in front of his wide-framed glasses.

However, during visiting hours, Ron became irritable again. This time, a patient called Lee was annoying him. As Steve Wraith sat drinking his tea, with Ron sipping his non-alcoholic lager, the sound of an out-of-tune whistle blasted through the ward.

'He's got to stop that,' Ron complained as the whistling became louder and even more out of tune.

Lee, obviously tone deaf, was wrecking 'Drunken Sailor,' as if the choice of tune wasn't bad enough; and, even worse, he chose to boost the volume with Ron in close proximity. As Ron's treatment was involving fewer drugs at that time he was more sensitive, more irritable and more likely to take exception to the appalling sound.

A few days later, newspaper stories recorded that Ron had tried to strangle the whistler. It took five nurses to calm Ron down. He was taken off the ward, lost his privileges and removed from gardening and kitchen duties.

Steve's role was to call the newspapers and say that Ron would take part in no more violent incidents. The out-of-tune whistler, all concerned agreed, would be the last to feel the fury of Ron's wrath. Ron and Reg needed to get down to business. Proper business.

Chapter 13

Making Money Behind Bars

Reggie and Ronnie Kray had a constant need to make money. They gave a lot of it away, infuriating close associates who helped to arrange an assortment of schemes – masterminded by the twins behind bars.

Their activities on the outside had included extortion, protection and fraud ... all grown out of operating snooker halls and clubs in the East End.

The most infamous criminals of the twentieth century were slowly adapting to prison life, and that meant fading into obscurity if they disappeared from the limelight.

It appeared as if the twins had been tamed by the prison system, but then a bestseller changed everything ...

Wilf Pine, Ronnie's business manager, explained: 'The whole situation with the twins would have died down like any other gangsters once they go to jail. When you're away for two or three years people forget, you know. But then John Pearson wrote his book, and you had that stark

David Bailey photograph of the twins on the front. Everybody bought it.'

And that was when the Krays began to forge a new legend, recreating their criminal empire from behind bars. The resurgence in the Kray brand proved to be an astonishing turnaround.

Wilf recalled their rackets on the outside: 'They had really only just got started when they were nicked. No matter where they went in London, they didn't have to demand protection money. People wanted to give it to 'em and say the Krays were looking after the place!

'I don't think they physically intimidated that many people to get their money. People were knocking on the door, asking to be looked after. The twins had built up such an aura, a reputation around themselves, because they had done some really nasty damage in fights. People were only too pleased to give them the bloody money.'

The twins, though not as smart as the Richardsons, operated so-called long firm frauds. Orders would be placed with wholesalers, and payment made on time. This meant that a good credit history was built up. The suppliers believed they were dealing with trustworthy people, and the orders became larger. Then a substantial order would be placed. The goods arrived, they weren't paid for, and everything was sold off. The villains receiving the goods also disappeared.

Chris Lambrianou's picture of London in the sixties: 'It wasn't ad hoc like it is now. In those days there were the firms. There was the heavy mob who would go out on the pavement as wage snatchers. They would meticulously plot different robberies from security wagons, which weren't as tight as they are today, or post offices and banks.

'In the old days two or three people took a bag to the bank and people would jump out on them, spray them with ammonia, and hit them with coshes. It was far worse than they did in the Great Train Robbery. Actually many of the train robbers were pavement artists as we called them. They didn't draw pictures but were out on the pavement getting money.

'And also you had the long firm men. The clever boys knew how to get in and do the long firm stuff, and they would open an office and shut it down. Everything was based on trust, and trust was the last thing these guys were thinking of.

'You had your safe blast men and you had your key men. There was a lovely guy named Johnny. Show him any door and he would open it. Prostitution was run by the Maltese. And there were heavy people, like the twins, who minded different clubs, gambling and all the rest of it.'

Residing at Her Majesty's Pleasure, and back in the public eye because of the Pearson book, the Krays realised the potential to start earning serious money once more, as Wilf explained.

'Some of the visitors that used to come to see them were like security firms. The Kray name was such a thing in the seventies. The twins were pinching two grand here, two grand there, from people who wanted to be able to say they were associated with the Krays.

'During one visit there was just me and Ronnie, and he said they needed to make some money. I thought, "Here we go," but he was very switched on. He thought they could make legitimate money.'

Ronnie had told Wilf: 'We just need these extra incomes to help with what we're doing.'

'Have you thought of T-shirts, saying *Kray Twins on Tour*?'

'Tell me some more,' Ronnie laughed.

'Mugs, posters . . . there's endless stuff out there. People would want to get involved. And you become mythical characters and icons of the underworld, right? I'm sure I can fix something up.'

'Do it, straight away,' Ronnie urged.

Wilf spoke to contacts in merchandising and, one by one, deals were done.

'So I spoke to a few people who I knew in merchandising and everything else. Everybody wanted to do it, but they all needed to meet Ronnie to make sure everything was sanctioned.'

The list of companies and individuals was endless. Wilf received call after call from people with ideas – and requests to meet the twins.

The resurgence of the Kray brand meant that the twins remained household names. At one stage they were earning £3,000 a week from Krays merchandise – a fabulous amount several decades ago. And that was only the beginning. They licensed their name for other companies to use too.

Patrick Fraser, son of enforcer Frankie Fraser: 'We've always thought they earned more money in jail than they ever did when they were out of jail.'

Professor Dick Hobbs described how many people looked back at what they saw as a golden age for criminals. Villains were starting to present themselves as celebrities. Various gangsters were coming out of prison and they were being interviewed on TV. But the Krays were the great icons – the big names.

'I don't think they had to do very much actually to sell the brand because there were other people doing it. Then we started to get more books on the Krays. Anyone who had any association with the Krays was writing a book. Anyone who visited the Krays was writing a book. There were TV programmes about the Krays and, of course, the film with the Kemp brothers.'

Professor Hobbs stressed that, if he worked with the police – talking about any kind of organised crime – the Krays' name would always come up. The twins were the epitome of old-school gangsterism. The Krays were really a benchmark: the gangsters to be compared with all others.

Security firms were attracted to the name. Could there be a stronger brand, promising a trouble-free operation? Would anyone really meddle with a company's affairs, knowing that Reg and Ron were involved? A few grand here, a few grand there; it all added up to a steady income stream behind bars.

And when their brother Charlie was released from prison, they had a man on the outside who could rebuild the Kray empire. He set up Krayleigh Enterprises which collected earnings from the twins' lucrative business ventures.

Krayleigh Enterprises offered bodyguards and personal protection. Reggie would write non-stop to his contacts on the outside, issuing instructions. On some letters he would mention the time of day he was writing. It could be the middle of the night.

The Krayleigh Enterprises operation offered 'personal aides to the Hollywood stars'. It's believed Frank Sinatra hired eighteen bodyguards from the firm for a trip to London. The twins did it their way . . .

Papers later released under the Freedom of Information Act show the authorities in Broadmoor were monitoring these business activities. There was no legal basis to shut it all down but, as usual with the Krays, it quickly ran its course.

Wilf explained: 'The few guys that they had on the books were knocking a few people out unnecessarily, not even for wages. And I just happened to say to Charlie at the time, "You gotta turn this one in, this is stupid for you." And he did – he wiped it down.'

And the merchandising?

'Nah, no more,' Ronnie told Wilf. 'I'm starting to feel like a clown.'

Wilf said Ronnie thought it was like coming to see the puppet or whatever.

'That put the blocks on it, but by then they'd accumulated a nice few quid each, believe me.'

The lack of money coming in meant that, as the years went past, Ron and Reg needed to have a rethink and revive the commercial activities.

Fred Dinenage's book, *Our Story*, was doing well as a bestseller with serialisation on the cards and offers from various newspapers. Reg and Ron wanted to appear respectable, and needed the authorities to regard them as serious figures.

'So what shall we do, Fred?'

'Well, the newspapers will offer you serialisation. Go for the most serious one.'

Just before publication, the publishers confirmed that they had had offers from the *Sun* and *News of the World*, the *Sunday Mirror* and the *Sunday Times*.

Fred advised: 'The smallest amount is from the *Sunday Times*. But go for that. Don't go for the big money initially. You'll get it in sales, anyway, in the end. Go for the *Sunday Times*. That's the most serious, the most respected.'

But no. The twins went for the *News of the World* and the *Sun*, and the extra money.

'I thought it was a shame. A week before publication Ron rang me up – they were both able to ring me from inside – and said, "They will treat it sensitively, won't they?" I reminded him that the story was going to be in the *News of the World*.

'Ron said, "Well, talk to them Fred, and make sure they do it sensitive, like."

'So I rang up the editor. It was a lady. I said Ronnie Kray was concerned that they might treat the story insensitively. She said it would be very sensitive.'

The following Sunday Fred spotted a copy of the *News of the World* in his local shop. Right across the top of the front page was a caricature of a madman with bulging eyes, trying to pull apart the bars in a cell. The headline said Ronnie Kray was mad and gay.

Within half an hour Fred had a call from Broadmoor. It was Ronnie.

'What the fuck is going on?'

Fred countered: 'Ronnie, I told you. You should have gone with the *Sunday Times*!'

Steve Wraith from Newcastle had kept in touch with Reg and Ron. Reg could see that Steve would be able to help on the business side. He phoned Steve, giving him addresses to help with mailshots. Reg contacted friends and supporters and gave Steve's contact details.

Steve gained Reg's confidence – enough to develop into a commercial arrangement. Reg wanted to develop that earlier interest in T-shirts, mugs and anything that could make money. Fred's book also had potential for extra earnings. The man who could help Steve, Reg said, was his old and trusted friend, Pete Gillett, who had come to the rescue during the Parkhurst football match.

He gave Steve the phone number of his pal who, he said, would supply the goods. The extent of the 'supplies' stunned Steve. On his doorstep: six large boxes from Pete.

'I took them inside and opened them up. There were so many T-shirts, I couldn't believe it. They had Reg's face on with the words "Enough Is Enough." There were also pictures of the twins and I noticed the price tag . . . £250. They looked like artist's impressions. There was a note from Pete that one of the pictures was for me.'

Steve dug deeper into the boxes and came across dozens of copies of the twins' autobiography. Steve had an idea to make more cash. He sent sticky labels for Reg and Ron to sign, then stuck them to the books. The 'signed' copies sold for £20 each and there was no lack of demand.

'I realised that although they were behind bars, the twins must have had lots of lucrative schemes like this. The merchandise was easy to sell. I soon had a tidy four-figure sum and sent the money off to Reg. He gave me a decent cut, and I was happy with that.'

At this point Steve was editing a Newcastle football magazine, *The Mighty Quinn*, named after legendary striker Micky Quinn, who joined the Magpies in July 1989 for £680,000. That was a massive fee at the time.

Micky scored four goals on his debut, when United defeated Leeds 5–2. He was the Football League's leading marksman in 1989–90 with thirty-four league goals. 'The

Mighty Quinn' was also a Bob Dylan song that became a hit for Manfred Mann in 1968.

Reg, well-versed on the fortunes of Newcastle, Quinn the footballer and also the song, asked Steve: 'What if we advertised our gear in your magazine? Would that be possible?'

'Yes, we can do that,' Steve told him. 'But could you do something for me?'

'What's that then?' a curious Reg wondered.

'I've heard you follow football and went to matches. I know that was a long time ago. Could you write an article for *The Mighty Quinn*, saying what the game was like in the fifties? If you can do that, I'll put an advert in.'

It was a deal. Reg, true to his word, started writing his article. Reg had often discussed football with Frankie Fraser, who was an ardent Arsenal supporter. Pete Gillett had also persuaded Reg to support Arsenal – the Gunners – but his memory was of a match at Tottenham Hotspur.

What a coup. One of Britain's most notorious gangsters, writing an article in a football club magazine.

Although I have never been a fanatic football fan, I have had the pleasure of seeing some of the great players. My earliest introduction was when I was about ten years old. An uncle took Ron and me to watch Tottenham Hotspur. There were thousands of people, packed together, and my first impression was that this could be dangerous if they weren't controlled properly. In those days they didn't have the same seating facilities as we have now.

I also noticed that the footballers wore very long and baggy shorts. I wondered to myself why they didn't have neat shorts, like boxers wore.

One of the greatest footballers I ever saw was Stanley Matthews. He dribbled past each player on the right wing until he was in a position to pass across the goalmouth. His dribbling was uncanny, and the way he swerved was a pleasure to watch. Another great player that I saw was the late Frank Swift. He was one of the world's greatest goalkeepers. I remember how he would pick up the ball with one hand and throw it to someone on his team.

I also witnessed the playing of the great Tommy Lawton, who could head a ball better than any other player I saw. I also remember the Compton brothers, Denis and Leslie, who played for Arsenal. Many years later I met manager Malcolm Allison at the Astor Club in the West End. Some time in the sixties I met Dave Mackay, the famous Spurs and Derby player. I used to buy ties at his shirt and tie shop.

When I was first convicted I spent some time at Leicester Prison where I met Frank O'Farrell, the former Manchester United manager. He was giving a lecture about football to the inmates.

Sad to say, some years after my first introduction

to football and my perception of the crowd dangers, there was a disaster at Hillsborough. On reflection, I feel that if a ten-year-old could foresee a problem, then the safety people should have thought the same.

On a happier note, I was pleased to see that my fashion consciousness did come into effect by the wearing of shorter shorts and better all-round attire.

I wish all football fans, regardless of which team they support, an enjoyable end to the season.

REGINALD KRAY

The press criticised Steve for giving Reg the publicity, but he couldn't care less. The more headlines – good or bad – the better, he thought.

As the fuss about the article died down, Steve cashed in by selling more and more merchandise. But one thing troubled him. The quality of the T-shirts left a lot to be desired, and several people had commented on the poor workmanship.

'Reg,' he said during one of his now regular calls. 'We could make a lot more money if the product was better. Believe me I can get the quality improved. What if the proceeds were seventy-thirty in your favour?'

'Deal,' Reggie agreed.

Steve organised higher quality garments with a more professional design on the front, and they sold quicker than hot cakes. Not only that, an entire range followed. There were towels, shopping bags, mirrors, mugs, and all with a jump up in quality that people were prepared to pay for. He mulled over the idea of Kray condoms, to provide ultimate protection, but thought that might be a step too far.

The twins made sure that Steve wasn't out of pocket and made regular payments to cover expenses. More money appeared, to send to boys in trouble or various charities. Steve kept a careful record of all transactions, bearing in mind who he was dealing with.

Not all of the schemes were successful. Reg was behind Campaign Cocktails to reflect his bid for freedom. These were red roses in plastic tubes with Reg's name on a card inside. Associates also came up with business ideas that nosedived.

For example, at one point the twins were asked to back a project where prostitutes dressed up as schoolgirls. They were to work in restaurants, offering more than just a main course. That one bit the dust before it got off the ground.

Other projects failed to materialise for a variety of reasons. Often there was no commercial viability; on other occasions the people behind the projects were undesirable in the extreme.

Reg was offered a share in a scaffolding business in Essex. He didn't need to do anything apart from agreeing to have his name used. Deeper investigations, however, revealed that the business owed money to some dubious people. Reg, as a silent partner, would be a good deterrent for any over-aggressive claims. The name 'Kray' on a letterhead would no doubt be a masterstroke for a business in trouble. The scaffolder was left to rebuild his business alone.

Reg, enjoying his regular 70 per cent cut from successful projects, provided Steve with a long list of contacts to take the goods and arrange more sales. It all snowballed. Steve admits that he took advantage of Post Office envelopes at his workplace to help with the venture.

Steve was still trying to get his head around the fact that the Krays, behind bars, were organising profitable businesses – and he was acting as something of a front man! And there was more to come. Reg was moved to Nottingham Prison, where he had another brainwave. Steve was told to pay an urgent visit.

As soon as he arrived, Reg described his latest money-making scheme. 'We had this book but it didn't do too well. It needs a relaunch. Now's the time to cash in. We're in the papers, I'm in your magazine and all that.'

'What's it called?' an intrigued Steve asked.

'*Thoughts, Philosophy and Poetry*. There are plenty of thoughts from me and some good poems by Ron. His poems are pretty good. Not a lot of people know he does poems.'

'Sounds interesting. What's the deal, if I can sort everything out?'

'You've moved on from the seventy-thirty. This would be fifty-fifty.'

It was a lot for Steve to take in, but he embraced the

project head-on. He had to sort out contracts, copyright issues and organise new proofreading. Reg's handwriting resembled a new type of hicroglyphics never seen before, which proved to be an arduous task for everyone involved in the project.

Steve called Reg at Nottingham: 'We're done. The final draft is ready. It's been hard work, but we're ready for the publisher now.'

Then, a bombshell. It was the last thing that Steve had expected after so many days, weeks and months flat-out preparing the manuscript.

'I've decided not to go ahead with it. I want us to work on a better book.'

Steve learned that the moods of Reg and Ron could change in an instant. One minute they would be all for something, and the next they would be totally against it. This was one of the most infuriating moments of his entire life. He had spent nine months getting the project up and running, and a Sunday newspaper had even run a preview. Now the material was destined for the shredder.

'This is a better book. It's called *Villains We Have Known*.'

Steve, beside himself with rage and totally flabbergasted, felt himself shaking. As Reg talked on the phone about a seventy-thirty deal, he'd had enough. He hung up on Reg Kray. Repeat: he hung up on Reg Kray.

But they made up. Meanwhile, someone else was selling T-shirts, and Reg and Ron weren't getting money out of it.

It turned out that Charlie was behind the sales of

merchandise. Reg contacted friends and supporters saying that Steve should be in charge of the business and not Charlie. Ron wanted to find out about Charlie's operation, but not to run him down. His letter to Newcastle ended, 'God bless, your pal Ron Kray' with two kisses.

Reg wrote to Steve: 'Any time you get word on Charlie, let me know. He does not help Ron or me at all.'

From behind bars, the Krays' charity work took off. But not everything was as it seemed, as Steve Wraith found out . . .

'I was asked to do many charity events using the Kray name. I went down to London to oversee some of these events. I noticed one of the guys in charge was putting money in his pocket. The cash wasn't going where it was supposed to. I took umbrage at the kid and pulled him about it.

'I said if he didn't put the money back in the pot I would let Reg know. He tried to set about me. He didn't realise about my self-defence background. The kid never bothered me again after that, and didn't run any events again.'

Steve told Reg about the incident, and he said they did have overheads which added up. However, Reg said that, if the kid was pocketing money, then it was wrong. Steve suggested staging an event in Newcastle for a young boy who had been badly burned in a bonfire accident. He'd been wearing a shell suit which went up in flames. He had 80 per cent burns. Steve asked Reg if he could use the Kray name and he said that would be acceptable.

'Charlie Kray and Tony Lambrianou came and it was

a great success. We charged £10 a ticket, there was a DJ on and the kudos of having Charlie Kray there. A tape from Reg wished the boy all the best, it was played during the evening, and around £3,000 was raised for the family.

'I didn't take anything out of it and neither did Reg. Six months later we decided we would do another event because the family still had issues and needed help. I went back to Reg and asked if he could help. He said he would, but things started to change when he said he wanted something out of it. He said it was all very well raising money for charity, but something needed to go into the pot for him. Things were a bit tight.'

Steve felt in a difficult position. He was twenty-four years old, clean-living and managing a sub-post office. Being involved with the twins was one thing. But running a charity event, taking money out and giving it to Reggie Kray, wasn't something he wanted on his CV.

'I got onto the venue and had a chat. Reggie was asking if he could have the bar money. He was trying to manipulate things and telling us how it should all be done. He was becoming quite agitated. He called me up, we had an argument and I put the phone down. He called back, we argued again and I put the phone down again.

'We left it for a day to cool off. He rang back and tried to persuade me. I said I would put the event on, with all the money going to the charity. He said I couldn't have Charlie Kray, I couldn't have Tony and I couldn't use the Kray name – so good luck with the event.

'I rang Charlie who said it was best if he didn't come. He said he would still do something for the child. Tony said he would come up anyway because Reggie couldn't tell him what to do. The event went ahead and it was another success, without Reggie's input. I recorded Reggie's conversations just to show that I had done everything above board.'

The 1990 film *The Krays*, starring Gary Kemp and Martin Kemp, was a money spinner for the twins, as David Fraser – son of Frankie – explained: 'Reg told me how much they all got for the film. He said they all got eighty-odd grand a piece. That's the three of them – him and his twin and his other brother, Charlie. So naturally I said that was handy, having that amount of money.'

Roger Daltrey had originally intended to produce a film about the Krays after reportedly acquiring the film rights to John Pearson's book, *The Profession of Violence*. He wanted Hywel Bennett as Ronnie and Gerry Sundquist as Reggie, Billy Murray as Charlie and Jean Alexander as Violet. The idea was abandoned when the Peter Medak version was announced.

In the end, Gary and Martin Kemp played the Krays with Billie Whitelaw filling the role of Violet.

Wilf recalled the hassle at the time: 'Oh, the film. That bloody film. I've gotta tell you, it was the bane of my life.

'It just went on for years. Somebody would write a script, submit it, and there was rubbish, right, left and centre. Charlie Kray even tried to get me to approach the yanks, because I was always in America. Then one day I got a call from Roger Daltrey. He said two young producers had come up with a great script.'

Apparently the film rights to the book were with Roger Daltrey and the film producer Don Boyd. Both were going up the wall with the twins' antics. They could say one thing, change their minds, decide something else and return to their original idea. Fred Dinenage had experienced all of that during his interviews with the unpredictable duo. Wilf was impressed with The Who frontman . . .

'Roger said to come down to the house if I had the time. It was a lovely place with a fish farm. He said we should talk about it.

'So I went down, because by that time I was Ronnie's business manager – well that's what he liked to call me. Roger showed me the script and it was very good. The last bit was very violent. I said it was a bit lively.'

And so a deal was on the table. It included a ten per cent payback to the Krays. The people who were putting the money up bought the ten per cent for £250,000. That was split between the three brothers, although Charlie was up to his eyeballs in debt and his share soon disappeared.

Reggie and Ronnie kept the money pouring in from their imaginative schemes. But, apart from helping sick children, what happened to the rest?

Wilf: 'They gave it away. Ronnie treated half of

Broadmoor to goodies. With Reg, he had friends on the inside – you know, they were earning off him. You draw your own conclusions on that one.'

Duncan Campbell's view: 'If you go through the cuttings of the time you'll see they were going to get a million pounds from the film being made about them, somebody had painted a portrait of the two of them that was going for £400,000 and so on.

'I'm sure they did make some money but there's not very much you can spend it on in either Broadmoor or Parkhurst. I know when Ronnie Kray got married to Kate Kray [in 1989], agents were asking for bids to start at £25,000 for a wedding photo and a brief interview with Ronnie and a brief interview with his new wife Kate.

'There were no Kray children to inherit anything. I think a lot of money was taken off them by people who were smarter. They were seen as earners for lots of people, who were either selling stories about them or pretending to be doing things for them.'

In the end, Duncan concluded, they would have been comfortable out of prison; people would have looked after them. But, in terms of the great Kray fortune, Duncan said they never made a lot of money when they were criminals, and there wasn't much left at the end.

Chris Lambrianou knew what happened to some of the money. Duncan was correct about the lack of spending opportunities, but Chris knew that Ron had one large expense – his bar bill!: he confirmed that Ron had once accumulated that bill of £7,000. He was always buying his non-alcoholic beers and cigarettes, as well as coffee and snacks for visitors.

'The cash was gone very quickly. I believe there was very little money left from the film. It just went.'

Fred Dinenage came to the same conclusion. He studied their operations closely. They did make thousands and thousands of pounds inside, but they spent it just as quickly and gave much of the money away. He believes they died virtually penniless.

Norman Parker saw the original Krays and the Krays brand as two completely separate entities. The 'brand Krays' were people who went around doing good acts and helping people. Perhaps they did a lot of that when they were in prison, Norman said; on the outside that didn't happen to the extent they made out.

Reg's second wife Roberta Kray, whom he married in 1997, was constantly in touch with her husband during the latter prison years. She described how Reg gave money away as quickly as it was received. He had a compelling need to provide for his friends. It was part generosity, part responsibility, but mainly the result of a deep-seated insecurity. He felt, sadly, that money might bind them in a way that emotion never could.

Chapter 14

Christmas with Jimmy Savile

The morning sun peeked through the forest as Christmas 1990 approached. The bare branches of a dense thicket of magnificent oak trees glistened, as the light dazzled on their frosty coating. Bracknell Forest was suddenly ablaze with lukewarm rays in the freezing temperatures.

The fine oaks stood like sentinels, harking back to another age. Their predecessors were mentioned as fine specimens in the Doomsday Book in the time of William the Conqueror. So many Decembers ago, in 1085, the oaks had been praised by that priceless manuscript, the 'great survey' of the country.

The modern landscape was similar, with so many trees competing for space. And yet, there was one prominent difference. Now the woodland ended abruptly when the concrete jungle of Broadmoor came into view. The incessant early morning chatter of migrating birds gave way to the human version inside . . .

'I recognise that face.'

'I've seen him on the telly.'

'Who?'

'Over there.'

'That bloke with the cigar.'

'Oh him? I've seen him here before.'

'Eh? Doing what?'

'He goes to the juvenile ward over in Somerset 2. I was there for a while and saw him.'

'What does he do there?'

'No idea. I kept well away. He's creepy.'

'Why does he always wear a tracksuit?'

'No idea.'

'Does he sleep with that cigar in his gob?'

'Unless he puts it somewhere else.'

'You what?'

'Joke.'

'All right, you lot, I heard some things were going on in Somerset 2,' Alan butted into the general chat. 'Young kids over there. I heard Mr Savile gives them plenty of attention. I've no idea what they do, but . . . you know . . .'

'He's coming to my cell today,' Ron said. 'I think he's going to see the Ripper too.'

'That's right,' the Ripper squeaked in the background, thrilled that another VIP was coming to see him.

Alan watched intently as Jimmy Savile, in his red tracksuit, mouth filled with the oversize cigar and wearing a Christmas paper hat, strolled around the ward, talking to patients. He handed out a few cards. Savile had arrived alone, and he appeared to move freely around the wards after being met by staff.

Those suggestions being talked about would never have been believed at the time. Given the mental state of some of the patients, any slight on Mr Savile would have been taken as an extra sign of their instability, considering all the charity work undertaken by the good chap.

Nothing could be said in front of staff or anyone in authority.

After his tour around the ward, Savile walked up to Ron, who was chatting to a couple of pals. He and Ron went into the Kray twin's privileged side room for half an hour or so, then it was the Ripper's turn. The Ripper was also allowed visitors in his room, and Savile went in there with Sutcliffe.

When Savile emerged back onto the ward, there was no mention of what had been discussed. Savile made for the dining room, sat down on a chair and a few patients followed. Alan, oblivious as everyone else to the predator's double life, wanted to chat about music.

'Just thought I'd say I like your *Old Record Club* show. I listen to it on Sunday afternoons. I like hearing all the old records from ten and twenty years ago.'

'Right,' Savile answered. 'That's been going a long time, but it was called something else in the seventies. It was the *Sunday Afternoon Double Top Ten Show*. Did you hear that one?'

'I must have been too young.'

'Well, I played records from two top ten charts and people were awarded points to guess the artists and the songs. It changed a bit with the *Old Record Club*, but people just like hearing good old music.'

Alan, wondering why Savile always wore a tracksuit or shell suit, watched as the VIP guest took a puff of his cigar and continued.

'One thing I must tell you. *The Old Grey Whistle Test* is making a comeback. That's the best show of all, better than anything I do. Look out for it.'

This was around the time of Savile's activities at Stoke Mandeville Hospital. He abused more than sixty people connected with that hospital in the seventies and eighties. There were several complaints about sexual abuse, but Savile was allowed to continue his reign of terror.

An investigation by the Department of Health and West London Mental Health Trust revealed that at some stage during his association with Broadmoor – between 1968 and 2004 – Savile received keys, allowing him access to wards, patients' rooms and day rooms. He could go into these areas unsupervised. Patients and staff making complaints feared they wouldn't be believed and could actually be punished for speaking out.

Lead investigator Dr Bill Kirkup: 'Savile was an opportunistic sexual predator who was placed in a position of power and influence at Broadmoor, and he consistently exploited his position there.

'Our analysis of how he came to be there, how he

behaved and what he inflicted on vulnerable patients and others reveals significant shortcomings in systems, processes, hospital culture, Department of Health practice, and the response to celebrity.

'These have all improved since the time of Savile's active association with Broadmoor, in some cases almost beyond recognition.'

There were eleven allegations of sexual abuse directly related to Broadmoor by Savile. Six involved patients at the time, two were staff and three minors. Two were male and nine were female.

Steve Shrubb, chief executive of the West London Mental Health NHS Trust: 'The abuse that Jimmy Savile perpetrated at Broadmoor Hospital may have happened several years ago. But it is only now that we know the full details and scale of his abuse. I and my colleagues at the trust are appalled that Savile abused vulnerable mentally ill patients and staff inside the hospital. On behalf of the trust I offer my heartfelt apologies to his victims. The suffering our patients and staff experienced at his hands and the lack of support they received at the time is unimaginable today.'

The medical press reported that a high-ranking nurse at the Department of Health questioned Savile's frequent visits to Broadmoor. The mental health specialist, who had supervisory responsibilities for high security hospitals, said Savile often roamed around Broadmoor and appeared 'voyeuristic'. Despite the concerns, no action was taken.

Savile didn't stay for any meals; Christmas Day

continued with one of the patients, Trevor, cooking a special breakfast. Trevor cooked eggs, bacon, mushrooms and toast. Trevor cooked in the scullery for about thirty patients, giving the chefs some time off.

After that, a couple of members of staff, in the festive spirit, offered Alan a drop of the hard stuff in his coffee. It was a gesture, well outside of the rules, but much appreciated.

There was another festive surprise for Ron, Alan, Charlie and friends at the breakfast table. A brown paper bag had been placed at each patient's place. A note inside said it had been supplied by the hospital's League of Friends.

The contents: a two-pound bag of sugar, half an ounce of tobacco, two first-class postage stamps, one packet of custard cream biscuits, one packet of bourbon biscuits and a packet of cigarette papers.

'Not much, but they've made an effort,' Ron said. 'I need more letters written, Alan, so the stamps will come in handy.'

The Christmas lunch was more of a normal affair, with menu choices A B and C, and turkey as one of the options, followed by mince pies.

For some reason, the event didn't have the atmosphere of breakfast, when Trevor was doing his own thing and the patients were wishing each other Happy Christmas. The format of the lunch, with its chosen diets, made it seem more formal.

After lunch, though, the staff brought videos to the day room. There was a happy mood as the patients watched *Terminator, Indiana Jones, Raiders of the Lost Ark* and *First Blood*.

Reg and Ron had spent so long behind bars that the festive season became an institutionalised, predictable affair. Turkey and all the trimmings, with fellow cons and prison officers, lacked a real festive atmosphere. At the end of the day, the warders or nurses headed off to enjoy a family Christmas, while Reg and Ron contemplated another dismal year in their cells.

Reg was moved again, to Blundeston Prison in Suffolk early in 1992. Previous inmates included John Stonehouse, the MP who faked his own death.

Blundeston (now closed) has a rectangular perimeter, with trees also bordering the complex. The prison opened in 1963 with four wings: A, B, C and D. It was steeped in controversy because of an escape in 1996. The six inmates who evaded their guards were said to be running a criminal empire inside the prison.

The jail was also in the headlines after a warder was sacked for making a comment about Osama Bin Laden. Staff had been asked to have continued sensitivity after the 11 September attacks. The prison had many Muslim inmates at the time. Also Muslim visitors may have heard his 'insensitive' comment. The officer won his claim for unfair dismissal.

On a more mundane level, during Reg's time, the fruit quota was cut due to the availability of prison-brewed hooch.

Reg wanted company for Christmas, because a family day was planned. As he'd got on well with Steve, he decided to invite him for six hours of quality time, starting at 10 a.m. and lasting until 4 p.m. There would be no hooch involved.

Steve, though, became anxious. Six hours? What would they say for six hours? Would there be awkward silences? What if he said the wrong thing?

'I was held up by bad weather. I called the prison, but the message didn't get through to Reg. The security checks held me up even more, and I was really worried about being late. Eventually I was escorted to the visiting area. They had made an effort to make it like Christmas, with decorations everywhere and children running around the room. Reg was sitting at a table in the middle with a vicar and a nun, so I held back a bit.'

After a few minutes the guests stood up to leave and bade their farewells to Reg. All in one movement, Reg strode across to greet Steve, put his arms around him and gave him a real bear hug.

'You're half an hour late. I've had to listen to those two for all this time.'

Steve tried to explain about the weather, the delays and everything but he could see that Reg had made his point. The visitor from the frozen north was late, he shouldn't have been late and that was that. No more discussion about the delay.

'It's something I really miss,' Reg confided. 'Families

everywhere are enjoying a happy Christmas and I can't get out to enjoy it. There is some good news, though. I've had a look at the menu for the day and the feller in the kitchen has pulled out all the stops.'

'What's for lunch then?' Steve asked, having missed breakfast and looking forward to whatever Christmas goodies the prison came up with.

'Wait and see,' Reg said. 'Turkey and all the trimmings. I reckon you'll be surprised how good it is.'

And so, at twelve noon, the visiting area was transformed into quite a cosy venue for Christmas lunch.

Families, unable to spend the big day at home with their loved ones, enjoyed vegetable soup, followed by turkey, sprouts, roast potatoes, parsnips and plenty of gravy, all served up by the staff. There was even jam roly poly and custard to follow. In Reg's world, Steve had become part of the family and both knew that, without having to discuss it.

There were no awkward silences. Steve, a boxer himself, was keen to find out more about Reggie's career in the ring, especially as he had been tipped for stardom.

'I wanted to get better at fighting when I was at school. I got into a few scraps with bigger boys and they won because of their size. I wanted to find out about technique, and how to box. Charlie was a great brother in that respect, showing Ron and me all the moves. He made a basic home-made gym for us to practise in.'

'When did you have your first fight?' Steve asked, intrigued.

'Well, it was actually against Ron. What happened was, a travelling fair arrived back home called Stewart's Boxing Booth or something like that. The idea was that you had to take on these huge guys and see how long you would last. No one wanted to take them on, but Ron said he would. Well, we were just kids, so that wasn't going to happen. In the end I fought Ron and we had a helluva scrap. We got paid 2s 6d, and that was a lot of money around the war time.

'I know I could have gone all the way. The only problem was, when I got into trouble, they didn't want me boxing.'

Steve was keen to know if Reg regretted killing Jack 'The Hat', the crime that led to his current situation. The answer came as a surprise.

'He got what he deserved.'

Steve realised that Reg was never going to show any remorse for his crimes. The Christmas visitor reckoned that the Home Office would have shown more compassion about an early release if he had. However, Reg stuck to his guns; there would be no apology and no movement from the Home Office.

Christmas meal over, Reg signalled to one of the prison officers, who disappeared for a few moments and returned with a brown box. Curiously, Steve unwrapped the box. It was packed with pens, pencils and boxing books. The books were by other famous fighters, and signed by Reg. These items had been sent in to Reg, but he had no use for them; it was the thought that counted.

Time to go. Steve stood up and held out his hand. Reg did the same, and the two men held the handshake for a few seconds. The sound of children's laughter began to die down; wrapping paper drifted to the floor from tables; prisoners began to shuffle out of the room towards their cells once more.

Reg stood at his table as Steve left, nodding and obviously feeling more than a touch of emotion. It had been a special Christmas Day. He had enjoyed good food, good company and a healthy chat.

For Reg and Ron, though, Christmas Days came and went. The twins would never apologise for what they had done. They could always justify their crimes.

Christmas became just a slightly happier window in a bleak year. Did it make any difference to their lives? None at all.

Chapter 15

Stars in their Eyes

Ron, preparing for a visit from a VIP, was determined to look his best. He had built up enough trust to have occasional visitors in his cell. He made the most of his privileged side room, unlike many patients who had to put up with the most basic of facilities.

His friend Alan, an expert ironer, ensured that everything was ready in time for an important visit. Ron had five or six suits, hung up in a cupboard in the side room. They were all expensive, with tailored shirts to match. As washing and dry cleaning services were minimal, Ron reused the same shirts for extra visits, although no one could tell, and he was always perfectly turned out.

The Krays' fan club included stars of stage and screen, politicians and sporting celebrities. There is a fine line between gangsters and showbiz. Judy Garland was a close friend in the sixties, as was Barbara Windsor. The twins received hundreds of letters in prison, and visits from the rich and famous. Reg and Ron were distraught when news of Judy's death filtered through. She had supported them all through their legal battles, but was found dead in her rented Chelsea house on 22 June 1969 due to an unintentional overdose of barbiturates.

Many friendships had developed in the only place Reggie and Ronnie felt safe – the East End.

In those days, the twins were the main men, the big noises in town, as Chris Lambrianou recalled: 'There were people who were fond of them because they were always polite, and not violent. They were never violent. They were only violent with the kind of people that might be violent to them or who had something that they wanted.

'The average human being, the average Joe, the average Jane, didn't have anything they wanted. So it was just a case of, "Oh there's Reg and Ron, hello Reggie, hello Ronnie." They were local boys and that's basically how it was.

'But walk into a nightclub with them and it was like the parting of the Red Sea. When they walked in that was it. In most places there would be a club upstairs and a private one downstairs for the Firm and the twins to entertain guests from all over the place ... from Scotland to America.'

Maureen was part of the colourful sixties scene with the Krays.

'They were completely out of their depth in the Knightsbridge places, because of the people there. But it was a very glamorous time. Women loved the hair styles, the clothes, the excitement, and the coffee bars in Soho. You'd go to the 2i's off Wardour Street and you'd see Tommy Steele or Cliff Richard. You'd know these people long before they were famous. Ronnie did like Cliff Richard. Then there was David Essex, who was rather beautiful and young.'

Maureen recalled Ronnie saying: 'Oh, who's that?'

The answer came back that, indeed, David Essex was starting out to be a singer.

'Oh, tell him he can sing in our club next week. See how he goes.'

From the early days, through the prison years, Ronnie and Reggie could count among their friends American singer Billy Daniels, Sammy Davis Jr, Sonny Liston, Judy Garland, Diana Dors, George Raft and Frank Sinatra.

Daniels was a favourite of the twins. He performed in the twins' club, the Kentucky, in Mile End Road. He went on to sell 9 million copies of *That Old Black Magic*. Like other showbusiness personalities he was intrigued by the twins' lifestyle. It is doubtful whether Reg and Ron matched his $26,000 weekly pay packet in Las Vegas.

George Raft, the American actor, became a loyal friend of the twins. He identified with them, having grown up surrounded by villains and narrowly avoiding a life of crime himself. Raft's family were German immigrants in New York, and one of George's young friends became a wheel man for the mob.

George played second lead in the 1932 film, *Scarface*, based on the life of Al Capone. There was a remake in 1983, starring Al Pacino, while Ron was imprisoned in Broadmoor.

Ron and Reg met George at the Colony Club in Berkeley Square during their heyday. George was in his sixties at the time, and full of stories about the highs and lows of his gambling career. At the end of the Second World War he lost $65,000 in a Las Vegas casino.

Ron and Reg clicked with George immediately, sharing similar backgrounds in a criminal environment; George also dressed immaculately. At one stage George was banned from entering the country because of his underworld connections.

Ron asked how George was in such good condition for his age: 'I'm very careful with my food. I don't drink and I have one meal a day – steak and salad. Keeps me in great trim.'

George talked about his love for the East End because it reminded him so much of New York. After his chat with the twins he presented them each with gold cigarette lighters.

Maureen met George at the twins' club, Esmeralda's Barn in Knightsbridge, owned by the Krays from 1960 until 1963.

George had been sent over by the Mafia when they were attempting to infiltrate London and trying, of course, to do it through the twins. But Ronnie messed all that up completely. He had a productive meeting, and it was all going to take place, but he laid down the law that nobody was going to come into their clubs, snooker halls and casinos – nobody except him and Reg.

Lita Roza, the singer mentioned by Chris Lambrianou as attending the Krays' trial, kept in regular touch. She had become friendly with the twins during the sixties club scene. Lita was the first woman to top the UK charts.

She made it with a song she hated, 'How Much Is that Doggie in the Window?' She was persuaded to record the song, but refused to ever sing it again in any shape or form – even in the Krays' clubs!

The first time Reggie and Ron saw Lita performing was while they were AWOL from the Army. The pair took a break from their spell on the run to visit the Royal Ballroom in Tottenham. Lita was singing with the Ray Ellington Band, and the twins were stunned by the quality of her voice.

Nothing was straightforward with the twins, though. A fight broke out, with Reg and Ron in the thick of it, and a scrum developed. Lita, always the professional, continued to sing as punches were thrown and feet flew on the dance floor. Eventually Reg and Ron, thanks to their boxing backgrounds, emerged from the heap victorious. And the band played on.

Diana Dors was a firm favourite of the twins. Reggie saw her singing in Room at the Top in Ilford. He told Ron that he had just seen a fantastic singer with platinum blonde hair. The brothers were also close to her husband, Alan Lake.

When Reg, Ron and Charlie were jailed, Diana and Alan went to visit them at various prisons. Diana was also a regular visitor at Vallance Road, bearing fruit and flowers for Violet. After Diana's death from ovarian cancer in 1984, Alan fell into a deep depression and shot himself. He loved her so much.

Even Violet Kray was starstruck in the early days. She had seen Judy Garland starring in *The Wizard of Oz*. Her favourite song from the film was 'Over the Rainbow'; little did Violet know that she would meet Judy in person.

And that is what happened; Judy performed 'Over the Rainbow' in one of the Krays' clubs.

'Judy was so glamorous,' a sixties clubber recalled. 'She was all sparkle with fur capes. If you wore fur now you'd be frowned upon, but we all wore fur then. The next week Violet had her hair done again and she was sitting next to George Raft.'

Maureen enjoyed fabulous nights at the Astor. Politicians, gangsters, celebrities and boxers all mingled there.

'American singer Billy Daniels came over and danced and sang. Sammy Davis went there, and Frank Sinatra too. Ronnie met Sinatra on many occasions, but the hand apparently went on the shoulder and you didn't touch Ronnie Kray.

'The twins both had this thing that they didn't like to be touched and didn't like to be hugged. If a woman just kissed them on the cheek that was OK. Now if you go into a club men hug each other and kiss on the cheek. I see it every time I go out. You could never have done that in the presence of Reggie or Ronnie.

'You shook hands, but never any cuddles. After Sinatra did that, Ronnie talked about it forever. He kept saying, "Who does he think he's touching?" He couldn't care less who it was! The twins also knew all the famous boxers. They brought over Sonny Liston when he was heavyweight champion of the world.'

A host of sporting stars and celebrities attended the Kentucky, a club in Mile End Road. The Krays opened the venue in 1962, spending a small fortune on fixtures and fittings. There were mirrors all over the walls with expensive carpets, lighting and furnishings.

Chairs and tables were given an antique look and sprayed gold. The Kentucky had its own claim to fame when it was used for some scenes in the film *Sparrows Can't Sing*, at the request of Barbara Windsor.

Along with Barbara Windsor, the cast included Brian Murphy and Yootha Joyce, who were popular in the Thames Television series *George and Mildred*, as well as Roy Kinnear, who was a regular guest on the comedy show.

One night there was a hilarious incident at the Kentucky, while Tex the Dwarf was providing the entertainment. His routine was to sing cowboy songs, playing guitar on the back of a donkey. Tex was tiny, and the bizarre sight of him plucking at the strings on an enormous guitar, astride the donkey, brought plenty of guffaws. Ron's role was to walk over to the donkey at the end of the act and lead it over to the bar.

The drama unfolded when Ron, as usual, took the donkey by its reins and headed for the bar, carrying a large gin and tonic. As he neared the bar, a familiar figure caught Ron's eye. It was a bookmaker who owed the Krays a tidy sum!

Ron gave the bookie a piece of his mind, yelling and shouting at him, while Tex the Dwarf looked on, bemused, with the donkey also displaying a puzzled expression. The audience cheered, possibly thinking this was all part of the entertainment; the startled bookie didn't wait for an encore and raced through the exit almost as fast as the favourite in the 2.15 at Chepstow.

There was an assortment of celebrities in the club that evening. And, either in Parkhurst or Broadmoor, those influential friends of Reggie and Ronnie kept in regular contact – with some well-known faces arriving to see the incarcerated killers.

The twins were not close to all celebrities. They were enraged to hear that entertainer Max Bygraves said they sat in his audience 'like a pair of dummies'.

Max also grew up in poverty in London, sharing a small council flat with five brothers and sisters, his parents and grandparents. He shared some boxing heritage as his father was a professional flyweight boxer, Battling Tom Smith.

The twins took umbrage when they heard that Max

claimed they had an air of menace about them and refused to clap. They came back with a short sharp response, saying they had never seen him perform and would never want to see him on stage anyway!

They also took issue with newspaper reports that they were close to Christine Keeler, the model and showgirl who was sleeping with John Profumo, the Conservative Minister for War, and a Russian naval attaché. The minister resigned in 1963 as the scandal became known as the Profumo Affair. Photographs of Christine enjoying drinks with the Krays circulated in the press.

The twins recalled meeting the 'very sexy' Christine at a pub in Whitechapel and at a restaurant in the West End. That was the extent of the relationship, they said. They also claimed never to have met her friend, Mandy Rice-Davies. Mandy and Christine were exotic dancers, as teenagers, in a club in Soho before they became household names.

Duncan Campbell is intrigued by the link with the stars: 'There was a symbiotic relationship, I think, between some parts of showbusiness and criminals like the Krays. Actors, photographers and singers were attracted to the dark side.

'People liked to be seen with them. So it was a glamorous thing. They had clubs at a time when the licensing restrictions in Britain were much, much stricter than they are today.

'Pubs had to close at a particular time and so these clubs became very seductive, exciting places to go to. If there were guys there, looking very smooth and wearing dark glasses, then it was even more exciting.'

Krays' biographer Fred Dinenage pointed out that Reg, in Parkhurst, could have any visitors he wanted from showbiz stars to boxers. People like Barbara Windsor were regulars. It meant that he had famous and infamous visitors crossing the Solent to see him.

'Ronnie's visitors in Broadmoor were more carefully vetted because it was a hospital for the criminally insane. It was more difficult, but again he had a lot of quite high-profile celebrities coming to see him.

'The communication both twins had with the outside world was quite considerable. We're talking about a time before emails and that sort of thing. The twins received a lot of fan mail, especially from women.'

Fred believed there was a sexual aspect. A visitor could be in the company of a potentially dangerous person, sitting at the table and even holding his hand. But at the end of the day everyone was completely safe. There was a thrill in being able to get that close, knowing that you weren't in any real danger.

Norman Parker, who knew the twins well from their prison years, explained why the public were obsessed with criminals. 'I think it's all about fame. Everybody nowadays, so they say, gets their fifteen minutes of fame. It surprises me in America when serial killers kill ten, fifteen or twenty women, that lots of people write in and want to become friendly with them!'

'I really think it is because they want to try to become notorious by becoming friendly with somebody who's notorious.'

Wilf Pine recalled that Broadmoor was like an 'open house'. Ronnie liked to take tea in the afternoon with his guests, and the amount of celebrities bordered on the ridiculous.

Wilf reinforced the statement that there was a very fine line between gangsters and some celebs. 'They both live in their own worlds, and they both want to know about each other's worlds. Ron had a lot of visitors from the world of showbiz. He was very popular.'

The most famous person to visit Ronnie in Broadmoor was Richard Burton.

It made sense for Burton to visit because he had played gangster Vic Dakin in the 1971 film *Villain*. The character Dakin is a London underworld boss who also has a relationship with a politician. Donald Sinden played Gerald Draycott, who is really based on Lord Boothby, Ron's close friend.

Burton's appearance was criticised for his attempt at a Cockney accent; perhaps Ron should have been involved in the early stages to tutor the world-famous actor in a gangster role.

Maureen had seen the film: 'I told Ronnie about it and he asked if it was based on him. I said it had to be. In the film Burton was homosexual, and in one scene he wakes up in bed with a beautiful dark-haired boy. When the boy turns over it's Ian McShane, I thought, "Oh God, this film is definitely based on Ronnie Kray." What gangster in London was openly homosexual? There wasn't one. He was the only one. I mean the Richardsons, the Nashes or whoever – there were no gay gangsters apart from Ron.'

Maureen asked Ron: 'What did you think about his beautiful speaking voice?'

'Oh, it was OK. I wasn't impressed. Anyway, I was taller than him.'

In a different environment, perhaps a nightclub in the sixties, Ron would have been telling everyone that he had Richard Burton at his table. But this was Broadmoor, and in that institution he had to be top dog – even if he was entertaining stars of stage and screen.

Ron was a big fan of his Broadmoor friend Charlie Smith's music. Charlie was a good guitar player, and attracted the attention of a record producer, Scott Pine. Charlie wrote his own songs, and sang them into a tape recorder in Somerset House. The album was called *Caught in Time*. Sadly Scott died, and Charlie was allowed to go to his funeral.

Ron was also fascinated by the singer Morrissey, who thought it was unfair that the twins were locked away for the rest of their lives. Reg and Ron were thrilled to be included in the lyrics of 'The Last of the Famous International Playboys'. Morrissey reached number six in the UK singles chart in 1989; Ron had a copy of the record and played it over and over again . . .

Chapter 16

Surrounded by Evil

'Reg, look at those oddballs.'

'You mean that feller with the headband?'

'Yeah, he is strange,' Charlie Richardson laughed as he opened his cell door for a better look.

Reg had popped in for a cup of tea and a chat. Two of the most notorious criminals in recent British history sipped their steaming prison-grade brew and gazed in amazement as a diverse group of characters ambled across the landing. The motley crew was led by a grimy-looking inmate who wore a headband around an unwashed, haggard face with visibly greasy hair.

'You know, Charlie, I've seen Dirty McSquirty come and go for years but I've never had a real talk with him. I tend to stick with people in the Firm. I'm sure he's a decent enough feller, but I've never got involved with these people.'

'I'm starting to study these strange types,' Charlie said. 'I mean, you get professors and everything trying to check them out, writing books and deciding what makes them tick. Now they are in front of us. We can study them here.'

'What's the point, eh?' Reg asked, puzzled.

'Well they're part of the human race – just – and I'm fascinated to find out about them. I've started holding loon nights. I had one last week. I get them to tell us their stories. It's a great laugh, understand?'

'I could see something going on in your cell.' Reg nodded. 'I overheard a feller saying something about angels flying around.'

'You should have come in. That was Lennie the Lid and his mate. Apparently an angel came down and landed in their cells. It had bronze feet.'

Reg almost choked on his cigarette smoke at the thought of an angel with bronze feet in the cell.

Charlie added that the angel also had fire coming out of its legs.

'Well, it breaks the monotony,' Reg conceded. 'Who else are you studying?'

'I'm looking at four or five, understand? You'll get the picture when I tell you. I'm intrigued by the Black Panther and the Teacup Poisoner.'

Reg took another gulp from his mug, put it down on Charlie's table, folded his arms and waited for the next instalment. As he did so, two more friends appeared in the cell, sat down at the table and poured themselves cups of tea from Charlie's large white china teapot.

The new arrivals were Gary Wilson, a blond-haired,

blue-eyed armed robber and Gaddafi's hitman in the UK, Ben Hassan Muhammad El Masri. Hassan must have been well over six feet, towering over everyone else, and he also had thick, black curly hair and dark, dark eyes.

'It seems you have a ready-made audience,' Reg grinned. 'What's that about the Teacup Poisoner? I know it's Graham Young – he used to be with my brother in Broadmoor. But he's over in the vulnerable prisoner's place now. He's been here for years. I saw him once when I was in "C" wing, so I know a bit of the story. He's a raving lunatic. You can't have that feller at your loon nights.'

'No, but I can study him,' Charlie continued, relishing the attention his remarks were receiving. 'In his lifetime he tried to poison seventy people. In here he could even make something nasty out of the moss on the windowsill.'

Gary Wilson knew sketchy details about the Teacup Poisoner, but wanted to know more; Hassan gazed at Charlie, waiting for more information; and Reg tilted his head to one side, anxious to hear every word.

'What is this about the tea poison?' Hassan said suspiciously, glancing inside his cup.

'No, we're safe,' Charlie assured him. 'What happened was, Young got a great thrill from poisoning people by slipping things into their tea or even their food. A few died in excruciating pain and he loved every minute. He even wrote diaries, keeping note of the symptoms and whether he should add extra doses.'

'You're having me on,' Gary spluttered.

'He is an assassin?' Hassan ventured, shaking his head and trying to understand the motives of the Teacup Poisoner.

'Not an assassin like you, Hassan. I've been reading up about Graham Young in the library. It's amazing that he's just through those walls. If he was in here we would be watching everything we ate or drank.'

'I followed my orders to kill the disloyal Muhammad Ramadan,' Hassan butted in, referring to the shooting, sanctioned by Libyan leader Gaddafi, outside Regent's Park Mosque in the spring of 1980.

Reg had more details: 'Tell you what I did learn. The vicar here, don't know the feller's name, had some sort of tea party for the Yorkshire Ripper and the other weirdos. They were having Bible readings and all that. The Teacup Poisoner wasn't invited!'

The Teacup Poisoner plotted his deadly campaign from a young age. Graham's father, Fred, noticed that he had a passion for science, and made the fatal mistake of buying him a chemistry set.

Graham Young didn't have the easiest starts in life; his mother died twelve weeks after the birth, so Young's father fostered him out to an aunt. But the foster placement wasn't successful. His aunt didn't particularly bond with him. Eventually his father remarried and the stepmother brought the family back together. But Young and the stepmother, Molly, failed to hit it off. The young schoolboy blamed Molly for breaking his toy planes.

Graham's solution was to make Molly suffer by poisoning her with a dangerous substance called antinomy. She developed flu-type symptoms as the totally inedible ingredients took hold. It appeared that Molly had flu or a vomiting bug.

Fred came home to find Molly in agony. She was dying. No one suspected poisoning. Graham was only fourteen at the time, so what could he have to do with it?

The budding young pharmacist poisoned his father, too, and also his sister. He put all sorts of weird ingredients in their food and drink. He took a shopping list to chemists, explaining that he was carrying out experiments at school. Graham kept notes on his father's illness. He attracted attention at school because of the health problems in his family, and eventually he was arrested for attempted murder. He even poisoned a school pal.

In the prison system, there was general wariness about Young. When he was sent to Broadmoor he browsed in the library, but most of the books he read were about poisons and toxicology. The joke was that he didn't read Mrs Beeton's cookery books unless he was going to put poison in a cake.

'Good, so he went to Broadmoor and that sorted him out,' Hassan said, looking relieved.

Charlie confirmed that was far from being the case; Young put toilet cleaner in the tea urn and people became ill. And a patient there died from cyanide poisoning. Young said he had taken poison from laurel bushes in the grounds. No one believed him, and the death went down as a suicide.

Gary picked up Charlie's newspaper cutting and read out loud: 'Young became the model patient. He fooled everyone and was allowed back into the community after eight years. He got a job at a photographic lab.'

'You can guess what happened next,' Charlie added.

'Ron told me that he got hold of a poison called thalium,' Reg told the group. 'It didn't have any taste, so he added it to their food and drink. One man at the lab died, they didn't suspect poison, and Graham suggested he should be cremated. So the evidence went up in smoke. Then another worker died. Graham enjoyed the power and control. He revealed his knowledge of chemicals and suggested thalium poisoning was to blame. He gave away too much and the Old Bill nicked him.'

Charlie was back on the case, quoting from Young's diary about poisoning a worker: 'I have administered a fatal dose of the special compound. He is surviving too long for my peace of mind.'

Charlie pointed at the prison walls, to show that Young was really only a few yards away.

One ex-Parkhurst prisoner later recalled the inmates' reaction to the poisoner: 'Young was deadly. We just avoided him. If he poured a cup of tea you couldn't have it, even if he drank some first. He would know how much to take so it wouldn't hurt him, and the other person would get a fatal dose. Nobody took any chances with him. I couldn't even sit at a table with him in case he dusted it with something. He made the Krays or any of the other bad men look like amateur streetfighters.'

Reg was also keen to display his knowledge about the Black Panther. 'You won't be able to have him at your loon night either. He's in the special security place or with the nonces. He wouldn't last long in here. He'd be cut to pieces.'

'What is this Panther, Reg?' Hassan asked. 'Is he like the tea poisoning man? Is he black?'

'You'll know that in our world we don't hurt women, children, old girls and people like that, eh? The Panther is different. They keep him well away from us. He's called Donald Neilson. He's under guard in the special security place over there. He robbed banks wearing a black outfit and balaclava.'

'Not a killer then?' Hassan cut in.

Reg confirmed that the Panther was the worst type of killer. He even murdered people running post offices, no matter who they were or what age.

Neilson kidnapped a teenage girl, Lesley Whittle, in 1975 and demanded £50,000 from her family. Their wealth came from running a coach firm in Shropshire. Neilson read in a newspaper that the Whittles had amassed a small fortune – and he wanted a share in it.

He broke into Lesley's bedroom, stripped her naked, placed a wire noose around her neck and a hood over her head.

The family tried to pay the money, but they were late, after a series of misunderstandings, and she was found dead at the bottom of a drainage shaft. The police were blamed for the 'cock up'.

Neilson was not to be confused with Dennis Nilsen. He murdered fifteen young men, strangling or drowning them in his North London flat. He bathed the bodies and dressed them again. He watched TV with the corpses and had sex with them. He cut them up and flushed the body parts down the toilet. The drains became blocked, and the company that came to have a look found a pile of flesh and bones. They called Nilsen the 'Kindly Killer' because he said he ended his victims' lives humanely.

The Kray twins were enraged by the Nilsen case. He killed all those young men and yet received a shorter sentence than the Krays! They also kept raising the case of the Ealing Vicarage rapists, Martin McCall and Christopher Byrne, who received ten and eight years.

Charlie reminded everyone that the Parkhurst Special Security Block opened in 1966, the year of his arrest. He was actually detained on the day of the World Cup final between England and Germany.

'There was another nasty bastard called John Straffen – he arrived at Parkhurst when the block first opened,' Charlie told the others. 'He was there just before six of the Great Train Robbers. Straffen preyed on young children, and he killed two in the city of Bath inside a month. He specialised in stalking local kids in the early fifties. Straffen had been sent to Broadmoor, but he escaped from there and kept killing.

'Straffen was sentenced to death, so I don't know why he received a reprieve. Maybe they realised he was mad after all. They said it was something to do with being "feeble minded", whatever that was supposed to mean. The bastard should have hanged. At any rate he was sent here to Parkhurst, then joined Ian Brady at Durham a couple of years later.'

Brady and Myra Hindley carried out their reign of terror in the Manchester area in the sixties. They murdered twelve-year-old Keith Bennett in 1964. The other victims: John Kilbride, twelve; Edward Evans, seventeen; Pauline Reade, sixteen; and Lesley Ann Downey, ten. Brady was moved around, with Parkhurst one of his residencies.

Everyone behind bars, throughout the land, hated Brady for not telling Keith Bennett's mother where the boy was buried. They thought that was wicked and 'beyond the pale'. Keith's mother, Winnie, never knew the location of her son's final resting place.

'I've seen Brady face to face,' Charlie said. 'I was in Durham. They were trying to keep him away from us, but they dropped their guard and let him walk in front of me. I was coming downstairs with a jug of hot water in my hand, so what a chance! I threw it all over him. Shame the water had gone off the boil a bit, so he didn't get the full effect.'

'Did they give you extra bird?' Gary asked as Charlie became more and more agitated, thinking about Brady.

'No way. I said I tripped, and anyway they should never have let him near me. After that they kept him away from everyone.'

During the twins' prison years, IRA members came and went. All of the IRA men were known as double Category 'A'. They were watched night and day, and often kept in the Special Security Block at Parkhurst. IRA people were moved around the country under the dispersal system and could find themselves anywhere from Leicester to Parkhurst. Female IRA prisoners were detained in Durham.

Reggie encountered many IRA people in his time. He was at Parkhurst when IRA commander Billy Armstrong arrived. Armstrong was one of those responsible for the car bomb attack at the Old Bailey in 1973. A bystander, sixty-year-old Frederick Milton, died and almost 200 people were injured.

At Parkhurst, Michael Gaughan, an IRA armed robber, went on hunger strike for sixty-four days in support of the Price sisters, who were also behind the Old Bailey bombings. His weight dropped from 160 lb to 84 lb.

In his final moments, the twenty-four-year-old issued a statement: 'I die proudly for my country and in the hope that my death will be sufficient to obtain the demands of my comrades. Let there be no bitterness on my behalf, but a determination to achieve the new Ireland for which I gladly die. My loyalty and confidence is to the IRA and let those of you who are left carry on the work and finish the fight.'

Over at Albany, Father Pat Fell was being held for planning an IRA campaign in Coventry while he was an assistant priest there.

Fell was convicted of being a commander in an active service unit, although he denied all charges. Fell was renowned for holding sit-down protests over the way IRA members were treated.

The death of Bobby Sands on 5 May 1981, and several other hunger strikers, boosted IRA recruitment in the early eighties. Throughout the UK, black flag vigils were held.

Bobby, held at Maze Prison in County Down, was protesting against the removal of Special Category Status for prisoners convicted during the Troubles. There was a three-day fast at Parkhurst when Bobby Sands died. The hunger strikers were taken down to the punishment block, as they would have engaged others in political talk. Ordinary prisoners were upset because at the end of the day they were inmates, too, behind bars.

During the Krays' spell on the Isle of Wight there were also so-called 'dirty protests', when IRA men covered themselves in excrement.

The infamously violent prisoner Charles Bronson, the man whose mum Ron had advised when she visited her son in Parkhurst, was another regular topic of conversation. Charles, later known as Charles Salvador, attacked thirty prison officers as well as taking part in ten sieges. He caused half a million pounds' worth of damage with his rooftop protests. Ironically, his first crime was a botched armed robbery at a post office on Merseyside when all he managed to steal was £26.

And yet he had such a normal upbringing, beginning life as Michael Peterson in Luton. His mother described Michael as 'the perfect child'. He was accidentally hit on the head with a bottle of tomato sauce in the family kitchen as a boy, and never seemed the same from that point onwards.

Charles Bronson shared the Krays' love of boxing. His father was a trainer and boxed for the Royal Navy – as did Charlie Kray. A boxing promoter, a friend of the Krays, chose the name Bronson for the young fighter. The determined Bronson proved to be a savage opponent in fierce fights, earning a brutal reputation.

Charlie Richardson and Reg reminisced about an occasion when Bronson took an interest in another football pitch at Parkhurst, close to the well-used tarmac area. Any player with even a modicum of ability would have struggled to make an impression on the rough, bare earth pitch. The halfway line comprised a trench. The pitch suffered from subsidence. Footballing inmates making a run on goal had to leap over the trench, displaying astute ball control.

The touchlines were also a hazard to life and limb. Enthusiastic players would crash into a bank on one side or a brick wall on the other side. Beyond the brick wall lurked a drop onto a concrete path. There was no shortage of broken bones on this pitch. This football area was, however, destined to suffer even more damage, and one day Reg looked on as a scenario unfolded, as he recalled to the others . . .

A governor at Parkhurst, called Marriott, was known to be progressive and had no problems talking to the prisoners. He visited them in their cells and even brought in an ice-cream van as an occasional treat.

He said to Charlie Bronson, who'd been in the punishment block for years: 'I'll let you use normal locations if you promise to behave yourself and not cause trouble in my nick. Is there anything you would like to do?'

'I'd like to do some gardening,' Bronson answered.

'All right, come up and do some gardening. Remember you said you wouldn't cause any trouble.'

Charles gave his word. Maybe he had the wrong end of the stick about gardening. He got his shovel and started digging up the middle of the lopsided football pitch.

'What the hell is he doing?' a group of confused cons grumbled. 'We're supposed to have a game this afternoon. We ain't playing around a hole in the ground!'

They drew cards to decide who would make a move and approach Charles and his new creation. Mickey, a murderer from Woolwich, went over to inspect the hole in the centre circle with his brother Danny.

'What are you doing, Charlie?'

'I'm making a fish pond.'

'This is the football pitch. This is where we play.'

'Football is a poof's game. It's just a load of geezers

chasing round in their shorts after a fucking ball. You'll love a fish pond. I'll make a really good one.'

While they were having the conversation Dessie Cunningham, a well-respected armed robber, was running past.

'All right, Dessie?' Charles asked.

Dessie ignored him, probably with other things on his mind, and not concerned with the appearance of a fish pond on the football pitch. But Charlie thought he'd been blanked and decided there must be a problem. He started saying a few things about Dessie.

Next thing, Charles was surrounded by the footballers and stabbed about eight times. He'd been cut with very thin blades so the holes weren't really showing.

Charles decided to run a bath in the shower area. He filled it up with cold water, and soon the tub was bright red. The screws called for a stretcher to take him to hospital. As they took Charles off the wing he suddenly sat up in the stretcher and shouted: 'I cut myself shaving!'

That was the last time he was ever allowed on the landings, and the fish pond was never finished. No one was nicked for the attack on would-be gardener Charles Bronson.

Hassan, who had heard the tales several times, was keen to move on. 'You people have been here much longer than me. I stay away from the dirty-squirty man because he is smelly. Did he kill someone? What happened, Reg?'

'They say McSquirty and a feller called Bulletproof

Jack robbed a shop and poured petrol into the shopkeeper's mouth. It was a horrible death. Frank insisted that someone else walked into the shop and lit a match. Eventually Frank won an appeal hearing and he was released. Once he won his appeal he became an innocent man. Jack was bulletproof because he survived several shootings.'

'Why does McSquirty smell so bad?' Hassan asked, screwing up his dark eyes and looking disgusted.

'You'll have to ask him that, if you can get close enough. I reckon he just can't be bothered. He spends most of his time persuading people who've lost their girlfriends to part with rings or whatever. He trades them in for gear, and gets stoned regularly.'

Hassan stood up. He had heard enough. This military man, an intelligence officer, had found out about new kinds of crime. All he knew was to act in a proper fashion for his great leader and execute opponents if necessary.

'I am going for a run and then I will take a shower. Persuade the squirty man to have a shower too? Just make sure it is well after me . . .'

There were other lighter moments. In the exercise yard, a dispute arose over money. A newcomer, a member of the IRA, became involved in an argument with Joe the Greek, an armed robber who took no prisoners. Joe decided to pursue the much larger new arrival with a blade.

Reggie's view was that the scene looked like something from the Benny Hill comedy programmes. Instead of chasing scantily clad women, Joe was pursuing an IRA man.

Reggie watched with Charlie Richardson and a few other so-called 'faces', totally bemused by the hectic chase. In the end, after Joe had aimed a few thrusts at the newcomer's backside, the warders intervened and led the frantic pair out of the exercise yard.

During Reg's time, Parkhurst opened its doors to Bob, an armed robber from Glasgow. He'd carried out some robberies up north and spent some time in Shotts Prison in Lanarkshire. He was given compassionate parole for a family illness, but that was the last they saw of him and he decided to try his luck in London.

Reg discovered that Bob had devised a very clever way of robbing places. He would pick out a small bureau de change, get the phone number and call up the manager from a phone box. He would say he was from the Flying Squad, and they were following a dangerous armed robber who was about to strike.

'He's looking at your premises at the moment. We've got twenty armed police out here and we're on his trail. He's going to come in and rob you. Don't cause no fuss, hand over the money and we'll get him on the way out.'

He put down the phone, once that had been agreed, and went into the place with a water pistol. He asked them to give him all the money. As he left the bureau he squirted water on the window with the pistol to prove it wasn't a real gun. He carried out four or five of these robberies, and he was getting eight or ten grand a time.

Still in London, Bob tried his luck at a bureau de change in Victoria. They'd just had a large delivery of foreign currency, so he got thousands of marks, yen, dollars and everything. It totalled nearly £100,000. He spent it all on hotels, prostitutes and drugs.

They arrested him at a posh London hotel. A security guard there who was an ex-policeman thought Bob looked a bit shady. He had already been sentenced to nine years in a Scottish jail. At the Old Bailey he was convicted of four robberies. They gave him a lot of 'bird' on top – around twenty years.

Bob ended up in a lower security Category 'C' prison. He took a criminology degree and asked the governor if he could be allowed out to collect his diploma.

The governor realised that Bob had four years to serve and this was a big turning point in his life. It was a matter of trust. Surely Bob wouldn't run off again. The governor decided to trust wily Bob.

Bob went out, collected his diploma and robbed several more banks. He was last seen in Whitemoor prison, just over thirty miles from Cambridge. He was serving another long stretch of bird, moaning about his bad luck as usual.

Reg concluded that the likelihood of another weekend pass for Bob was remote. In fact, the chances were zero.

Chapter 17

Parkhurst Prepares for War

Ron Kray was alone in his privileged side room. He had a colour television. Velvet curtains and matching bedspread created a comfortable background. His list of contacts, nationwide, ensured that he lived as well as possible under the circumstances.

True, he couldn't go anywhere. Ron was alone, with his thoughts. Reg, he knew, was becoming friendly with arch rival Charlie Richardson; it was time to write a letter.

As usual, Ron was dressed to kill. He wore his favourite sky-blue suit with silver and diamond cufflinks. A matching tie, crisp white shirt and black Gucci shoes completed his outfit. Ron sat on his leather upholstered armchair, looking like a businessman about to make a key decision. His mind was made up.

All in one movement, he picked up a notepad and pen from his table and moved quickly across the room to open his door. He could see Patient P chatting to Merv, Mike and Jamie. Den the trustee was mooching around, circling them near the charge nurses' office.

'Could I see you for a minute?'

It was more like a military order, carefully said, rather than a request that could be dealt with at a future date. Patient P left the other patients and headed for Ron's side room.

'I'm getting a letter done. I don't need you to write it out for me. It's to Reg. I just want to make sure it makes sense. I need to get some points across. I'm upset with a feller down at Parkhurst.'

'Who are you upset with?' Patient P asked, prepared for whatever Ron had in mind.

'Have you heard about Charlie Richardson?' Ron answered, posing another question.

'Was he a torturer or something?' Patient P came back with yet another query. 'I remember reading about the case in the paper.'

'Yeah. We've had a few run-ins. Cornell was one of his. It's a long story. But I'm hearing from Reg that he and Charlie Richardson have cups of tea and chats. That's not on. I'm going to have to do something.'

'I can't see what you can do here in Broadmoor,' Patient P said after digesting Ron's comments. 'Parkhurst is on an island, right? You can't get there. Maybe writing isn't the answer. Why don't you try to phone and say you have an urgent message? Tell Reg not to have his cups of tea if that's what is bothering you.'

'Reg will get the picture when he sees my Colonel Biff.'

Patient P and Alan had dealt with many a 'Colonel Biff'. A 'Biff' was a letter from Ron. The origin of the phrase was unclear. Ron, still known in many quarters as 'The Colonel', had added the 'Biff' part to his letters.

Ron spoke softly, slowly and with definite intent as he clutched his notepad and started to write: 'Now hear this. I want you to do Charlie.'

'Is that it?' Patient P asked, sounding confused.

'Well, I'll add my greetings and sign it off as usual with "God bless" and all that, but that was the message. Charlie is going to be whacked. I don't think I'll write any more, after all. Reg will get the picture.'

'Killed?'

'Reg will see to it.'

'Ron, this is serious. I don't think you should be sending that letter. Can't you move on?'

'We've been at war for years. Haven't you heard what happened at Mr Smith's? I'm going to win the final battle.'

'I don't know about Mr Smith's,' Patient P admitted.

The fracas at Mr Smith's on 8 March 1966 was a messy affair. Neither the attackers nor the attacked had the full picture of what was happening. Mr Smith's was a gambling casino at Rushey Green in south-east London. The club was owned by a Manchester businessman and a former heavyweight wrestler.

The story goes – and there are a few versions – that the club owners met with Eddie Richardson and Frankie

Fraser to work out a deal for protection, and to install gaming machines. Eddie and Frankie departed after business had been concluded, although they were invited back for something to eat and a drink or two.

Eddie, Frankie and associates returned, although they were expecting to be fed and watered rather than end up in a violent confrontation.

Other South London gangsters in the club included the Hayward brothers and Dickie Hart, who was a member of the Krays' outfit. Billy Hayward, believing that things were about to get ugly, sent out for weapons. Apparently fighting started after Eddie asked the Haywards and their companions to leave as it was past licensing hours.

Gunfire broke out, Dickie Hart received a fatal shot, Eddie Richardson took a round in the rear quarters, and Frankie Fraser was hit in the leg.

Ron told Patient P that the main people in the Richardson firm were arrested. Cornell was still free, and he shot him the next day in the Blind Beggar.

'Crikey. But that's all in the past now, Ron. What you're doing now will only make things worse, especially as there seems to be peace at Parkhurst.'

'Reg will see to it that the Firm is all tooled up.'

'The Firm at Parkhurst?'

'Yeah, we have plenty of supporters there. Charlie Richardson doesn't know what's going to hit him.'

'Don't send the letter,' Patient P pleaded.

Ron took no notice, sealed the envelope, marched out of the side room and strode off in the direction of the charge nurses' office.

'You can't send something like that in the mail,' Patient P said, raising his voice slightly to be heard. 'Anyway, your mail will be opened.'

'I thought mail isn't opened?'

'Well, I reckon that would never get to Parkhurst.'

'I've got a visit later. Someone close to Reg. He'll take it for me.'

'Well, you can do that, but . . .'

There was more to the Mr Smith's story, as Chris Lambrianou recalled: 'It all kicked off at Mr Smith's with two firms. But no one knew exactly who it was at the time. It came up that the Richardsons were involved. I knew Charlie Richardson wasn't there because he was in South Africa. It could only be Eddie Richardson and Frankie Fraser. I know Frank got shot in the leg, and I know Eddie was hit as well, and Dickie Hart got shot. There was rivalry going on about protection. It was a whole thing that had gone on and finally kicked off at Mr Smith's.'

Frankie Fraser's recollection: 'It just so happened that another little gang was in there, looking for trouble. They went for us. That was their mistake, because we went for them then.'

Frankie said he was lucky to survive; although being injured, he won the fight. Hart was unlucky and he lost. Frankie said Dickie Hart died as a result of a 'bit of everything'. Hart was shot, but a hammer and a knife were also involved. Police suspected that Frankie had shot Hart, but evidence was in short supply. In the end, Frankie and Eddie Richardson received five years each for affray.

Wilf Pine stressed that the real reason for the George Cornell killing, the night after the Mr Smith's tragic episode, was a previous beating handed out to Ronnie.

'This from Ronnie's lips. He was legless drunk. He went to a little spieler, a card game place, with a boyfriend. They were a little loudish or whatever. George Cornell kicked seven bells out of Ronnie. He gave him a beating like you can't believe. In normal circumstances, you would think that the next day there would be repercussions. But Reg said to Ronnie, "Hold up there, we've got interests here, there will be a time and there will be a place." Ronnie told me that when he heard Cornell was at the Blind Beggar it was nothing to do with the Richardson revenge thing. It was his chance to kill him.'

Lenny Hamilton, a jewel thief, described a series of events that built up Ronnie's hatred.

'George did call Ronnie a poof. I was behind the Krays coming out of the Astor Club one night and George Cornell was going in with the Richardsons. George went, "Oh, look who's coming up here . . . that fat poof." That led to a fight at a pub called the Brown Bear in Aldgate.

'George was in the pub one night. Someone must have phoned the twins, but Ronnie got to hear that George was in there. Ron was driven to the pub by one of the Firm.

He asked the driver to go in and see if Cornell was still there. The driver reported back that George was having a drink with a feller.

'Ronnie said to go back in and say George was wanted outside, but not to say who it was. George walked outside and he was confronted by Ronnie. They had a fight and George knocked him out. That's where the needle was with Ron and George. Ronnie came unstuck, because George could really fight on the cobbles.'

Lenny had good reason to detest the Krays' methods of controlling people and getting what they wanted. He was at the wrong end of a red-hot length of steel, like a poker, held by Ron Kray with the potential to blind Lenny.

He had accidentally offended a friend of the Krays, with an innocent remark in a bar. Ronnie wanted to see him at Esmeralda's Barn in Knightsbridge in 1962.

'I knew how Jack "The Hat" felt when he walked into that house in Evering Road. The gambling tables were closed, and people were standing on either side as I walked in. I was shown into a kitchen and Ronnie Kray was standing there. He said everything was all right and I was to sit in an old armchair.

'Ronnie started mumbling and I couldn't make out what he was saying. All of a sudden, two fellers got hold of me, the gas was on and things that looked like pokers were heating up. They were steels, used to sharpen knives. They were getting white hot on the gas. He went to pick one up and it was too hot. He dropped it and got an oven glove. He came over to me. I had thick black curly hair then and he started burning it. He started to burn my new suit. I started to piss myself. He went and got another of the steels and put it across my eyes, burning my eyebrows off.'

'Now I'm going to burn your fucking eyes out,' Ron snarled.

Someone at the back shouted, 'No, Ron, not that . . .'

Ronnie just switched off and said: 'You can go now.'

After the Krays' arrest several years later, Lenny Hamilton gave evidence against Ron. He said he wasn't a grass, but had to act when he received a note saying: 'If the Old Bill comes round, keep your mouth shut or we are going to shoot your kids.'

Whatever drove Ronnie to write the letter to Reg at Parkhurst, he made sure that it had a safe journey over the Solent. Bobby Cummines was in the high security 'B' wing at Parkhurst when Reggie received the letter, delivered by an associate.

'The communications in prisons during my time was better than BT. We all knew what was happening. When Reg received the letter, his people got to know about it quickly. Ron had actually written "Fucking do Charlie", so he wasn't messing about. I could see it ending up as a bloodbath, because those loyal to Reg were getting tooled up, and Charlie's firm were getting tooled up, too. Another prisoner gave me a tip-off, to see if I could do anything about it.'

Bobby was running businesses in Parkhurst and didn't need the aggravation. Also, he was getting on well with Reg and Charlie, and could see no future in a full-scale war on the Isle of Wight. How could he be 'true to two'? Another issue was the fact that some of the prisoners were coming to the end of their sentences, or needed good behaviour for their record. A battle at Parkhurst made no sense at all.

Bobby decided to tackle the issue head-on. He knocked at Charlie's cell door. 'Come in.'

That was a good start. Only trusted people were allowed near Charlie, and his firm kept a good eye out. Bobby was one of the trusted group and, even if he'd been seen walking along towards Charlie's cell, no one would think anything of it.

Charlie was casually dressed, in T-shirt and shorts, sipping from a mug of tea and drawing on a cigarette.

Perhaps Charlie had made the first move: 'Have you set anyone up to whack Reggie? There's been a letter from Ronnie.'

'I haven't done anything. Ronnie is off his head. Fucking sort it out.'

Next step, along to Reggie's cell, a few doors away. 'Reggie, I've heard about this letter. This could become a bloodbath. Everything is sweet at the moment. I need to sort this out.'

Reggie wasn't giving much away. Bobby reckoned he knew Charlie had many loyal, ferocious supporters who would probably win the day. Also Reg knew that Bobby, as the fixer, would ensure that Reggie received steaks, whisky and many other goodies, with ample supplies of dope. The screws would turn a blind eye for the sake of a quiet life; everything was at risk here.

Back Bobby went to Charlie's cell to keep up the communication and show that he was determined not to give up.

'I've got an answer, understand? Tell Reg I'll meet him down in the gym. Block off the doors and I'll give him a straightener.'

Back to Reggie's cell, then, with the offer of a fight in the gym.

'You know I'm not afraid of Charlie Richardson, Bobby,' the ex-boxer said sharply.

'And I know he's not afraid of you!'

Neither of the main men wanted to back down. However, they both wanted to retain the status quo, keeping all of their benefits without losing face. There would be no winners. If Reg was whacked, or the same happened to Charlie, long sentences would be added to existing bird. Members of both firms would suffer at the hands of the authorities, if they survived the fighting.

Bobby had an idea: 'Reg, what if you sort it out when you're both released?'

Reg said one word: 'Yeah.'

Back to Charlie's cell then, with news of the suggested compromise. Two words from Charlie. 'Any time.'

That was that, then.

On the landing, the prisoner who had tipped Bobby off signalled: thumbs up or down? Bobby gave him the 'thumbs up'.

'Thank you,' the man with the tip-off mouthed across the landing.

The next thing Bobby knew he was clutching a bottle of Irish whisky.

Reggie and Charlie both realised that their reputations were intact, members of their firms were intact, and it was time to move forward. Ronnie may have been the dominant twin but, on this occasion, his orders were ignored. And, no doubt, several lives were saved as a result.

Chapter 18

Dreams of Freedom

Freddie Foreman recalled getting into the prison van, leaving for the Old Bailey, with Ronnie dreaming about his freedom.

'We used to get into the meat wagon with dog handlers and stuff, and we had screws all around us. Ronnie said when it was all over he would get himself a young boy and go on a world cruise. One of the prison officers, who knew Ron faced a long stretch of bird, said if he saved up his canteen money he might have enough cash to do it!'

Fred Dinenage holds the view that, when the twins went down for a colossal amount of time, they accepted that the game was up but, deep down, they had dreams of freedom.

'Both of them had this dream that, one day, they would be free, and Ronnie Kray used to talk to me about his hopes. He said that he and Reg would go and live in Morocco. They would have a house each on a beach overlooking the sea. That would be their life in the future.

279

Ronnie had this dream, a vision of freedom. Ronnie, I think, always believed that one day he would be free, and I think that's also why he got married to give him as much credibility as possible.'

On the landing of 'B' wing at Parkhurst, Reggie confided in his fellow prisoners. He had definite plans for the future.

'When me and Ron get out we'll have a big house with a swimming pool. We'll have lots of land and we'll feel the wind in our faces. Some firms will get together and we'll have a Mafia-type of operation going on.'

Reggie's plan was to form a gangsters' union. There had been talks with Mafia people. The various firms, Reggie thought, could come together. They would be 'Mustache Petes', old-school villains, maintaining values of respect and dignity. The younger gangsters would be the Godfathers. Surely, Reg thought, people like Charlie Richardson and the Nash family could get together and make the scheme work?

But no. The British underworld was ticking over, with all sorts of different firms running their own manors and not treading on each other's toes. Also, Charlie Richardson was keen to start up various business ventures and make straight money, using his inherent skills and education qualifications, gained in prison.

In Parkhurst, for example, he had an idea to recycle instead of throwing so much away.

'A mound of newspapers and lots of other stuff comes

in here every day,' he would say. 'Tons of it can be used again. They could do this in every prison. Good for the environment, too, reusing things instead of throwing it all away. All the paper can be compressed to make bricks for barbecues or people's fires at home.'

It was a great idea, well before its time. However, the authorities were worried about the king of the long firm building up a business in Parkhurst. No doubt, they thought, he would be taking over other areas of the prison's business!

In 1989, Reg felt that freedom was on the horizon. He was told that he would be able to leave the dispersal system within the confines of a lower category prison. A move to the Category 'B' prison at Lewes in Sussex was on the cards. Everything seemed definite apart from the date; Reg had no idea when he would be moving. February came and went, and in March, Reg was under high security at Gartree. At last, on 19 April 1989, Reg was driven south to Sussex.

Lewes was a different environment completely. He was close to the Sussex Downs and rolling countryside. He even played football, went to the gym and kept up his letter writing.

The town of Lewes had a fascinating history. Lewes Naval Prison held 300 Finnish grenadiers during the Crimean War. A large number died from tuberculosis, and they were buried at the Church of St John sub Castro. Tsar Alexander II of Russia had a monument erected to the twenty-eight who perished. It stands in the churchyard.

Perhaps Ron could join him in this much quieter place?

With Ron's schizophrenia always an issue at Broadmoor, the answer was a resounding 'no'.

In 1990, for the first time in twenty-five years, Ronnie had windows without bars. Patients from Somerset House had a new home – Oxford House – where the windows were unbreakable. It was a new building in the hospital. That meant a packing and moving operation. The destination for Ron and his friend Charlie was Henley ward. The patients were thrilled with their new surroundings. In Somerset House none of the cells had a toilet or washing facilities. However, in Oxford House there were washbasins and toilets in the patients' rooms. Ron even splashed out on a range of yellow and peach furnishings.

Ron was pleased to see two televisions available. One was in the dining room and the other in a dedicated TV room. A 'quiet' room for deep-thinking patients was an added bonus and proved to be a place of solace for the more thoughtful types. Ron often went in there for a good think.

He was thrilled with his new surroundings. He also took on board the warning that misbehaviour would lead to smaller rooms, and serious misdemeanours would result in a return to the old block.

Ron, realising that this was to be his home for the foreseeable future, became proud of his room. He added ornaments and photographs, read books and listened to his record player.

In the same year, Reg's hopes of more downgrading

and eventual freedom received a body blow. In the early hours one Saturday he was moved to Nottingham, apparently after the discovery of a weapon. It did seem unlikely that Reg, having served twenty-two years, would jeopardise everything with an escape attempt at gunpoint. Nonetheless, an inquiry continued and, after Nottingham, Reg was moved back to Gartree and into the dispersal system again.

Later it transpired that Reg would be cleared of anything to do with a firearm; however, he was returned to Nottingham and not Lewes. Then he was shifted to Leicester for a short time and on to HMP Blundeston.

But even after all these moves it seemed he was destined for another. While he was still settling in at Blundeston, Reg was horrified to hear that he might be transferred to Albany on the Isle of Wight, the high-tech prison beside Parkhurst.

He was upset because he had spent so long on the island and a return would have been such a retrograde step. Also, he was concerned about the number of sex offenders at Albany. If he went there, he would have to be segregated. The authorities listened to his pleas, and Reg was transferred to Maidstone Prison in Kent. In March 1994, he was placed in Weald wing. This Category 'B' prison was what he had been hoping for; the regime was easy-going, and prisoners could cook their own meals and wear their own clothes.

The only drawback for inmates was the amount of time locked up. They were confined for twelve hours at night, plus lengthy spells in their cells at lunchtime and late afternoon.

At Maidstone, Reg discovered a new form of currency: phone cards. He continued his early-morning letter writing, but he was also able to use the official prison cards to make calls.

Inmates could buy as many as eight cards. Reg could buy them from his £5 a week pay as a cleaner, although friends also brought in cash for him.

The new phone cards proved a formidable rival to tobacco in the prison's black market. They were sought after, and used mainly in the evenings when it was cheaper to make calls.

Reg became friendly with a younger prisoner, Bradley Allardyce, the armed robber and later killer, who told the BBC about his intimate relationship. Reg ensured that Bradley had enough phone cards, and bought him a gold cross and chain to recognise their friendship. Bradley was transferred to Whitemoor prison in Cambridgeshire, much to Reg's disappointment; the crestfallen Kray concentrated on preparing chapters for future books.

Soon after, Reg revisited some old memories when he was actually allowed into Parkhurst as a visitor – to see Charles Bronson. Charlie was serving another sentence at Parkhurst then and invited Reg for a meeting. Reg said the prospect of seeing Bronson again after so many years was frightening.

Twenty prison guards surrounded Bronson's cell when the meeting took place. But it was a light-hearted affair, full of laughter, and Reg even received a pair of signed boxing gloves. Even in the nineties, the prospect of freedom for both men appeared to be as bleak as the Parkhurst midwinter skyline. Reg, Ron and Charles Bronson had no interest in botched escape attempts themselves, but they were all intrigued by a foiled effort at Parkhurst.

At Parkhurst, just a few weeks before Ron's death, a trio of prisoners made their bid for freedom. They were Keith Rose, forty-five, a murderer and kidnapper; Andrew Rodger, forty-four, a burglar who killed a night watchman; and Matthew Williams, only twenty-five years old, who tried to cause explosions and poison people.

Keith Rose shot Juliet Rowe, the wife of a wealthy supermarket owner, six times during a kidnap attempt. He tried to take her from her home in East Devon in 1981. He shot Juliet four times in the back with a pistol, and then finished her off with bullets in the head and heart.

Rose escaped justice for several years until in 1990 he was convicted at the Old Bailey of kidnapping the deputy chairman of a food wholesaling company, Victor Cracknell, at his home near Guildford, leaving a £1 million ransom note.

Rose bound and gagged Cracknell's parents and threatened them with a sawn-off shotgun. The thirty-one-year-old subject of his attentions was blindfolded and gagged and taken to a secluded Devon gully. He spent four days handcuffed to a tree branch with a wire noose around his neck.

A substantial ransom of more than £140,000 was paid by his family. The money was left on a footpath near Farnham. The Old Bill kept Rose under surveillance and followed him to Devon. Mr Cracknell was able to break free, while Rose was arrested.

Rose was sentenced to fifteen years for the Cracknell kidnap, then later a whole life sentence added when he was convicted for the Rowe murder. Now, destined to spend the rest of his life in Parkhurst, he wanted out.

After darkness fell at Parkhurst, the potential escapees finished their usual exercise and hid in the gym. Back on the wing, the warders didn't notice that ten prisoners had become seven. Old Gold Top wasn't there to count them out and count them in, so something went seriously wrong.

Off they went, opening lock after lock with a copied master key, until they came to a wire fence. They cut their way through that. Alarms hadn't been installed in the fence, and the prison officers watching the cameras didn't see anything.

The escapees were wearing their own clothes, not prison uniform or anything like that, so they were able to walk to the nearby town of Newport and hail a taxi to Sandown, about eight miles away.

After getting dropped off in Sandown, the three made their way to a small private airfield between Sandown and Shankhill. They knew that, in the middle of winter, the airport would be very quiet.

Rose had a good look round for available aircraft; all were secured in a large hangar apart from a Cessna 105. It was a two-seater trainer – not ideal for three blokes. Could the Cessna have left the runway? Rose never found out, because he couldn't find a key. He attempted to turn the lock with a piece of metal, but failed.

Perhaps they had given up hope of leaving the island. They were walking, just like normal pedestrians, on the road between Newport and Ryde when they were spotted at about seven o'clock in the evening. Despite the darkness, an off-duty prison officer, Colin Jones, recognised Williams from the way he walked. He phoned the police, and the game was up.

Reg analysed the facts with great interest; it all seemed a complete waste of time, and a dream of freedom that became a nightmare.

Norman Parker believed that Ron knew he was never going to be released. Once he'd been sentenced, that was that. Norman said Ron should have been found unfit to plead at his trial because he was so ill; they made a criminal out of a sick man. Under those circumstances Norman thought release could have been an eventual possibility.

'Poor old Reggie did thirty years and died. I think in the later years it affected his mind. He didn't know what he had to do to get out.

'In some ways the twins were their own worst enemies. Films and documentaries were made and books written. I suppose the Home Office would have been worried about them appearing on *Panorama* or another film and this, that and the other.'

Duncan Campbell believes that Reg had so many people going to see him because he hoped it would show the outside world he was ready for release.

'He would never say that Ronnie had been the dangerous one. But the feeling on the outside was that, had it not been for Ronnie, Reggie might never have been involved in that particular world. Ronnie was always the one who was more aggressive and more active and anxious to create this image of them as feared creatures.

'Reggie would talk about the books he was wanting to do, the poems he'd been writing, the charities he'd been involved in, the donations of his art to raise money at auctions and things like that. He was very polite, well spoken, very calm and everything like that.

'I think probably at the back of his mind was the feeling that he might one day be allowed out and I think, towards the end after he had married again, there was a feeling that he might be allowed out. In the end he was, but only for a very short amount of time.'

Duncan pointed out that the Krays were fairly well behaved in prison, whereas people like Frankie Fraser were involved in riots and disturbances.

'The Krays seem to have kept their noses pretty clean. You didn't see them on the roofs of prisons complaining about conditions. I think Reggie believed that, if he behaved himself, he might one day be allowed to come out. Ronnie was heavily drugged most of the time and therefore not in a combative mood.'

Wilf Pine recalled Ron's sense of humour, even in dire circumstances. The conversation went something like this:

'If by some miracle, Wilf, if they ever let me out, I wanna throw a party.'

'That ain't a bad idea.'

'I want you to listen to me carefully, Wilf. You get along with everybody. So I want it to be your party, in a big suite in a nice hotel. I want you to invite everybody there. I'll be the guest of honour, but they don't know that. When the last guests arrive, greet them, shut the door and don't come into the room.'

Wilf: 'Why's that?'

''Cos I'm gonna have two hand grenades, one in each hand. And I'll take the lot of those bastards with me. BOOM.'

Reg had a longing to experience the exciting innovations of the outside world. He was only familiar with life on the other side of the wall in the sixties. The internet, mobile phones and all the other technological advances in society that had appeared since the Old Bailey trial intrigued him.

He was also aware of the increase in traffic, the shape of new cars, the spread of motorways and the impact of massive new developments.

Reg yearned to go round a supermarket, choosing his

items and placing them in his trolley. In prison he was always told what to do, and when to do it.

The thought of making his own choices was always just a dream, with the vague possibility of coming true on a distant horizon.

It was a dream that could never become a reality.

Chapter 19

Ron and the Monkey

The more Ron got to know fellow patient Alan, the more he trusted him to perform mundane but necessary tasks. The normal payment in tobacco was a welcome gesture.

'At one stage I was in solitary isolation for four days out of each week. When I came out of isolation each day for a wash and shave, I was allowed a cigarette and Ron supplied the tobacco for me by leaving it in a locker outside the isolation room.

'Someone recommended to Ron that, because I was educated, I could do a lot for him. I was given four ounces of tobacco each week by Ron and eventually became totally trusted.

'I ironed a shirt for him after he saw me press a shirt of my own, and he often asked me to iron his shirts, so I never ran out of tobacco.

'Ron could not read or write fluently, but he wrote a scribble that could be read and make sense to just close a letter. He always ended any message with, "God bless,

Ron Kray." After I had done a few of his letters to his male friends or whoever, I advised him of a better way to express himself, and he took that on board.'

The ironing and clerical duties continued unabated. As Alan ironed or tidied up Ron's letters, the ex-gangster would get various matters off his chest.

'Ronnie would regularly give me even more two-ounce pouches of tobacco to listen to the exploits of his illustrious criminal past, and I wrote it all down to keep a record for him. He was saying things like his Firm had steered people down an alley. Ron was hiding in the alley and appeared with his pistol. He aimed the gun at two people and it didn't go off. He thought that was a sign from God, and the ones about to be shot became friends of his!'

That was similar to the fate of Albert Donoghue, who was shot in the leg by Reg. Because he didn't grass, he became a trusted member of the Firm until he felt forced to give evidence against them at the trial.

Ron also told Alan how much he had hated his time in the Army. The one bright spot, according to Ron, was that he learned how to make a man lose consciousness by choking him with an arm lock from behind. People who annoyed Ron found themselves struggling for breath, then flat out on the deck as Ron perfected his choking technique.

Alan suspected that Ron and Reg were responsible for more deaths than the two they had been charged with.

'Ron said he found it a problem to dispose of the slags

that he and his brother had taken care of. He never liked to advertise that someone had been seen to, and getting rid of slags was a nightmare.'

'I'm going to give you a monkey,' Ronnie said one day. 'It's what you deserve for all your hard work.'

'A monkey? Right, er . . . thanks, Ron . . .'

The offer of a monkey confused Alan; he felt he had to go along with the offer for fear of upsetting Ron, especially as medication had just been consumed.

'Well, you're doing a lot for me. You're helping with my letters, sorting out paperwork and doing lots of nice things. Good, good. Look at all the ironing you do for me.'

'Well, I'm just keeping legible notes in case anyone wants to tell your story. It's a gruesome tale, but I'm sure people will want to know all about it one day.'

'I've done worse things than I've told you. I'll make a fortune.'

'What worse things?'

Ron just smiled. It made Alan think of the numbers that must have been led up an alley, and how unusual it would be for a gun to fail. He kept thinking of that gun not going off.

An associate from the time said people could take that smile two ways; it could be because you were going to get hurt, or a smile because he liked you.

Ronnie walked into one of his clubs one day. He said 'hello' to everyone, went to his pocket and pulled out a Beretta pistol. He walked up to one of the people there and took aim. He pulled the trigger twice and nothing happened. Everyone thought it was a joke. Ron took two bullets out of the gun and said: 'Here's your birthday present.'

Fast forward to Broadmoor: 'Anyway, it has to be a monkey. You've been so good to me that it can't just be a pony.'

Again, Alan kept playing along, smiling at Ron and listening to his bizarre offer. Could it be some sort of gay connotation? Ron often talked about a banana in someone's pants. Alan wasn't an East End boy so this talk of ponies and monkeys was confusing. Alan pursed his lips as he tried to work out what Ron was on about.

'You know my reading and writing is hopeless and I need you to help me write to people all the time. I have another important letter to write tomorrow.'

'I'm happy to help, Ron, and I appreciate all your offers, but I'm confused. How are you going to give me a monkey?'

Ron grinned, patted Alan on the back and produced a shiny black wallet from the inside pocket of his jacket. He held up a pile of notes and laid them out on a table in his room.

'That's a score,' he said, pointing at a £20 note. 'Add a fiver and it's a pony. I don't have enough cash on me to pay you, so I'll arrange to get you a monkey.'

'You still haven't described a monkey,' Alan pointed out. 'What the hell is a monkey?'

'It's £500! That's what you're worth to me. A ton is £100. Oh and by the way £1,000 is a grand. You'll have heard of that one.'

'Ah right, a grand. But you can't add anything into my account here. It's not allowed. Honestly, I'm happy just doing the work. Give me some more tobacco some time. Don't worry about the monkey.'

'Would you like the money delivered to your brother Bill in Gateshead or your other brother Ian in Poole?'

Alan was shocked. He had never mentioned his brother in either place. Ron had obviously carried out careful research through his contacts.

A couple of days later, Bill, on leave from the Forces, was in bed with his wife Jane. It was 2.30 a.m. There were footsteps. A knock at the door. A click of the letterbox. Bill flicked on the light and carefully crept downstairs. The footsteps tailed off, a car door slammed and a powerful-sounding engine burst into life with a growl.

Bill picked up the brown envelope and studied the writing: '£500 to be paid into Alan's account. Compliments of the Krays.'

A week later, Bill appeared in the visiting area. He sat down, had a look round and breathed more easily. There was no sign of Ron, who was obviously still in his room relaxing after breakfast.

'Tell you what, it's all a bit scary. I paid the money into your account, but I didn't like the idea of some gangster coming to my door early in the morning with a brown parcel. We're moving house soon. Make sure you don't tell a soul, especially your gangster friend with the monkey!'

Ron mentioned a monkey again while referring to compensation in the Lord Boothby case, when the Tory peer received a £40,000 libel payout.

'Lord Boothby adored me,' Ron said. 'He did me favours by keeping people away from my business. But he got tens of thousands. And all I got was a monkey.'

Chapter 20

Wedding Bells at Broadmoor

'I'm going to get married, Reg,' the scribbled letter from Broadmoor declared. 'I'm going to be respectable. I'm going to be a respectable married man.'

Reggie, 'banged up' in his Parkhurst cell, couldn't believe the news from his homosexual twin. He wrote back. 'Getting married? Who the hell are you marrying?'

A reply. 'Wait and see. I'm going to move fast.'

Those were drastic steps by Ronnie to secure his freedom. Money was becoming less important to Ronnie and Reggie. They had their books and a film deal. All they needed was a new lease of life – freedom.

Even though Ronnie was openly gay, he surprised everyone by announcing his marriage in Broadmoor.

Fred Dinenage, who interviewed them on countless occasions: 'Ronnie had this dream – a vision of freedom we mentioned earlier. He always believed that, one day, he would be free. That's also why he decided to get married.'

Gang member Chris Lambrianou understood Ronnie's

thought process: 'His mind was alert enough to know that, if he could convince the authorities he was sane and no longer a danger, not a homosexual and in a proper man-woman relationship, then he had a chance of getting out.'

That plan was clearly in Reggie's mind, too. He spent years mourning the death of his first wife, Frances Shea, who took her own life in 1967, aged only twenty-three.

He asked sixties model Maureen Flanagan to marry him on three separate occasions over the years. Maureen divorced her first husband; she later married again, but sadly her second husband died after a heart operation.

'I keep asking her to marry me and she hasn't said "yes" yet,' Reggie complained.

Charlie Kray had the answer: 'What does she want the aggravation of being married to you for? You already give her enough to do. You have her off buying this, buying that, going to see this person, writing that letter and asking for parole.'

Reggie proposed to Maureen in front of other inmates and the guards. They were all offering to be best man.

Maureen reminded Reggie that he had vowed never to marry again. Reggie said that, if he was going to marry anyone, it could only be Maureen. His mother had loved her, her brothers loved her, she was loyal to the family, and had to be the natural choice.

Maureen thought back to what had happened to Frances and how she couldn't cope with the whole situation. Also, Ronnie became jealous if anyone became too close to Reggie.

Maureen believed Reggie was looking for a second mother figure, to replace Violet and take care of his laundry and all his wants and needs. It wasn't a tempting prospect.

Ronnie's chance for romance came sixteen years into his sentence, and Maureen played the role of Cupid. Elaine Mildener, who was intrigued by the aura surrounding the twins, became the unexpected bride. Elaine had actually written to Reg first after reading a book about the Krays. She travelled to see him in Parkhurst. Reg said she 'must go to see Ronnie, he'll really like you'.

And that is what Elaine did. This very homely, motherly lady, always immaculately dressed, travelled to see Ron in Broadmoor. She even took her two children along. Elaine worked as a secretary in the East End; perhaps her organisational abilities would satisfy Ron's long list of needs.

Elaine may have been expecting bulletproof glass screens and a heavy lock and key environment; this, however, was a hospital and not Parkhurst. Ronnie, though, was still being watched like a hawk.

He appeared in a sober grey suit, crimson handkerchief neatly arranged in his top pocket and impeccably shiny black shoes. Ronnie had a thing about shiny shoes; fellow inmates provided the shoeshine service. All visitors had to display the same detailed attention to their footwear – any failure in that area could cut the visit short.

Ronnie and Elaine got on very well. They chatted

about everything from Elaine's children to Ron's hopes for freedom.

One visiting day, Maureen was asked to pick up his new friend on the way. Of course Maureen could drive Elaine to Broadmoor. They arrived, met Ron and sat around a table in the visiting area eating strawberry tarts. Elaine smoked one or two, while Ron had cigarette after cigarette after cigarette . . .

'Are you all right, Elaine?' Ronnie enquired, peering over the thick tortoiseshell frames of his glasses.

'Er . . . I'm fine, Ron,' a nervous Elaine mumbled as she gaped in awe. 'I'm fine.'

'Right,' Ronnie answered, not shifting his gaze. 'Are we going to get married, or what?'

Elaine was staggered and looked desperately at Maureen for advice.

'Uhh? Maureen?'

'What are you looking at her for?' Ronnie continued softly. 'It's me you've got to answer. Is it "yes"?'

'Um . . . yeah. OK. Yes.'

'I wanted you to say "yes" because I'm going to get the papers involved and they'll give us a lot of money.'

'Um, yes,' Elaine gulped again. 'OK, yes.'

Maureen grimaced; was this a marriage just for the money?

'Who have you talked to, Ron?'

'I'm going to get twenty grand from the *Sun*,' Ronnie announced proudly.

A brief, intimate ceremony inside Broadmoor was attended by close family and friends in 1985. Pictures were taken, the money was paid, and that was that.

Roberta Kray, who married Reg later, said it was difficult to explain exactly why women married lifers. She fell in love. Other women benefited from a feeling of emotional or physical safety, with the prisoner under lock and key. Any dangers associated with living together as a couple did not exist.

Ron, she said, enjoyed being around women even though his sexual preference was for male company. The loss of his mother, Violet, had left a void in his life.

With Elaine, he could enjoy the company of a lady, benefiting from the companionship, without any requirement to have sex. Elaine's children gave the relationship a 'family feel'.

After four years, Ronnie divorced Elaine so he could marry his next wife Kate, a kissagram from Kent. Would it be 'Kiss me Kate' and another whirlwind romance? Patient P spent time in Broadmoor, studying the lead-up to the new romance. Ron had been keen on a lady from the hospital's League of Friends, but that friendship fizzled out as Kate appeared on the scene.

'Ron showed me a picture of a girl wearing a red leather jacket, and he told me she was Kate. She was attractive and had nice boobs. The picture was of her topless. I said to him that she would turn any man straight, which he laughed at, as he had never attempted to disguise his sexuality with me, but Kate and Ron did marry shortly afterwards.'

Fred Dinenage, who regularly met the Krays face to face in their respective establishments for his exclusive interviews, couldn't wait to ask Kate about the new relationship.

An eager Fred fired the questions. Kate, with blonde shoulder-length hair and wearing a lacy white top with a black jacket, answered every word. Fred noticed that she wore a dazzling, chunky gold and diamond ring on the little finger of her right hand.

'He's a real gentleman,' Kate explained. 'Ronnie is one of the old school. Not many of them about.'

Fred was intrigued: 'But what sort of marriage will it be, as far as you're concerned? How often will you see him?'

'I see him twice a week, but I'm in contact with him every day. I ring him every night.'

Fred was even more intrigued: 'But what about the future? How do you see things developing?'

Kate was honest enough, as the wedding day approached: 'Well, it would be nice if they let him out. Hopefully they will. But if they don't, I'll take what I can get.'

Wilf Pine recalled: 'Kate was a good laugh. I think she treated the whole thing as a laugh as much as Ronnie did. She originally got in touch with Reg, who fobbed her off to Ronnie. Ronnie liked the lunacy of her because she was funny, funny, funny. She was a strippergram – successful and very good looking.

'More than anything, to my mind, they became mates. And the next thing I knew Ron was saying to me that he wanted to marry Kate. I told him that he couldn't marry Kate. For God's sake, I told him, he was still officially married to Elaine.'

And there was another delicate matter to be addressed. Wilf thought that the whole thing was ridiculous. 'You're gay, Ron!'

Ronnie explained that his sexuality wasn't an issue: 'That's all right, she don't mind that, you know.'

Wilf put it all down to Ronnie's 'devil may care' attitude. The next thing he knew, the couple were engaged!

Ronnie's complicated marital situation required Wilf's help.

'Wilf, you gotta do something for me. Go and see my lawyer. I've gotta get a divorce.'

'So I've got to explain that you're already married, and you've gotta get out of this marriage because you want to marry another woman!'

Ronnie: 'You can do it, Wilf. I know you can do it.'

Looking back, Wilf reflected on his unexpected mission. 'To be fair, Ronnie hadn't seen Elaine for a couple of years. It sort of just drifted away. But nobody could get hold of her. I had people going looking for her to get a quickie divorce. The only recourse was to go to court.'

Wilf found himself in Portsmouth Crown Court with Ron's lawyer and a judge.

'I don't think this has ever been done before,' the lawyer

instructed Wilf. 'But I want to use you as a material witness.'

Wilf remembered that the judge looked as if he was intrigued by the bizarre goings-on. He also recalled that he'd actually dealt with the judge in a previous court case.

The judge announced that he would hear from the material witness. Wilf stepped into the dock. The judge stared at Ron's determined business manager. Wilf also looked the judge up and down. Wilf certainly did recognise the judge from that previous encounter. Perhaps the witness before him was also logged in the judge's memory bank.

'I told the truth, that Ronnie and Elaine hadn't seen each other for years and so Ronnie wanted a divorce. I said all of this wasn't helping with his treatment in the hospital.'

The judge made up his mind: 'Thank you, Mr Pine, please sit down. This is not going to set a precedent, but I have listened to what Mr Pine and Mr Kray's lawyer have to say.'

And so the divorce was granted. No sooner had Wilf got his breath back and regained his composure than TV cameras appeared outside the court. He gave a round of interviews, and then headed for Broadmoor to tell Ronnie: 'You have your divorce.'

Kate and Ron had to make it clear that they were serious, and it wasn't just a gimmick. Kate was told by a specialist at Broadmoor that Ron was a chronic paranoid schizophrenic, although his illness was now controlled by medication. Ron's behaviour depended on his drugs. If he took them, there should be no major issues in the future.

The doctor did offer some hope that, in time, Ron would be curable; he might be moved to a less secure hospital. It was possible that he could be released into a home environment with less supervision.

But nothing was set in concrete, and no one knew what the future held. The way things were, Ron Kray had to be locked up. On the positive side, it was accepted that Ron would not be able to cope with a prison environment, so that was out of the question. Ron would never revisit the horrors of Parkhurst.

The Broadmoor authorities asked Kate and Ron to think long and hard about the step they were taking, considering the strain on both of them and the difficulties in making the relationship work. They did take their time looking at the pros and cons, but nothing would change their minds. Broadmoor gave permission, and the wedding date was set for 6 November 1989. The Broadmoor chaplain and catering manager gave their blessings. The only proviso was that they would have to pay for everything! And there could only be eight guests, including the photographer.

Ron wanted to invite Charlie Richardson, despite previously wanting to kill him. The reason was, although there had been gangland feuds in the past, it was all still business. Another key factor was that Charlie Richardson had visited Ron at Broadmoor. Charlie was released but the authorities didn't want him as a guest.

What about Reg? Surely Reg could come? Yes, he could. Reg was in Gartree at the time and accepted Ron's invitation. However, the brothers had a disagreement over a minor issue and Reg said he wasn't coming. They made up again, as they always did, but the Home Office had cancelled the travel arrangements and that was that.

The twins were both upset. However, Ron and Kate carried on, working out who should be invited. In the end, the list read: Charlie Kray; Wilf Pine; artist Paul Lake; boxing promoter Alex Stein; Joey Pyle and Ron's friend Charlie Smith. Kate's best friend Sharon Denley, who was maid of honour, completed the guest list. Charlie Smith was chosen as best man.

What about the wedding photos? Ron was desperate to have David Bailey, who had taken those iconic images of the twins many years ago. The unique pictures had adorned newspapers and magazines since the sixties. David, though, was abroad, and couldn't come, so a local photographer was recruited.

To make up for the absence of Mr Bailey, Ron arranged for Kate to have a photo session in London with Lord Lichfield, the Queen's cousin. The results were spectacular; Ron bought the copyright to the photos and made sure they belonged to Kate.

Kate bought her wedding dress and also purchased a suit for the groom. It had to be the highest quality, to suit

Ron's requirements. She also bought him an expensive gold watch. Ron provided dazzling engagement and wedding rings. The engagement ring contained thirty pure white diamonds. The wedding ring caught everyone's eye with a circle of rubies and diamonds. Kate also received Ron's gold signet ring with the initials 'RK'.

Kate and Sharon arrived at Broadmoor in good time for the wedding to take place at a quarter past five. Ronnie was waiting in the chapel, quickly delivering a tender kiss and squeezing Kate's hand. It was a moving and emotional service, with Ron smiling and enjoying every second. Kate said later that she found it difficult not to cry.

Ronnie looked more than a million dollars in his grey suit, blue tie with white spots and matching handkerchief. A blooming carnation rested neatly above the handkerchief; surely Ronnie was the best-dressed groom ever to emerge from Broadmoor and take his vows.

It was no surprise to see Ronnie dressed to kill. He loved exquisite, hand-made suits. Top Italian tailors visited him at Broadmoor to measure up. Armani ties and gold, premium-brand watches were everyday items for this 'legend' of the underworld.

Ronnie's bride wore a strapless pink silk dress, with gold necklace, ornate headpiece, and dazzling earrings. She carried a beautifully arranged bouquet of flowers.

The Broadmoor kitchen had made a heart-shaped wedding cake on two tiers. The small party of Ron's loyal friends were treated to lobster, caviar and champagne.

The ceiling was covered with a hundred pink and white balloons and a myriad of flowers. Best man Charlie Smith footed the bill as his present to the couple.

The small gathering spent a precious two hours together at an event which surely could never be repeated.

Eventually, Ron and Charlie Smith had to be left behind, though. Kate felt sad, having to leave her new husband, but he urged her to enjoy the reception. Next stop: the Hilton.

Dozens of cameras waited outside Broadmoor and captured Kate leaving; dozens more were waiting at the nearby Hilton Hotel in Bracknell, flashing and clicking non-stop. About 200 of Ron's old friends attended the reception . . . drinking toasts to an absent friend. Shadowy, gangland figures wearing sunglasses and weighty, high-value gold jewellery caught the eye of onlookers.

TV News producer Kim Hewitt was working as a local newspaper reporter in Bracknell in 1989. She remembers the Hilton reception as if it happened yesterday. Kim wore a trouser suit and comfy flat shoes – ready to follow her stills cameraman in the rush to get shots through the wedding car windows and throw questions to the new bride.

'It was just so unusual. When you look back, you think . . . did that really happen? Of course, Ronnie and Kate married in the hospital itself. The press pack was camped out at the reception, no more than a fifteen-minute drive away. It was such a shame they wouldn't let Ronnie attend.'

Kim recalled that Kate had her blonde hair highlighted, and it swept up from her face. She grinned from ear to ear. As she went into the hotel, there were the usual quick-fire questions from the press:

'What's it like being Mrs Kray, Kate?'

'What's happening on the wedding night?'

Kim could see that Kate had ample experience of the press and retained her dignity. To be fair, the new bride had played everything by the book. Kim noted the heightened security arrangements that accompanied the celebrations.

'Journalists from TV, radio and newspapers mingled with police and minders. A wedding in Broadmoor . . . a reception at the Hilton, minus the groom. Who would have thought it? It was amazing! And Kate looked every inch the bride. She was an incredibly attractive woman who glowed with pride on the day she married a Kray!'

That evening, Kate called her new husband from the hotel. Normally she could only pass on a message; now she talked directly to him.

Duncan Campbell analysed why two women would want to marry Ron Kray: 'It's well established that lots of people in prison get fan mail from women who are perfectly happy to wait for them and even marry them. I'm sure, for some women, it's much more attractive to have a husband locked up indefinitely than to have them around the house.

'I think a cynical person might say it was a nice little

earner all round and certainly there was money made from the actual weddings and the publicity around them. And I think, for somebody like Ronnie, it was something to do. It was a way of dealing with the monotony of being locked up all the time.'

Roberta Kray believed that Kate was more outgoing and enjoyed making the most of the attention from the press. Roberta said that, despite the claims of a marriage of convenience, Ron and Kate did hit it off and were really fond of one another.

Eventually, the pressures told on Ron and Kate. She said she was picking up parcels, delivering them, waiting for instructions and running Ron's life outside Broadmoor. Ron was struggling with the relationship, as he became more and more paranoid.

And Ron's black moods returned. During a visit to Broadmoor, Ron's appearance concerned Steve Wraith. Normally the dapper Kray wore a suit, tie, cufflinks and smart shoes. But clearly something had upset Ron this time. He was wearing a jumper and trousers, his hair was dishevelled and things were definitely not right.

'I want Kate killed.'

There he was again, enveloped by a dark mood and upset about his wife. Steve had heard that she was very funny, a good laugh, a woman with soul and not someone who deserved to die.

'It's the book,' he muttered.

Ron explained that Kate's book, *Murder, Madness and*

Marriage had revealed details about a 'sex pact', allowing her to have relationships with other men. Steve had read about it in the papers, gaining the same knowledge as a large percentage of the population.

The revelation to the press meant that Ron sat in the visiting hall, calling Kate names and clenching his fists tightly. He stared and stared at Steve. 'She's a slag, she's a slag,' he growled.

Maureen also had a taste of Ron's displeasure over the sex revelations. When she went to see Ron, he stomped over towards her with an expression like thunder. The whole world knew that his wife was allowed to have relationships with other men.

Maureen pointed out that the agreement had been made, and it was the truth, but Ron said he was made to look like a fool.

Eventually, Ron began to calm down. He took several weeks to unclench his fists, and the death sentence was never mentioned again.

The marriage ended in divorce in 1994.

The next year was filled with sorrow for all who had known and loved Ronnie Kray.

Chapter 21

Farewell to Ronnie Kray

The strong bond between the brothers was finally broken forever in 1995.

The close connection had been illustrated earlier in the month of March when Reg felt dizzy, with pains in his chest. He was examined, although a doctor at Maidstone could find nothing wrong with him. Was it a warning about Ron's health in Broadmoor?

Nine days after that, on 15 March, Ron was admitted to nearby Heatherwood Hospital for tests. He had collapsed and was complaining about acute tiredness.

Reggie was allowed to call Heatherwood Hospital to talk to Ron. His twin seemed to be all right; however, Reg was far from convinced and wanted to travel to the hospital. His request was refused, and Ron was returned to Broadmoor. Reg felt restless, desperate to see his twin, and spent hours pacing around his cell.

Almost immediately, Ron was taken ill again. He was taken to Wexham Park Hospital, Slough, where he died from a massive heart attack. It was 9 a.m. on 17 March. Shortly afterwards, Reg was informed by the staff at Maidstone. Some of the inmates knew already because they had heard the story on the radio news. They felt that they couldn't tell Reg after hearing in that fashion, and offered their condolences when he returned from a meeting with senior staff. Reg was allowed to call his distraught brother Charlie, who had also been informed.

Alan was saddened by the circumstances surrounding Ron's death.

'He'd been involved in an altercation during his dinner, but when he collapsed he was removed from the dining area to be placed in a cell. That was so that a doctor could see him as he had complained about chest pains.

'The sad thing was that the lunatics had all been giggling and shouting – as the lunatics they were – while Ron struggled to breathe with a doctor tending to him. However, I don't think the staff could have done more for Ron. I felt sorry that his good friend Charlie Smith was denied a last chat with him before he went to meet his maker.'

Reggie was devastated. He was in pieces. Prisoners close to the surviving Kray twin were allowed to see and console him.

Feared associate Freddie Foreman recalled: 'Reg was in a different wing to me at Maidstone at the time, but the governor let me go to see him. We just talked and reminisced. Sometimes he'd have a little cry. They let me stay with him all day, just to keep him company.'

Maureen Flanagan heard the news from Charlie Kray. He phoned her to say that Ron had had a suspected heart attack, and she thought it would have been from taking so many tablets.

'Ron had been a good inmate in there. He never caused any trouble apart from the first six months. The only upheaval he had in there was when they told him that the Yorkshire Ripper was coming.

'I had already spotted Peter Sutcliffe in Parkhurst. Ron applied to see the doctor and the governor of Broadmoor, saying not to put him in his house. They had all of those places there, like Somerset House.

'Ron said not to put him in his house because he wouldn't be responsible for his actions. The doctor asked why he was so against Sutcliffe, when he didn't even know him. Ron said people saw the Krays as bad, but the Ripper killed women.'

Professor Dick Hobbs wrote an obituary: 'I was just struck by the reaction of the media. They had become fans of the Krays.

'A typical newspaper of the day would have a huge picture of the twins, describing Ronnie's death and stories about what terrible people they were. Then, inside, there would be more stories about the Krays on pages 4, 5, 6 and 7. The twins sold newspapers.'

Reggie, ever the Krays' PR man, threw himself into arranging his brother's final farewell. Three days before the service, Reg was allowed out to pay his respects at English's funeral parlour in Bethnal Green Road.

His every waking moment was spent organising the funeral. Ron had expressed the desire to have his coffin pulled along by six black plumed horses. That was going to happen, despite brother Charlie's concerns that they would take too long to cover the six miles from St Matthew's Church, Bethnal Green, to Chingford Mount Cemetery. Reggie's first wife, Frances, and his parents were also buried there.

'We've got twenty-five limos,' Reggie declared to Maureen on the phone. 'Ronnie is going to be buried like a king. I want you to be the person in the church who seats the people.'

The wreath from Reg declared, in large letters formed from white chrysanthemums, 'To The Other Half of Me.'

Reg was driven from Maidstone prison in a police car. He was handcuffed to a tall, bespectacled prison officer during the journey and all through the service. Inside the church, the mourners greeted and hugged Reg, one by one, while he was still attached to the prison officer.

Reg also said a few words: ' I'd like to thank all our friends and supporters. Very nice people. I wish it had been under different circumstances, but it's still really appreciated that they are supporting us.'

Maureen had read in the press that Ronnie's funeral would rival that of Winston Churchill.

'Winston Churchill didn't have twenty-six cars,' Reggie pointed out.

Professor Hobbs: 'It was an enormous service in East London. It was on an unbelievable scale – as if a king had died. People like Frankie Fraser were waving to the crowds as they drove along in the funeral cortege.'

Maureen: 'Reggie had worked out everything – who went in the first car, second car and so on. He mapped everything out and it all ran according to plan.

'The whole of the East End was at a standstill. Helicopters were above us. Police on motorbikes rode alongside our cars as we were driving along.

'We slowed down in traffic and I looked out at Walthamstow Dog Track. There were men with hard hats who had been working, and they were sitting with their legs dangling, you know, and their hats off.

'These were just workers who never knew Reggie or Ronnie. They were just young guys in their twenties or thirties. Of all the funerals, Ronnie's was the biggest. Charlie's was the smallest. The last one, Reggie's, was the saddest because the pall bearers weren't allowed to be the same people who carried Charlie and Ronnie.'

Freddie Foreman was asked to help carry Ron's coffin: 'I was finishing off a sentence in Maidstone and they said they wanted me to carry the coffin so I said "OK." They wanted me to go in handcuffs, so I asked how I could carry a coffin with handcuffs on. I asked them to give me a bit of a break. The Parole Board gave me time off my sentence so I could go to Ronnie's funeral and carry the coffin.

'It was an emotional day. The funeral was a big turnout. There was a coach and horses through the East End of

London to the cemetery. It took forever to get there, you know, with the horses and all that.

'We had a drink, and in the car they were breaking their necks to go to the loo. They were saying they would have to do it out of the window or something. Some people were starving and jumped out to a pie and mash shop on the way. I would say the funeral went off as sweet as a nut.'

Freddie's memory was of an upset Reg, but Ron's twin was trying not to show it.

'The funeral was over the top with the press and all that. People were there who never knew the guy and never met him. And they all wanted to turn up for the showpiece event. All these funerals are the same now, aren't they? Like with Ronnie Biggs and Bruce Reynolds.

'You go there to show your respects but there are people you've never seen before in your life. They think they can get their picture in the paper so they all turn up, you know? I hope it's not like that when I pop me clogs.'

Joining hands inside the church around the coffin for a minute's silence: Charlie Kray, Reg, Freddie Foreman from the south of London, Teddy Dennis from the west and Johnny Nash from the north, each representing their particular areas of the capital.

A message was read out: 'My brother Ron is now free and at peace. Ron had great humour, a vicious temper and was kind and generous. He did it all his way, but above all he was a man, and that is how I will always remember my twin brother Ron. God bless, Reg Kray.'

Prayers were said, and the congregation sang 'Fight the Good Fight' by John Samuel Bewley Monsell.

Ron's coffin was sprinkled with holy water. A trickle of smoke, from incense, drifted through the air.

Everyone stood as family friend Sue McGibbon read the poem, 'Do Not Stand at my Grave and Weep' by Mary Elizabeth Frye. Whitney Houston's song, 'I Will Always Love You', played from the church's loudspeakers.

At the front of the coffin, a floral portrait of Reg and Ron took pride of place. The ornate coffin was touched by the hands of mourners as it passed, ever so slowly, carried by the pallbearers. Candles were lit by the shrine of Our Lady.

Outside, the streets were packed. The service had been broadcast by loudspeakers, and so the atmosphere reflected that inside the church. The coffin was loaded into the hearse, and a procession of limousines headed, ever so slowly, towards Chingford Mount Cemetery. There were many, many wreaths and flowers with poignant messages. Kate Kray wrote: 'Tears in my eyes, I can wipe away. But the ache in my heart will always stay.'

Duncan Campbell was intrigued at the sheer scale of the event: 'They read some of "Invictus" by Henley: "I am the master of my fate, the captain of my soul." We had "My Way" sung and it was an enormous event. Then we went to the cemetery, and Reggie arrived with prison officers.'

Duncan described how men in dark glasses and suits embraced each other. It was like a scene from a *Godfather* film. Again, Reggie was mobbed by his supporters as they mingled in the churchyard. Reg was there, at the graveside, as the coffin descended into the earth.

'I think, by the time Ron died, the whole Kray publicity machine was so cranked up. The books were coming thick and fast, and the stories were all coming out. So when Ron died, it wasn't really the end of an era at all. It was just part of another East End tragedy.

'It was a strange story. The way he lived in Broadmoor, the wives, the boyfriends and everything. When he died, more stories came out, so it didn't really end with Ron.'

Professor Dick Hobbs believes that, if the Krays were around today, they would be on shows such as *Celebrity Big Brother* – and winning it. They were so good at public relations, especially Reg.

'It was a showbiz funeral on a huge scale. It didn't really look like a gangster's funeral at all. Whether we like it or not, the Krays were celebrities.'

Frankie Fraser knew Reg and Ron when they were very young; he knew their father well, too.

'Out of the two I liked Ronnie better because he was so honest. If he liked you, he told you. And if he didn't like you, he would tell you.'

After Ron's death, there were suggestions that Reg had lost the will to live. Roberta Kray says 'nothing could be further from the truth'.

She wrote: 'The death of his twin, although devastating, made him even more determined to carry on.'

Chapter 22

A New Bride for Reggie

Would Reggie Kray ever get married again? Could he ever recover from the emotional strain of his relationship with Frances Shea, or the loss of his twin? Perhaps a new marriage, with the stability he needed, would further the case for parole?

Entering the scenario: Roberta Jones, thirty-six, an English graduate. In 1996, Reggie, in Maidstone Prison, was making a film about his late twin. Reg wanted to make a tribute to Ron by means of a video. His emotions were transmitted onto tape.

Roberta agreed to step in and help with publicity, although she was nervous about going into prison and meeting Reg.

Maureen Flanagan recalled the early days of the relationship: 'One day I got a call from Reggie. He used to ring me at eight o'clock in the morning. He asked if I was coming up on Friday. I said I was. He asked if I could pick someone up – a girl who'd been writing to him for six months. I found out that she lived two minutes away from me.

'So I picked her up in my car and took her to Maidstone. She was very quiet. She asked me how long I'd been visiting Reggie and what he was like. I told her she wouldn't believe his energy, that she should forget it was a prison and imagine she was meeting a top businessman. I told her he would hug her, give her a kiss, ask her to sit down and say what he wanted to do.'

When Roberta arrived and saw some of the visitors, she realised that many were young, bare-legged and high-heeled women, sporting plenty of cleavage. Not knowing what to expect, Roberta had donned a grey woollen jumper and trousers of the same colour, matching the exterior of the prison wall. She felt 'like a house sparrow in an aviary of exotic birds'.

Reg did make a good impression. He proved to be fascinating for Roberta, who wondered how he had survived so long in jail without going completely mad.

Roberta reported that there were no sparks flying, it wasn't love at first sight, but she was surprised by his abundance of spirit and energy.

Maureen confirmed: 'They got on like a house on fire. She kept going back and they became extremely fond of each other.'

On the return journey, there was little conversation. It had been a momentous occasion in Roberta's life and she needed to reflect on the day's events. The Blackwall

Tunnel under the Thames came and went in a blur, and soon the newly acquainted friends of Reg were in Hackney and outside Roberta's flat.

Whatever she thought about Reg, the visit that day or any future visits, he would not be escaping from her thoughts any time soon. As she settled down in her flat, the phone rang. It was Reg.

Wilf Pine, one of the Krays' associates, described the relationship: 'Reg was having his boyfriends in there, but I genuinely believe that he did fall in love with Roberta. Out of the blue, he rang me one day. I never heard Reg Kray cry, but he was crying on the phone. He thought Roberta had dumped him.

'So I rang Roberta and pleaded with her to speak to Reggie. She said she would. And, after things were patched up, they were married.'

After many successful visits, the bond between the two became strong, and Reg proposed over the phone. He assured his future bride that he was down on one knee.

Those close to Reggie thought there was an ulterior motive. If Reggie married, perhaps it would give him a more respectable background – which would lead, eventually, to freedom.

Roberta's friends and family, in turn, greeted the news of the forthcoming wedding with incredulity. Had she lost her mind? Was she really going to marry a man jailed for life after a brutal murder? There were some who simply could not digest the news, and they moved into other circles. Her family, while finding the entire scenario difficult to take, stayed on her side.

The day before the 1997 wedding, in the chapel at Maidstone Prison, a thirty-minute laser show lit up the prison walls. The names 'Reggie and Roberta' appeared in the sky beside an image of wedding bells. Red, blue and silver colour created a spectacular, unique scene at the jail. The couple's friend, John Redgrave, organised the display. The prisoners gathered around their windows, cheering, despite the efforts of prison staff to calm everyone down.

On the wedding day itself, on Monday 14 July, Southport-born Roberta wore an ivory beaded dress. She arrived at the visitors' gate, driven in a black Jeep. Relatives gathered in a nearby pub, where flowers arrived including a dazzling bouquet from brother Charlie. He was beginning his own ten-year jail term on drugs charges.

The best man was Bradley Allardyce, the close friend of Reg. Bradley had been married at Maidstone a year earlier, with Reg doing the honours. Bradley's wife, Donna, acted as bridesmaid for Roberta.

The guest list was limited to twelve and included Tony Burns, a friend who had known Reg since childhood. Tony ran the Repton Boxing Club in Bethnal Green, where the twins used to train. Tony knew the twins so well that friends joked he was the only person who could call Ron 'a fat poof' and get away with it. In the ring, future world lightweight champion Ken Buchanan said Tony gave him the fight of his life. Tony attended the wedding with his wife, Barbara.

Also present were Reg's solicitors, Trevor Linn and Mark Goldstein, who were constantly on the case for parole.

At first, the authorities decided that there could be no photographs. After intense negotiations involving Mark Goldstein, a camera was allowed in. However, it could only be a prison photographer and the pictures would remain as Crown Copyright. The couple had no choice but to agree, although a dispute continued because Roberta said some pictures were being withheld.

After the wedding, the new Mrs Kray walked out of the main prison entrance and climbed into the jeep again. The vehicle drove off, with photographers jostling for position. The driver was distracted by all the photographers' flashes going off and put her foot down.

One of the photographers was struck by the vehicle, receiving what Roberta described as 'a glancing blow' in the melee. She apologised, hoping the photographer wasn't badly hurt, but didn't feel responsible as everyone could see the vehicle was trying to leave.

Married life, with Reg confined to prison, was fraught with difficulties. Roberta always felt that their future was in someone else's hands and they could never make any key decisions about life in the years to come. The relationship depended on phone calls and letter writing. Reg, as at Parkhurst, put pen to paper in the early hours of the morning and kept going. They actually managed to speak five times a day.

Like any married couple there were disagreements. Reg could wake up in a bad mood and provoke an argument. Roberta also became frustrated if Reg did anything to affect his chances of parole. After all, she was busy campaigning for his release as he was moved around the country, from jail to jail. Roberta even helped him to write one of the books about his life.

Roberta believes that, by getting to know someone slowly, as with Reggie, solid foundations can be built. Today, she says, there is too much emphasis placed on physical relationships, and the whole thing can collapse in a few weeks; people get carried away by the intense, often short-lived, passion.

Reg would have seen Roberta as someone to talk with, write to, respect and harness dreams of a brighter future. She helped him to break the monotony of the prison routine. And he fell in love.

He confided in Roberta completely, telling her when things went wrong. One day, for example, he was sent on what is called a 'laydown' in solitary, to Wandsworth, but was unsure of his offence.

'I lay down on the bed for twenty-three hours and switched off like a corpse,' he told her.

Roberta, in constant contact with Reg, discovered the real person. When he dropped his guard, Roberta found out the truth.

'I witnessed his many faces: the businessman, the entrepreneur, the sociable host, the criminal, the gangster, the dreamer – he could be all things to all men.

'Like a mirror image, he reflected exactly what his visitors wanted to see. Reg was the perfect chameleon. He knew instinctively exactly what was wanted and what was required of him. The real Reg, the man behind the mask, was someone very different. Full of private fears and anxieties, he struggled to make sense of his life.'

Roberta also knew how close Reg was to his mother and how he had felt such a sense of loss after her death. She reflected on the long, difficult journeys made by Violet to see her sons. People who had a grudge against the Krays even lobbed the odd brick through the mother's window.

Roberta's view: 'Violet spent the rest of her life being punished for the crimes of her sons.'

Roberta and Reg's marriage was a relationship that could have worked away from the prison walls, the cells, the bars and the intimidating atmosphere of a prison.

But happiness, for innumerable reasons, was never given a chance.

Chapter 23

Memories of Frances Kray

Reggie's prison wedding to Roberta wasn't the first time he'd been married. He walked down the aisle in April 1965 to wed Frances Shea – who was a mere twenty-one years old.

They'd met several years earlier. Reg went round to the Shea home in Bethnal Green to see one of his drivers, Frank Shea. Frank was out, and Reg was greeted by his sister, a teenage beauty. Frances Shea had dazzling red hair and big brown eyes. He was blown away by her charming smile and long, long eyelashes. The bisexual Reg had found the love of his life in the form of a female who was ten years younger and knew nothing about the Krays' evil deeds.

Reg wanted to make a good impression, although he wasn't exactly sure what to say; he was totally lost for words. He asked if he could see her again, even though he had only just seen her in a normal day-to-day situation. Reg was befuddled.

Frances sensed that Reggie's intentions were more than returning to say hello again when Frank was in. She asked where he wanted to take her. The offer of a ride in his car would have to do for the moment.

Reg was attracted by the fact that Frances was a decent type, unlike some of the one-night-stand ladies who frequented clubland. This old-fashioned girl, with old-fashioned values, had bowled Reg over. Reggie Kray told everyone. He was in love.

The venue for the first date? The twins' Double R club. There was no dancing and smooching during the evening. Instead, they sat and gazed into each other's eyes.

Maureen Flanagan could see Ron becoming jealous of Reg's relationship. One day she was in the Vallance Road kitchen with Violet and Frances. The twins' driver, Ronnie Bender, was waiting to go on a mission. Ronnie Kray remarked that it was like a mothers' meeting. Frances held Reg's arm and asked if he would be out for long.

Ronnie's eyes developed an extra bulge. He was absolutely furious. His glare was almost tangible.

Ron hissed: 'He will be as long as it takes. We've got business to do.'

Reggie and Frances went overseas on holiday in the early sixties. They travelled to Milan and saw *Madame Butterfly* at La Scala opera house. They also spent some time in Barcelona, where they watched a bullfight. One thing they agreed on: that gory confrontation was a horrible experience.

At home they visited West End clubs. Frances was a big fan of Noel Harrison, the son of actor Rex Harrison. Noel wasn't successful in the charts during their time; he had a minor hit with a number called 'A Young Girl of Sixteen'.

Several years later, Noel made his name with 'The Windmills of Your Mind', a song from the film *The Thomas Crown Affair*. When Noel spotted Reg and Frances, he often went over for a chat after his performances.

Frances was a deep thinker, intelligent and gentle. Reg was 'spooked' when she predicted that she would never reach old age.

According to Reg, the angel of his life predicted that she would die in her twenties. Reg told her that was nonsense; he never imagined that his gorgeous lady would be taken from him and no doubt transported to a better place.

Reg was transported to a worse place, Wandsworth, as the new decade dawned, for demanding money with menaces. Reg went into a shop to claim cash he said he was owed. No money was forthcoming. The police had had a tip-off and were hovering inside the building.

That meant six months without his beloved Frances. She accepted his sentence, still wrote to say that she loved him and looked forward to making their breakfast again when he was out.

Frances also stood by Reg during the next 'money with menaces' episode, the Hew McCowan club case, and the logical step was marriage.

David Bailey took the wedding photographs at St James

the Great Church in Bethnal Green on 19 April 1965. The best man was Ron, of course, with a star-studded guest list and telegrams from the likes of Barbara Windsor and Judy Garland.

But the marriage was faced with challenges from the very beginning . . .

Maureen Flanagan: 'Like a bird in a cage – that's how I saw her.'

Frances was on show to the underworld.

'It started off as a wonderful love affair,' Maureen recounted. 'I know there was a big difference in age between them, which didn't seem to matter because she obviously liked the experienced man who took her to nightclubs and dressed her up. She was sitting with all these glamorous people.'

Reggie's friends from the time recall that Frances was faced with a premier collection of film stars, politicians, TV celebrities and famous boxers. She sat, on display, like a princess in a palace.

Then all of a sudden Reggie wouldn't take her to these places, or outings were restricted to once a month. Business came first.

'Frances wasn't allowed to go out and buy a dress because a dozen would be delivered on a rail,' Maureen reflected.

Eight weeks after their wedding, Frances and Reggie were living apart . . . and Frances became more withdrawn. A tragic young life was about to draw to a close.

Charlie Kray broke the news to Maureen in a late-night phone call. Her husband Patrick, who hated the Krays, was out. Any communication from the Krays would have resulted in a bitter mouthful of abuse.

Charlie, on the phone, simply said that Frances had gone. Maureen, wondering what he meant, asked where she had gone.

'Frances is dead. Some sort of accident with pills. Reg is going potty.'

Maureen said Frances just went to bed and took a lot of tablets. Her brother looked in, brought a cup of tea and went out. When he returned, the tea was untouched.

He shook her, but it was too late. Frances was dead.

Frances's mother and father were screaming and shouting, calling Reg a murderer; they said she'd killed herself because of Reggie's behaviour.

When Maureen went to visit Violet, the devastated mother started crying. Bizarrely, the tears were for Reg. There was no thought of the Shea family losing Frances. Violet said Reggie was a broken man.

Everybody loved Frances, Violet told Maureen, but she was never cut out to be a wife. She couldn't even make a proper cup of tea, never mind cook anything. She wouldn't know how to wash a shirt. Violet said Reggie should never have married Frances and he needed a girl to look after him.

Looking back, Maureen said: 'How tragic. A young, beautiful, vibrant girl. And she took her own life.'

Since Frances's death, questions have remained about the exact nature of her passing . . .

Fred Dinenage: 'I spoke to Reggie in Parkhurst about what happened to Frances. He was never very keen to talk too much about it. He said to me he was very much in love with her, and tried to protect her. He tried to look after her.

'There were all sorts of rumours about what happened to Frances. You know, the fact that she was very depressed, and she felt repressed in her life. She was very unhappy. Reggie denied all of that to me. There were all sorts of rumours going around about what happened to her, some of them quite ugly, but I don't know exactly how it turned out.'

Frances's death haunted Reggie for the rest of his life. Alone in his cell – in his concrete tomb – he could only brood over a tragic love affair.

Albert Donoghue thought that his job on the day of Frances's funeral was 'sick'. He had to go around, taking a careful note of who hadn't sent flowers.

Freddie Foreman: 'It was tragic what happened there with Frances. Lovely, beautiful girl. She was a trophy wife and I just don't know how anyone – any woman or girl – could fall in love with him. She could have had anybody. She was beautiful. So sad.'

Chris Lambrianou: 'Reggie was so full of grief. I saw him one day, leaving the Carpenter's Arms and he was walking down this street, coat collar turned up and I asked him if he was getting a lift home. He said he was going to walk, and I thought there was one of the saddest men I had ever seen. But then he'd lost a lot as well, you know. And he had his dreams and his hopes and I think they all died really, when Frances died.'

In Parkhurst, Bobby Cummines noticed that Reg was looking melancholy. His downbeat appearance came on all of a sudden.

'I've been thinking about Frances a lot lately. Can't seem to get her out of my mind,' Reg told him. 'These things come and go. It was the anniversary of her death the other day. It set me off.'

Bobby was having tea in Reg's cell. It was a June day, close to the anniversary of his wife's death fifteen years earlier.

'I tried to give her everything. She had mental problems.'

'Really sorry, Reg.'

In one of his own books, *The Parkhurst Years*, Bobby wrote: 'Frances was only twenty-three when she died in 1967, and the thought of it all haunted Reggie. In reality Frances had entered a world that she couldn't live in. Reggie bought her everything, but he owned her. He expected her to do whatever he wanted. Frances was trapped in a world that she knew nothing about.

'All around her, people were getting hurt. She wasn't used to that lifestyle and couldn't get out of it. Violet Kray was very protective of the twins, so if Frances had the hump about something she couldn't go to her mother-in-law.

'Reggie, in his own way, couldn't see that he was doing anything wrong. Frances received everything she could wish for, apart from real love. She wasn't allowed to have a mind of her own; she was controlled from the moment she met Reggie. That was the truth, and I knew it, although the entire romance had been a disaster. I felt for Reggie, whatever the rights or wrongs about how he had treated his wife.'

Franie's niece, also Frances Shea, has followed her aunt's life down to the finest detail. She is upset with some recent publicity, saying key facts were not checked out.

When asked to write a few words about my darling aunt Frances, I find it hard. I want people to know that she wasn't bullied and browbeaten, and that she lived her very short life the way she wanted to. Dying was her aim.

She had a death wish from a young age and was convinced that she wasn't meant to live past the age of twenty-five. I was told so much throughout my life. What I read in Franie's diaries will stay with me because it was so very private; she's entitled to some privacy.

The press have never taken her family's feelings into consideration and have continually printed rubbish about her and other family members. I was enraged by one book with my aunt's suicide notes (there were many written) in which I am mentioned a few times.

Franie says the family has me to compensate for her and that she wanted me to have her things. What hurt so much was that people felt no need to get my input. They knew there was a living relative who had been there, yet chose to take the word of strangers instead of coming to the source.

I was very young but I have very clear memories of time spent with my Uncle Reg and Aunt Franie. I was confused when Franie died. Reggie disappeared out of my life and Mum and Dad split up. Nan and Grandad were more than heartbroken and I saw that heartbreak first hand for years to come.

My dad carried a lot of guilt regarding his sister's death. That was uncalled for. It wasn't his fault. It was nobody's fault. It was something that couldn't be avoided. Frances was very strong-willed. There are some dark diary entries that she wrote when she was in turmoil. I doubt that, when she wrote it, she ever dreamed that her thoughts would be sold to the highest bidder at auction, and then put out there for the world to see.

I've written my darkest thoughts down and would be devastated to think that could happen. Frances is not here to defend herself and I see that as my job. The press have been quick to print whatever they want to. I had a bad experience with one of the newspapers. I was mortified to see what they published. According to the article I'd called Reggie a 'monster'. I never did.

I don't blame the Kray twins for Franie's demise. She took her own life. It's been said that Ronnie Kray forced her to take an overdose. Untrue. Another story is that Violet Kray, mother of the twins, paid someone to kill Franie because she was pregnant with Reggie's child. More nonsense. Totally false.

I've been very angry and frustrated for a long time. I suffer from mental health problems myself. The film *Legend* didn't help my mental state. It upset my daughter, Bonny, very much. We both cried our eyes out after going to the premiere of the film at Leicester Square. Who were those people up on the screen? My family? My backside.

I'm writing my truth, and it's much harder than I expected, but given the fact I've been shunned by the media world I will carry on regardless.

Franie's death taught me a huge lesson . . . one that still applies today. She died and I've survived because of her. Had I not seen the aftermath from her death I may have been another suicide statistic. I've fought suicidal tendencies throughout my life. My dad attempted suicide several times. He eventually took his life aged seventy-one when diagnosed with throat cancer. It wasn't long after he died that a book about Frances came out, followed by the film *Legend*.

Talk about feeling helpless. How could I fight an American director? I had a little go but didn't get very far. That's why I'm writing away now. I need to get some truth out there and get the closure I need for me and my grandchildren.

The bitterness stops here. Although there are things to be bitter about, it is pointless. The twins were incarcerated for life. As far as I'm concerned there are far worse crimes committed by far worse people. I can't hate. It doesn't help. It just doesn't help anyone at all.

Chapter 24

In the Shadow of his Brothers

Charlie Kray moved in the same circles as the twins, and yet he operated in the shadow of his brothers. He handled a lot of their business interests, had his disputes with them and, in many ways, was his own man. He was an affable character, tainted by his imprisonment over the Jack McVitie affair, but he had the ability to keep bouncing back from adversity.

Nipper Read always thought that Charlie was more involved in crime than he let on. In fact, Nipper believed that Charlie was the brains behind the operation. Nipper noted that, when the twins were in trouble, they turned to Charlie.

Charlie always claimed to be a background figure. He was not the type to walk into a pub and shoot someone, or produce a meat cleaver in a public place with the genuine threat of using the weapon. He saw himself as more of a front man, acting as an agent, looking after business interests and booking acts for the twins' nightclubs and bars.

Charlie became close to stars such as Judy Garland and Christine Keeler, although the twins maintained they saw Christine on very few occasions.

Charlie was a quiet, easy-going Cockney, although deep within him some said there were volatile Kray traits. One night he displayed that side at Esmeralda's Barn in Knightsbridge. Charlie's role was to meet and greet gamblers who enjoyed a flutter on the second floor while their children danced the night away on the first floor.

One evening, Ron Kray spiralled out of control. He was chatting up young males, making a nuisance of himself, and upsetting patrons at Esmeralda's. Charlie asked him to stop and even Reg stepped in, but Ron continued unchecked. Charlie had had enough. He picked up a chair and threw it at the bar, declaring that they may as well smash the place up.

Reg and Ron tried to calm him down, though it took a lot of doing. Charlie was affable, easy-going, friendly and smiling most of the time. That night he showed that he could mix it with the best, or worst of them. He was a Kray through and through, and his reputation underwent a slight change on that evening. Ron had to think twice before making dodgy moves of any description in Esmeralda's.

Charlie appeared on *The Frank Skinner Show*, looking like a showbiz star himself. The eldest Kray brother still had long hair, and wore an immaculate suit and tie. Frank asked Charlie about Jack 'The Hat' and Charlie said he received ten years of bird because of his name. He said on the show that he should have been found not guilty.

Charlie explained on the programme that Reggie received some high-profile visitors such as boxing champions Joe Louis and Rocky Marciano, as well as singers Frank Sinatra Junior and Tony Bennett. In the sixties, he said, they were friendly with superstars like Judy Garland. Viewers knew only too well that celebrities such as Diana Dors were close to the twins.

In 1996, Charlie was arrested and accused of being part of a multi-million-pound cocaine-smuggling ring. He was trapped by a police sting operation at a Newcastle hotel, offering to supply the drug.

There was a video of Charlie and undercover police at a party. The national news bulletins carried the story, showing the damning evidence.

Wilf Pine was aghast. In his book, *One of the Family*, Wilf said he was baffled by news of the arrest, because drugs 'were never Charlie's thing'. It was so unlike the Charlie that Wilf knew. He assumed it had been the result of old age and the fact that he was still grieving after the death of his son, Gary. It was sheer stupidity on Charlie's part, and he should have been more careful.

Wilf believed that Charlie had never been a serious criminal; he had suffered all of his life from having the Kray name. 'He wasn't violent, but he was a Kray.' The judge may as well have put a black cap on, Wilf said, and sentenced him to death.

Charlie, protesting his innocence, was taken to Belmarsh Prison, beside Woolwich Crown Court. Although an OAP at seventy years old, Charlie was detained under the highest possible security and locked up for twenty-three hours a day. Yet he was still confident of getting bail, and was cheered up when Dave Courtney, known as a self-styled gangster and close friend of the Krays, was cleared in a separate case.

Was Charlie guilty? Steve Wraith, who entertained Charlie in Newcastle several times, thinks not. But he was naïve and careless getting involved. Charlie believed that, even if he was caught, he would be in the clear because he was only introducing two parties. The law would say that is setting up a drugs deal.

'I personally went into the court and gave a good account of Charlie. I told them that he would do anything for charity. He wasn't a man who would deal in drugs. I never saw him handle or take drugs. Charlie was never found with any on him. All they had was a recording of Charlie saying he could put them in touch with people.'

Frankie Fraser: 'Charlie was absolutely innocent, 100 per cent. I would swear to God on it. He thought they were people who just wanted to go for a drink with him, and at the end of the night they would give him £500 or whatever. He thought they just wanted to be with someone from the Krays.

'When they asked if he could get them a load of cocaine . . . well, if they had asked for a load of gold he would have said "yes." He never dreamed they were undercover cops. And even if he had known, he would have still said it 'cos he was doing nothing wrong.'

When Frankie gave his evidence he told the judge it was the first time he had left the court a free man. Steve felt that having Frankie as a character witness helped to condemn Charlie to what was, eventually, a death sentence.

In court, Charlie's defence said the oldest Kray brother was made out to be something he was not. In reality he was anti-drugs, against crime and with a heart of gold. He was described as 'an old fool, a pathetic old has-been and an utterly washed-up figure'.

None of that made impression on judge and jury. Charlie was jailed for twelve years.

The length of the sentence angered Wilf Pine. He was also furious because Charlie was treated as a Category 'A' prisoner in maximum security. At seventy years old, he was the oldest prisoner of his type in the country.

Everything went from very bad to disastrous for Charlie. An appeal in his drugs case was turned down; at the same time his health deteriorated. Charlie was moved to Parkhurst, where he collapsed with a heart condition. Reg realised that his brother might well end his days on the Isle of Wight, where his own nightmare had begun so many years ago.

Reg learned through friends that Charlie had lost a lot of weight, could hardly walk and there was considerable swelling on his legs. Reg, in Wayland, was kept informed about Charlie's condition. A trip to the Isle of Wight became inevitable.

Reg was driven down to the coast, onto the ferry, and then to St Mary's Hospital. Encased in handcuffs and chains, he was led into Newport Ward. There were four prison officers on duty during the half-hour chat.

Despite his own health issues, Reg was shocked and distressed at Charlie's condition. He was heavily drugged and attached to an oxygen supply.

Reg was returned to the Parkhurst psychiatric unit where he had spent time in the past with Ron; he was allocated Charlie's cell.

Roberta Kray crossed the Solent on 24 March 2000 and arrived to see Charlie with Wilf Pine. Neither could believe the desperate condition of the oldest brother. Roberta had only talked to him on the phone previously; now, during this unfortunate first meeting, Charlie looked dreadfully ill.

Breathing heavily, he clambered into a wheelchair and carefully manoeuvred himself into a day room, with the prison officers doing their best to allow some privacy.

On 3 April, during the evening, news came through from St Mary's Hospital that Charlie's condition had deteriorated. Reg was escorted from Parkhurst during a mini monsoon while press photographers grabbed any images they could. All Reg could do was hold his brother's hand and maintain the close bond of brothers.

The next evening, three officers arrived at Reg's cell

and broke the news: Charlie Kray was dead. He passed away at 8.50 p.m. on the evening of 4 April 2000. Reg was even more upset because Charlie's son, Gary, had already died from a terminal illness in 1996.

The next day, Reg returned to Wayland under heavy escort. He was now without his mother, father and two brothers. He had lost his entire family as well as the young bride Frances. He needed Roberta more than ever.

The funeral ceremony, traditionally for the Krays, was held at St Matthew's Church in Bethnal Green. Reggie was allowed to attend, handcuffed to a female prison officer. Supporters cheered as he arrived.

Reg was allowed to mingle with mourners inside the church, and talked freely to associates from the underworld.

The funeral was a much smaller affair than the massive gathering after Ronnie's death in 1995; although closely associated with the twins, the eldest brother never shared their notoriety or legendary status.

Maureen Flanagan has a vivid memory of Charlie, when he was released after seven years for his role in the McVitie case.

'Violet had a little party for him in a pub in Old Street. We all went. The place was packed. He looked the usual Charlie Kray, tanned as usual because he used sunbeds. He always wanted to be tanned.

'We had a wonderful night. Violet was dancing, singing and cuddling him. Charlie gave me his views on his brothers' futures. He told me he didn't think Ronnie would ever be allowed out of Broadmoor, but there was a chance with Reggie as he'd never been declared insane and had been a good prisoner.'

Jewel thief Lenny Hamilton, who operated at the same time as the Krays: 'Charlie Kray was my friend. He was my friend until the day he died. He was a nice man. You can't blame him for what his brothers did. If you were having a drink in the pub and Charlie Kray was there, you couldn't swear in front of any women.

'Charlie was well respected in the East End, whereas the twins were feared. They were jealous of Charlie because people respected him.'

Charlie was buried in the family plot at Chingford Mount cemetery. The cortege, laden with flowers, was adorned with a boxing ring, made from red and white carnations . . . provided by Reggie, of course.

Chapter 25

Reggie's Last Breath

Reg celebrated his sixty-fifth birthday within the confines of Wayland. It meant, with thirty years of service, an end to his cleaning duties.

'Do I qualify for a gold watch?' Reg enquired on a request form.

The governor pointed out that, technically, Reg was not an employee of the Prison Service and, unfortunately, his request would have to be declined. Reg did appreciate the humour in the response.

There had been no mention of a release date; no suggestion of parole for Reg during his thirty-year tariff.

He depended on his wife, Roberta, for moral support, love and friendship. All they had: phone calls and a few visits a month.

Extract from letter, written by Reg to Roberta on 25 December 1998:

Rob –

Thanks to you I had a good night. Without you, I would have been shattered. My thoughts are with you. Hope you have a good night and we have a good day tomorrow.

Goodnight
God bless
All my love

Reg xxxxx

Days drifted into other days, into weeks and months . . .

In July 1999, though, Reg and Roberta experienced one particularly happy day at Wayland. The prison organised a 'Lifer's Day' event, where long-term inmates were allowed to spend much longer than normal with friends and family.

What a day for the lifers. It all started at 9.30 a.m. in the visiting hall with tea and chats. At lunchtime, everyone ventured outside into the prison field. Roberta and Reg had only breathed in the outside air together once before, when photographs were taken at the Maidstone chapel on their wedding day.

A marquee had been put up, and a buffet-style lunch provided. Children played football, the sun shone in a vivid blue sky, while Reg and Roberta revelled in each other's company. Music played in the background.

Reg couldn't resist the question: 'Shall we dance?'

They began a slow waltz between the tables, with other couples joining in. Families enjoyed the day of their lives in the grounds of a prison.

'I'll never forget today,' Reg said as the precious minutes ticked past.

All too soon, it was time to return to his cell.

A year later, in mid-July 2000, Reg, in Wayland, was struggling with stomach pains. Tests had not revealed any cancer; he was taking mild painkillers that did little to ease his agony. Later he told Roberta that he rang the emergency bell, but no one came.

On 27 July, Reg was moved to Norwich Prison Hospital for observation. When Roberta visited him there, he spent the entire time holding his stomach. A nurse gave Reg paracetamol and he took the pills without a hopeful expression.

On 3 August, Reg phoned Roberta to say he had been coughing up blood. He was taken to the Norfolk and Norwich Hospital, where a small camera was inserted in his stomach.

The specialists delivered bad news to Roberta. Dark liquids on his stomach had been hiding a large blockage in his intestine. After a short operation, the surgeon said it did not look like cancer, although that was not definite.

One main issue at the time was whether Reg's handcuffs should be put back on. Senior members of staff from

HMP Prison Norwich visited regularly to check on his condition and decide whether the cuffs should be reapplied. A reprieve was granted because of the number of wires, drips and tubes attached to the prisoner.

Although Reg started to feel better and the wound began to heal, there was more grim news to come; a consultant confirmed that the growth had been cancerous after all.

Maureen Flanagan's memories: 'Reggie was treated with Milk of Magnesia over a period of about nine months until he got worse and worse, then Roberta insisted on another doctor taking an X-ray and he was diagnosed with cancer.

'We kept applying for parole which they agreed when he had not long to live. He was taken out to a hospital for two weeks, and Roberta was by the bedside all the time. I think she really, really loved him. He was put into a nice hotel in Norwich, and he was in a little top room for the last two weeks of his life. Roberta never left him. So she was very good for Reg.'

In bed, enjoying his brief spell of freedom, with not long to live, Reg said he liked to hear the sound of children playing; a sound he had not heard for more than thirty years. He thought everything on the outside would be beautiful. It was just a case of getting used to it all. Reg thought that it would be a complex environment, with so much going on, and he would find it all really interesting. But his wish to enjoy the outside world with Roberta would never come true.

Freddie Foreman said he died in his arms. Other well-known gangsters of the time were there for the final moments with Roberta.

They included Joey Pyle, Wilf Pine, Jerry Powell and Johnny Nash – not the singer but an educated criminal who won a scholarship as a young boy.

Freddie, his voice trembling with emotion, described Reggie's last days: 'He had a nice room and a view out onto water at the back. A least he had some pleasantness in the final days of his life.'

Reg, though, looked terrible. He was like a skeleton and nearing the end of his time on Earth.

'He was asking how we got there and all that. We were having a chat in a way. It was a real effort for him but he was trying to be sociable, you know. Then all of a sudden a doctor came in and said we had to leave the room. It was time for Reg to have his injections.'

The visitors went off to the bar for a drink, after assuring Reg they would return shortly. Reg kept asking if they were coming back. Perhaps he knew the end was near.

When they returned, Reggie's condition had deteriorated. He was semi-conscious and struggling to breathe. He couldn't speak.

Freddie recounted the final moments: 'There were people all around him, but I propped him up with my arm. I said, "Don't fight it, Reg, let it go, let it go, I'll see you another time, another place." And then I became all emotional because I'm a bit of an emotional person.'

Fred said he took his arm away and told the others in the room: 'He's gone. He's gone, you know.'

But Reggie, a fighter all of his violent life, wasn't quite finished.

Freddie said he couldn't hear any breathing and Reg was making no noise at all. Then all of a sudden, Reg gave out a loud cough and everyone jumped.

'It must have been the last air expelling from his body. It made such a loud noise that everyone jumped.'

Roberta Kray described Reg's final moments: 'Reg's breathing stuttered, stopped and then suddenly started again – one last tiny half-breath. And then there was nothing. Silence. It was the worst moment of my life. I took him in my arms. His skin was warm, his eyes closed as if he were still sleeping. I put my hand on his forehead and stroked his hair. It couldn't be possible. Not this man I had known and loved. It couldn't be over.'

Reggie passed away on Sunday, 1 October 2000.

Once again the East End came to a standstill as the Krays' manor said farewell to another notorious son.

Reggie's supporters turned out in strength for his funeral at St Matthew's Church in Bethnal Green – the setting for Ron's funeral, five years earlier. A procession of six black plumed horses pulled the hearse. The words 'Reg' and 'Respect' stood out on the hearse as crowds watched the cortege pass. 'Legend,' some of them shouted.

At the church, mourners recognised the unmistakable

tones of Frank Sinatra's song, 'My Way'. Reggie had planned his own funeral and chosen his own music. The twins' favourite record was an essential feature at both funerals.

Actor Steven Berkoff, who played George Cornell in the 1990 *Krays* film, said: 'It's because they represented not just the villain. The pair of them were so unique, being twins. There was something mythic, rather strange about them, and it brought people back to an older time.'

When Reg passed away, Roberta talked in the newspapers about 'an awful emptiness'. She thought about him all the time. She said she didn't want to avoid speaking about Reg. She wanted to come through the grief and find good memories.

She said that she found solace in her writing; it helped her to rebuild her life. She received masses of correspondence detailing Reg's life in prison and that inspired her to become an author. Without meeting Reg, she would never have chosen that path.

Reg was laid to rest at Chingford Mount Cemetery, close to his former wife Frances, twin brother Ron, elder brother Charlie and his parents. Roberta was surrounded by wellwishers as she paid her final respects.

Frankie Fraser was there, too. He paid his respects and even mentioned his alleged role in the Charlie Richardson torture trial, when he was alleged to have pulled out teeth with pliers.

'In many ways I am the link that links us all together. In

the public's eyes they are making me an icon as well. As long as I go down as the best dentist, I don't mind.'

For those who go to Chingford Mount Cemetery to pay their respects, an ornate headstone stands, with a picture of the twins on either side of it. Beneath the headstone, flowers are regularly replaced.

The headstone reads:

In Loving Memory

RONALD KRAY
Born 24th October 1933
Died 17th March 1995

REGINALD KRAY
Born 24th October 1933
Died 1st October 2000

Grant them eternal rest, O Lord;
and let perpetual light shine on them.

Chapter 26

Legends or Failed Criminals?

Was it all worth it? What did they achieve during their lives? Did crime really pay for the Krays? Did it pay for the Richardsons? What was the point of it all? What was their legacy?

Our true crime books were shaped, several years ago, when we met Charlie Richardson. We were filming a documentary and at the same time writing a book about Charlie; a similar situation to *The Prison Years* scenario.

Now Charlie was an interesting case in the criminal world. He told us how he tried to stay ahead of the law with his imaginative schemes. He described the Krays more as bulls in china shops, drawing attention to themselves and becoming marked men. In another world, Charlie would have gone on to become a successful businessman. As a clever criminal, despite so many attributes, he was always going to be incarcerated.

The fact that the Richardsons and the Krays had put their rivalries behind them was reinforced at an historic meeting in Maidstone Prison in the mid-nineties. It was organised by Dave Courtney, who adored Charlie Richardson and Reg Kray but hated Frankie Fraser. The guests, settling down in a room that doubled as a canteen, included Dave, Frankie, Charlie Richardson, Christian Simpson – who was a close friend of Freddie Foreman – and boxing promoter Alex Stein.

'Legends' in the criminal underworld assembled around tables in the middle of the room and waited on Reggie. Soon enough the main man appeared, wearing a blue and white pinstripe prison shirt. A gold cross with ample dimensions could be seen glinting beneath his undone top buttons. A new pair of white branded trainers and fashionable Levi's completed his outfit. Reggie certainly didn't have the appearance of a down and out old lag. With a broad smile, he embraced each of his visitors one by one.

Other prisoners and their visitors fell silent as the group took their seats in the middle of the room. The faces were all recognised, although people could hardly believe that Frankie Fraser and Charlie Richardson were about to chat to Reg Kray in front of their very eyes.

An account at the time said the meeting was an emotional time as they caught up with the news, who was alive and who was dead. Most of all, it was firmly established that they were all at peace; there were to be no more gangland wars.

There was dark humour too. When refreshments were requested, Frankie Fraser asked what sort of biscuit Reg would like: Penguin or McVitie's? The death of Jack 'The Hat' McVitie at the hands of Reg and Ron was no laughing matter, although several smirks had to be suppressed.

Professor Dick Hobbs believes that the Krays were important figures of their time for a number of reasons.

'They are icons of the sixties. If you talk about the sixties, you have to talk about the Krays and their impact on society and the way we think about crime. They became the stereotypical gangsters. If you talk about British gangsters, the Krays come up time and time again.

'I think we can remember them as icons of the old white working class as well. Many people look back at the twins and they say they were wonderful people, and a lot of crime now wouldn't have happened in the time of the Krays.

'A lot of today's crime didn't go on then anyway. You didn't have internet crime and we didn't have the likes of DVD recorders to steal. There is an awful lot of glamorisation about the Krays and what they were about. They weren't Robin Hoods. They were villains. They were old-school villains who looked up to the gangsters from the twenties and thirties and took their lead from them.'

Professor Hobbs says prison did give the Kray brand a mystique that they wouldn't have had if they'd stayed outside. It's very difficult, he stresses, to see how the Krays would have adapted to an evolving East End and changes to crime.

'The year 1968 was big, not only for the Krays, but for the East End. Youth unemployment went up for the first time since the Second World War. The area was redeveloped, new populations came in and the old Cockney population started to move out.'

The twins were already talking about retiring when they were arrested, he pointed out. And it would be difficult to see how they could have maintained their status outside. Prison put them in a 'freeze frame'; the myth was able to expand and the brand was allowed to develop while they were behind bars.

Duncan Campbell's view suggests that the Krays should have followed the example of gangs who skulked around in the shadows, going about their business without making a fuss.

'The legacy of the Krays is that, if you're a criminal and you want to have a very large profile, you may have that very large profile – but it will end up with you being a target for the police and you will end up spending a long time inside.

'I think the Krays should be remembered as a strange phenomenon of British culture. We're very grateful for the fact that we didn't have Chicago in London. The Krays, and to a lesser extent the Richardsons, were the nearest that we had to it.

'The nearest equivalent to the Krays today in terms of publicity is people who become famous through reality television or through being in soaps, and who are happy to be photographed in clubs. Now, there is not a criminal equivalent to the Krays or the Great Train Robbers. One of the reasons for that is smart criminals today don't want anyone to know their names and they don't want to have their photos taken.'

Duncan points out that modern villains aren't keen on anyone sniffing around, writing books and making films about them. The last thing they want is to be part of a musical or have someone selling boxer shorts with their faces imprinted on the garment.

'I think one of the reasons that the Krays are still well known today is partly because they wanted the publicity themselves. They had their photo taken by David Bailey, and they liked to model themselves on those Chicago gangsters with the suits, ties and white shirts.

'The Krays always said they never hurt women or children and I think that is probably largely true. I think that the violence was with people who fell out with them or who weren't prepared to pay their protection money.'

Wilf Pine says that the legend of the Krays will never end.

'There'll be a million stories and a million lies. But look at what it's done. It's made nearly everybody an author.

'But they're dead and they can't answer questions any more. America's had the likes of Al Capone, John Dillinger, Charles Luciano and Vito Genovese. We got the Kray twins and for all time that's exactly what it's gonna be. You know when your daughter is fifty years old she'll be reading something or seeing something being filmed about the Krays.'

Chris Lambrianou found out to his cost that crime doesn't pay. We found Chris to be a highly intelligent individual, with a strong sense of right and wrong even though he chose the wrong path in life. His loyalty cost him so much. His life was ruined because of those efforts to clean up after the Krays.

'Reggie Kray died in prison, apart from those last few days of his life, Ronnie Kray died in prison and Charlie Kray died in prison. Whatever they achieved in life was such a small amount compared to what they might have achieved. They sold themselves cheaply, and that's what I believe. There was so much more they could have done. On the criminal side, they could have been more professional. And as for doing good, they could have reached the heights, but their lives were dashed. We lost everything. We gave up everything for them. . . . our future, our lives.

'I wasn't grateful that the Krays were in my life, to be honest with you. I had fifteen years to regret it. But you know, I don't think I ever wished them ill or anything like that. My regret is that I let my family down. I wasn't the perfect human being that I should have been.'

His brother, the late Tony Lambrianou, said after his release: 'I had a wife and a young child, but you don't realise it at the time. I didn't see my child until he was sixteen. I had a daughter who was nearly six, and she was twenty-two when I came out of the nick. My father became an old man, never really knowing what had happened. There was tragedy and heartache for the families. What good came out of it? Where is the glamour in all that? There was no glamour at all.'

Alan the Broadmoor patient got to know Ron Kray at close quarters. He saw Ron in all sorts of situations, and can give a unique insight into life with the highly unstable twin.

'If I had met Ron on the outside, then I would have steered clear of him because of his brutal crimes, protection rackets and all the rest of it. But I gradually got to know him, living in the same environment every day for a long time. He was a very ill man and he could change moods just like that.

'However, he was a generous and loyal type and he would support someone in trouble. Putting everything into perspective, and the background he came from, I actually quite liked him. His legacy would be a type of criminal, found in the sixties and never to be repeated; a criminal who had feuds with his own kind, but not members of the public.

'I am sure that, with all his medication, he became more erratic in Broadmoor; he lashed out at the patient eating dinner after allegedly flicking peas, for example. I have to say, though, I never felt threatened by Ron.'

With the passing of the twins, Steve Wraith felt an empty space in his life.

'The era of the Krays had finally drawn to a close. It had drawn to a close so quickly. I had gone from having three infamous brothers as friends and associates. Now they were all gone. I felt as if the whole thing had been a dream. No more East End gangster shouting down the phone at me. No more arguments over who was going to get money from any particular party. I was just shocked that the end had come.

'Everything has changed nowadays. If two people in the East End wanted to take over the odd snooker hall or the local clubs they would be met by the Triads, the Yakuza or the Yardies. There are too many now. The Krays are history. The Krays are a legend. The Krays are something now you can only read about or see in films.

'So what is the legacy that the Krays leave behind? For me it is a mixed one. As criminals in the 1960s they were unique, one-offs. Like Capone across the pond before them, they courted publicity and mixed with celebrities and gave interviews to the media, raising their profiles to such a height that the authorities had to take action and put them out of business and ultimately behind bars.

'If you do a survey in the UK and ask people to name an English gangster, then you can bet your last pound that 99 per cent will say Ronnie or Reggie. They earned their place in history. That is their legacy . . .'

Fred Dinenage believes that, in the end, prison took its toll.

'It broke their health and, in the case of Ronnie, broke

his spirit as well. Half a lifetime inside. It would break most men. There was no hope and no light at the end of the tunnel and they both died sick, unhappy men. The Kray twins represent proof that crime doesn't pay. It might have paid in their heyday, but then came all the stress, aggravation and time in prison. Finally, came the ill health and deaths with hardly a penny to their names.

'The Kray twins in many ways were bad men who committed bad deeds, but you have to speak as you find and I caught them at a stage in their lives when they were, if you like, senior citizens. They were older, wiser and calmer than they had been for a long time.'

Fred found Reg more difficult to deal with. He was always on edge. Ronnie, Fred discovered, was a gentle type despite his appalling crime. He was full of medication though, so how much did Fred see of the real Ronnie? He'll never know.

'The Kray twins still have this incredible following, not only amongst older people, but also in the younger generation. I get emails and letters from all age groups, asking about Ron and Reg.

'The Kray legend, if you like, lives on. The books still sell and the films still sell, years after their deaths. It's extraordinary. The Kray twins did have that image about them, inasmuch as they would never hurt children – or women or older people – or indeed anyone who wasn't involved in the criminal underworld.

'That was the image, along with the idea that if you

lived in the East End you could leave your front door open and not worry about being burgled.

'I'm not sure how much of all that is actually fact, and certainly if you talk to former criminals, or ex-criminals who've fallen on the wrong side of the Krays, you'll get a very different story. But I do think there is a certain amount of substance to the Robin Hood image.'

David Fraser, son of Frank: 'They'll become Robin Hoods like my father has become. The Krays, my dad and all the other guys like Freddie Foreman will become like Robin Hood and the Merry Men.'

Pat Fraser, son of Frank. 'I think they should be remembered as two stand-up guys. They were never grasses.'

Freddie Foreman backs up the Robin Hood reputation: 'If people were in prison, they would send money round to their wives. It was a nice thing to do, helping out the families and kids. There was only one money earner, and women weren't working like they are today. It was a different scene then.

'Yeah, they did raise money for their charities. I went to a few of the charity things and I know it was genuine. In Newcastle, there was a little boy with a hole in the heart. The twins, especially Ronnie, were very generous. If you said to Ronnie that he had a nice watch he would want to take it off and give it you.'

Bobby Cummines remembers the twins with affection. 'In a place of brutality, when my mother was dying, they showed humanity to me and my family. They were there for me. It's the same as all the guys in our world who have lived our lives. We have our differences, like any family. We fall out. One minute we love each other, and the next minute we want to go to war with each other.'

Norman Parker recalled that it was sometimes better just to leave the twins alone and not get involved.

'You had to be very careful what you said to Ronnie. But he was never on the main location. He was only in the high security wing, or the psychiatric wing and then he was in the hospital. He was a man best left alone because we can all say things that we think are humorous and funny, and you'd really upset the man.

'With Reg, he pretty much had people's respect. He held his head up. He did his time like a man, as best you can do your time over thirty years. But again he would keep people at arm's length, otherwise he'd have a constant stream of mugs coming in and out of cells driving him mad. Anyone who knew Reg would give him a little bit of space.

'For those people who turn round and say the Krays have left a legacy, I can't see it. I think if there is a legacy it's not to be an unsuccessful criminal. Whatever else they were, they were very unsuccessful criminals.'

Maureen Flanagan's view? 'Prison was the best thing that could have happened to the Krays. It meant that nothing deteriorated, and still hasn't up until the present day. There are still books, there are still films and there are young rappers rapping their name in songs. At the trial they only had to admit to certain things, but they wouldn't because they wanted to keep up that celebrity lifestyle.

'They knew that several famous people would still visit and they thought, later on, that more films would be made, and books and songs would be written. Their paintings sell all the time, and poems sell as well as autographs.

'It goes on and on. It's like an ongoing Robin Hood thing you know, like folklore. They are the folklore of the East End, that's for sure.'

Reg's wife, Roberta, says her husband was a man of contradictions and complications, capable of immense love and compassion but also, in his past, of great hate and violence. This was partly because he was a product of his environment, partly a victim of his own personality, and partly, inevitably, a victim of the personality of his twin.

'He paid the ultimate price for the terrible choices he made. To say his life was wasted would be a denigration of his incredible spirit and of the joy he brought to me and to others.

'But what he lost through the years was more than he could ever gain. If there is to be one enduring legacy, then Reg would wish it to be this: that no one should ever again take the same long and painful road.'

And the prisons?

The name Parkhurst was lost in 2008. The two other prison names, Albany and Camp Hill, were dispensed with too. The new 'super prison' was called HMP Isle of Wight. Albany, next to the jail, forms part of the complex.

Camp Hill eventually closed altogether in 2013. The building was decommissioned 'as part of an ongoing programme to modernise the prison estate and further reduce the costs of prison'.

Now HMP Isle of Wight, opened in 2009, is a category 'B' male training prison. The jail holds around 1,100 prisoners, mainly sex offenders, on two sites. A third of them are serving life sentences, or jail terms with no definite end date.

Parkhurst itself is used to house the prisoners, while the former Albany jail is the centre for healthcare.

At Broadmoor, a massive development project is taking place. It's costing more than £240 million.

The work to build sixteen new wards at the high security psychiatric hospital in Crowthorne, Berkshire, will end in 2017. The new hospital will provide accommodation for 210 patients. Current patients will remain on site throughout the redevelopment.

At the time of writing, the Grade 1 listed gatehouse, with its clock tower, is set to remain. It is a gateway to the future, with a stark reminder of the past; through the ages it has stood, bearing silent witness to the good, and the evil, that has dwelt within the walls of Broadmoor.

The Krays are gone but, like their legacy, many of the institutions that housed them live on.

The legend of the Krays and their prison years will always survive. It will last forever.

Acknowledgements

Ajda Vucicevic; Huw Armstrong; Trudi Gough; Matt Blyth; Jan Beal; Jenni Day; Frank Beal; Discovery Channel; Daniel Korn; Adam Jacobs; Louise Hulland; Marianne Benton; Bob Benton; Fred Dinenage; Duncan Campbell; Professor Dick Hobbs; Wilf Pine; Freddie Foreman; Chris Lambrianou; Maureen Flanagan; Patrick Fraser; David Fraser; Norman Parker; Dr Liz Yardley; Roberta Kray; Steve Wraith; Alan (Broadmoor patient); Bobby Cummines OBE; Ronnie Richardson; Luigi Bonomi; Noel 'Razor' Smith; Frances Shea (niece).

This book is based on the documentary, *The Krays: The Prison Years*, produced by Woodcut Media for Discovery Channel.